D1447353

When is it correct to say that a person's freedom is
restricted? Can poverty constrain freedom? Can you
constrain your own freedom, for instance through weakness
of the will or self-deception, and are you not truly free
unless you act on a rational choice? Kristján Kristjánsson
offers a critical analysis of the main components of a theory
of negative liberty: the nature of obstacles and constraints,
the weight of obstacles, and the relation of freedom to
power and autonomy. Through this discussion, which
examines much of the contemporary work on political
freedom, he develops his own theory of negative liberty,
the so-called 'responsibility view', which meets many of the
goals of advocates of positive liberty while retaining its
distinctive 'negative' nature. He also argues for and
implements a method of naturalistic revision as a way of
solving conceptual disputes in social philosophy.

SOCIAL FREEDOM

SOCIAL FREEDOM

The responsibility view

KRISTJÁN KRISTJÁNSSON

CAMBRIDGE
UNIVERSITY PRESS

Published by the Press Syndicate of the University of Cambridge
The Pitt Building, Trumpington Street, Cambridge CB2 1RP
40 West 20th Street, New York, NY 10011–4211, USA
10 Stamford Road, Oakleigh, Melbourne 3166, Australia

First published 1996

Printed in Great Britain at the University Press, Cambridge

A catalogue record for this book is available from the British Library

Library of Congress cataloguing in publication data

Kristján Kristjánsson.
Social freedom: the responsibility view / Kristján Kristjánsson.
p.   cm.
Includes bibliographical references and index.
ISBN 0 521 56092 6
1. Liberty.   2. Authority.   3. Social values.   4. Choice
(Psychology)   1 Title.
HM271.K75 1996
303.3 – dc20   95–25298   CIP

ISBN 0 521 56092 6 hardback

For my beloved wife,
Chia-jung

Contents

Acknowledgements

This book has its origin in my PhD thesis, 'Freedom as a Moral Concept', on which I began work in 1987 and which I submitted to the University of St Andrews in 1990. I would like to thank Andrew Mason for his helpful advice and encouragement towards the beginning of my project and ever since. Special thanks must be extended to Gordon Graham who supervised my thesis and provided me with incisive comments, and to my friend and mentor Mikael M. Karlsson for his generously extended criticisms of a draft of my thesis and most of the articles which were to grow out of it. I am indebted to many others who have read drafts of particular sections of this work at various stages, including Christopher Bryant, Peter Dalton, Guðmundur Heiðar Frímannsson, David Miller, Peter Morriss, anonymous referees of some of the journals listed below, and two readers for Cambridge University Press. My thanks are also owed to my student Björn Sigurðarson for his important secretarial work. Most of all, I am grateful to my wife, Chia-jung Tsai, for her invaluable encouragement and assistance.

My original thesis was written while I was supported by an Overseas Research Studentship from the Committee of Vice-Chancellors and Principals of the Universities of the United Kingdom, and a research studentship from the University of St Andrews. Later, I received a generous grant from the Icelandic Council of Science to continue with my research. Finally, a grant from the research fund of the University of Akureyri, Iceland, where I am currently employed, helped me to add the finishing touches to this book. I am most grateful for all this support.

The book incorporates revised versions of previously published or presented papers: chapters 1, 2, and 6 include paragraphs from 'For a *Concept* of Negative Liberty – but which *Conception?*', *Journal of Applied Philosophy*, 9 (1992); chapter 3 is a re-worked version of 'Freedom, Offers, and Obstacles', *American Philosophical Quarterly*, 29 (1992); a large part of chapter 4 is taken from 'Social Freedom and the Test of Moral Responsibility', *Ethics*, 103 (1992) and is reproduced by kind permission of the University of Chicago Press; chapter 5 is partly edited from 'What is Wrong with Positive Liberty?', *Social Theory and Practice*, 18 (1992); sections of chapter 6 originally appeared in '"Constraining Freedom" and "Exercising Power Over"', *International Journal of Moral and Social Studies*, 7 (1992); and chapter 7 is based partly on a paper I delivered at the 10th Inter-Nordic Philosophical Symposium in Finland (1993), and partly on 'Social Concepts: Normativity without Relativity', *Res Publica*, 1 (1995). I am grateful for permission for reprinting material from the above articles.

CHAPTER I

Introduction: freedom from Berlin onwards

This book aims to expound and defend a certain view of social freedom which I shall call *the responsibility view*. Arguably, for reasons of methodology if not human psychology, a study of this kind is best begun by laying down some provisional theories or hypotheses which are then put to the test: substantiated, amended, or discarded as the work progresses. But, as this book presents a conceptual analysis and not an autobiography, I see no reason to preface it by describing the basic ideas with which I started and the story of my struggle with them,[1] nor does the plan of this work reflect the order in which I reached my conclusions. Rather, I shall present and develop my account in what appears to me, on afterthought, to be the most logical order. For example, while it was plain from the start that a multitude of methodological questions would have to be addressed, discussion of them is postponed until chapter 7.

My line of argument may appear to follow a somewhat circuitous route, at least to those not versed in the regular twists and turns of contemporary accounts of freedom, touching on many issues whose interrelations need not always be immediately clear. Thus, while chapter 2 focuses on a host of different versions of so-called negative liberty, chapter 3 introduces the problem of the necessary 'weight' of potential freedom-restricting obstacles and brings the discussion to bear on a long-standing controversy regarding the nature of threats and offers. Chapter 4 then canvasses the notion of moral responsibility for obstacles. In chapter 5, we move on to the realm of so-called positive-liberty

---

[1] The preceding Acknowledgements indicate some of the 'chapters' in that story.

accounts, highlighting the way in which 'internal bars' can or cannot curb our freedom. Chapter 6 looks at the relationship between freedom and power, and chapter 7 is, as already mentioned, devoted to questions of method. By the end of the book, however, all these apparently different strands – none of which can, I believe, be neglected with impunity in a comprehensive analysis of social freedom – will have been drawn together, with chapter 8 containing a summary of the main results of the study.

Introductory chapters, which reveal so much of what the author is about to do, how he does it, and what his conclusions are that reading the rest of the book does little more than fill in a few missing details, are a diet I have grown increasingly weary of. Let it, therefore, suffice to say at the beginning that the *responsibility view* I aim to defend is that variety of a conceptual negative-liberty theory according to which an obstacle counts as a constraint on the freedom of an agent B if and only if another agent A can be held morally responsible for the creation or non-removal of the obstacle, i.e., if and only if the onus of justification can be placed on A, whether or not A imposed the obstacle intentionally, and whether or not he can ultimately be held culpable for its existence.

I hope my responsibility view will be found to contain some novel and original features. There is no use, however, in trying to make light of my debt to numerous predecessors in the field. For example, some sort of a responsibility view has already been suggested by other authors, from whom I take my cue.[2] Still, I am led to dissent from, and hopefully improve upon, certain elements inherent in all these previously presented views. Of necessity this work will contain much polemical matter. But then, stating and arguing for a position on the issue of freedom without any relevant interaction with the ongoing debate would

---

[2] A 'responsibility view' of freedom was first suggested by S. I. Benn and W. L. Weinstein, 'Being Free to Act, and Being a Free Man', *Mind*, 80 (1971) and later worked out in more detail by Benn and various other authors; see, e.g., W. E. Connolly, *The Terms of Political Discourse*, 2nd edn (Oxford: Martin Robertson & Co., 1983), D. Miller, 'Constraints on Freedom', *Ethics*, 94 (1983), S. I. Benn, *A Theory of Freedom* (Cambridge University Press, 1988), and D. Miller, *Market, State, and Community* (Oxford University Press, 1989).

be less than stimulating. At the risk of bestowing on some sections of the book the cursory character of a survey article, I deliberately try to comment upon the views of as many participants in that debate as space allows me to. I hope this will be of particular use to readers who have not yet been initiated into the intricacies of the freedom-debate.

As noted above, discussion of methodological issues will, for the most part, be shelved until chapter 7. On the one hand, this is done for the sake of convenience of exposition: the reader will presumably want me to get on with an analysis of the book's main topic, social freedom, as quickly as possible. On the other hand, I firmly believe that a tree is best known by its fruit, namely, that it is more convincing to 'deliver the goods' first before explaining the method by which – to quote Pindar – the tree was 'fed by the green dew' and 'raised up . . . to the liquid sky'. Nevertheless, I think it is necessary at this point to make a few comments about the method implicit in the ensuing argument, if only to forestall certain objections that might be pressed against it.

After reading a plethora of conceptual studies, I would venture to claim that the most fruitful ones, namely, those which move the discussion of a given concept in the right direction, tend either *explicitly* or *implicitly* to presuppose a plausible methodology. What does such a methodology involve? Arguably, it satisfies four main conditions: it (*1*) respects *common usage* as much as possible; (*2*) yields *coherent* definitions, both internally and with respect to other related concepts, by honouring morally important distinctions; (*3*) yields *serviceable* and *non-relative* definitions in the sense that they commend themselves to any rational thinker irrespective of their community or philosophical persuasion; and (*4*) accounts for *conceptual contestedness* – that is, it explains why people have hitherto disagreed about the extension of the given concept, and why they may still continue to differ about particular cases.

The invocation of these four conditions, especially the highly controversial (*1*) and (*3*), may seem blatantly question-begging. However, my claim is not merely that good conceptual studies have tended to pass these four hurdles, but, more importantly, that plausible reasons can be given which suggest *why* and *how* such studies could, at least in principle, be expected to do so. Those reasons will not be discussed explicitly until chapter 7, but hopefully by that time the reader will have found the arguments given for my proposed specifications of 'freedom', 'power', and various other terms persuasive in themselves.

This book purports to argue for a definition of social freedom, satisfying the four conditions laid down above, a definition employable in political theory as well as in ordinary discourse. I realise that the mere mention of a *definition* may raise an eyebrow or two in our post-Wittgensteinian, post-Quinean age, which does not speak easily of the quest for definitions. However, rather than rushing my fences at this early point, I hope such worries about the ultimate viability of my quest will gradually disappear once the reader comes to understand the kind of *open-textured*, *naturalistic* 'definition' at which I am aiming (secs. 7.2–7.3).

To anticipate another, if related, objection: it might be urged that all too often in the course of my argument competing accounts and even whole moral theories are over-hastily disqualified on the basis of a counter-example or two. To alleviate in advance the force of this objection, let me make it quite clear that, although *one* of the touchstones by which a sound conceptual inquiry is to be judged is its respecting common intuitions, all satisfactory inquiries into the nature of social concepts will be *critical* ones. What we should be aiming at in such an inquiry is conceptual *revision* rather than mere *analysis*. It must be shown why the point of the given concept *is* or *should be* of interest to people; how the term designating the concept must be defined so as to correspond to this point; and how its meaning is to be distinguished from different concepts, with other (but perhaps related) points. We need to investigate both what people say and what they had better say to capture this point. Thus, although alternative accounts may, at an early stage in my book, seem to be dismissed on the basis of a 'thin' intuition, more substantial reasons will in most cases, I hope, manifest themselves in the course of the discussion why the rejected account is inferior to the one I have proposed (not as serviceable, not supported by as sound a metaphysics or psychology, etc.). This way of arguing is indeed the fulcrum around which the method of *naturalistic revision*, employed in the sequel, revolves.

Now, there is an element of truth in the discouraging, if somewhat sardonic, remark at the outset of Felix Oppenheim's *Dimensions of Freedom* that when one speaks of freedom, La Bruyére's words come to mind: everything has been said and we come too late to add anything.[3] Yet, philosophers evidently do not see discussions of social freedom as the flogging of a dead horse, for in recent years articles and books on the subject have appeared with almost dreary regularity. If there ever was a feeling in philosophical circles that 'everything has been said' on the issue of freedom, the publication in 1958 of Isaiah Berlin's Inaugural Address to Oxford University, 'Two Concepts of Liberty', created enough stir to dispel any such illusion.[4] Berlin placed the notion of social freedom firmly on the agenda of current debate and paved the way for the spate of publications that was to follow.

The aim of this introductory chapter is to set the stage for the ensuing discussion by laying a part of its conceptual foundation. To do so, let me next make some basic observations about the different kinds of freedom and rehearse briefly a number of the fundamental problems characterising the discourse about social freedom from Berlin onwards.

I.I. KINDS OF FREEDOM

At the outset of his essay *On Liberty*, John Stuart Mill announces that the problems he means to tackle are those of political or social freedom, not those concerning the 'so-called Liberty of the Will'.[5] Mill was quite right in making this distinction: *freedom of the will* and *social freedom* are logically distinct in the sense that people who hold the same view of the former may hold different

[3] F. Oppenheim, *Dimensions of Freedom: An Analysis* (New York: St. Martin's Press, 1961), p. 3.
[4] Reprinted with Introduction in I. Berlin, *Four Essays on Liberty* (Oxford University Press, 1969).
[5] J. S. Mill, *Utilitarianism, Liberty, Representative Government* (London: J. M. Dent & Sons, 1931), p. 65.

views of the latter. Moreover, few would deny that social
unfreedom[6] is compatible with freedom of the will. On the other
hand, there is a strong case for saying that determinism, whether
'hard' or 'soft', excludes the possibility of social freedom and that
such freedom presupposes an underlying metaphysical view of
human beings as free and responsible agents. This is, for
example, Berlin's opinion in his *Four Essays on Liberty*. Now, it is
tempting, when writing about social freedom, to deal as
succinctly with free will as B. Crick does: 'I take "freedom of the
will" for granted – what else can one do?'[7] Indeed, the free-will
problem will scarcely be of more concern for my book than it is
for Crick, although it will be briefly touched upon again in
connection with an analysis of the notions of *autarchy* and
autonomy (sec. 5.5).[8]

   There are discordant opinions as to how many concepts of
freedom are abroad in everyday and/or philosophical discussion
apart from the two already mentioned: freedom of the will and
social freedom. Oppenheim locates and defines a number of
these;[9] but he may be too generous in his enumeration, for some
of the concepts he distinguishes seem to be nothing but variations
or metaphorical extensions of others. Thus, what Oppenheim
calls 'feeling free' may be little more than a metaphorical
counterpart of social freedom: when I take off my heavy,
woollen sweater, I feel as if I had been let out of jail, but there is
hardly a reason to exalt this feeling to the status of a special
concept of freedom. Still, as Oppenheim rightly shows, there are
various *kinds* of freedom and many freedom-concepts which
have nothing to do with social freedom.[10] However, searching

---

[6] Notably, the word 'unfree' (and 'unfreedom') is rarely used in everyday English. That
might be little more than a linguistic coincidence since the equivalents 'unfrei' and
'ófrjáls' are, e.g., current words in German and Icelandic. For reasons of style, I shall
sometimes be tempted to use 'unfree' in the sequel, but then merely as a short for 'not
free', and 'unfreedom' as a short for 'the state of not being free', i.e., 'the state of being
constrained'.

[7] B. Crick, 'Freedom as Politics', in P. Laslett and W. G. Runciman (eds.), *Philosophy,
Politics and Society*, III (Oxford: Basil Blackwell, 1967), p. 202.

[8] All references in parentheses in the main text refer to pages, sections, or chapters in this
book.

[9] Oppenheim, *Dimensions of Freedom: An Analysis*, pp. 139–78.

[10] There are also freedom-concepts abroad which *do* relate to social freedom, but which
are more restrictive than the general concept of social freedom under discussion in this

for the exact number of these does not seem to be a very fruitful endeavour and will not be pursued further here. Let it therefore be clear that, unless otherwise stated, the words 'freedom' and 'liberty' will be used interchangeably in the sequel to refer to *social freedom* and nothing else.

Students ploughing through some of the current elementary literature in social and political philosophy may get the impression that there are two contending accounts of social freedom. On the first account (the one embraced by 'right-wingers') freedom can be restricted only by legal rules and occurrences of force and fraud, while the second account (the 'left-wing' one) claims that, since freedom is not only freedom *from*, but also freedom *to*, it does not merely depend upon the absence of such restrictions, but also upon the presence of effective alternatives for action. However oversimplified and misleading this distinction is, it draws to some degree on Berlin's influential analysis of *negative* and *positive liberty* in his previously mentioned paper.

It is common knowledge that there Berlin distinguishes between two 'political senses of freedom' as answering two logically distinct questions. In the *negative* sense, the question concerns the extent of 'the area within which the subject . . . is or should be left to do what he is able to do or be, without interference', and the answers to that give rise to a concept of liberty as the absence of external constraints: as 'the area within which a man can act unobstructed by others'. In the *positive* sense, the question is 'what, or who, is the source of control or interference that can determine someone to do, or be, this rather than that?'[11] There, we are no longer concerned with the conception of a vacuum in which nothing obstructs us, but rather with the notion of self-direction or self-control, which relates to our deeply rooted desire to be masters of our own destiny. But, as Berlin is quick to point out, although the desire to be governed by oneself may be as deep a wish as that of a free

book and in most other studies of liberty. An example is the notion of being a 'free person' in the sense of not being a slave or a prisoner of the state (irrespective of other dimensions of social freedom). This concept is discussed, *inter alia*, by I. Hunt, 'Freedom and its Conditions', *Australasian Journal of Philosophy*, 69 (1991), 290.

[11] I. Berlin, *Four Essays on Liberty*, pp. 121-2.

area of action, and even historically older, 'it is not a desire for the same thing'.[12]

Although Berlin's terminology is now, by and large, accepted as common ground, there is still ample room for dispute. Three of the most vexing questions are: (*a*) whether positive and negative liberty constitute different concepts or only variants of the same concept, (*b*) what kind of a nature or history an obstacle must have to be a possible candidate for a constraint on liberty in the negative model, and (*c*) how weighty or efficacious such an obstacle must be to count as a constraint.

Unfortunately, Berlin himself is not particularly clear on any of these issues; indeed, he never directly addresses (*c*). As for (*a*), he sometimes speaks as if positive and negative liberty have a common root or source and that they 'start at no great logical distance from each other'.[13] This has led John Gray to conclude that 'when Berlin speaks of two *concepts* of liberty, he intends us to understand this as a reference to what Rawls would call two *conceptions* of liberty'.[14] But elsewhere Berlin clearly states that these are 'not two different interpretations of a single concept, but two profoundly divergent and irreconcilable attitudes to the ends of life'.[15] I find this latter contention more in line with Berlin's general view, according to which the notion of positive liberty has suffered a historical transformation, to the detriment of its original nature. In the light of his detailed description of its abuse in political discourse, it is difficult to see it simply as a variant of the same concept as negative liberty.

Concerning (*b*), Berlin's own view is even more equivocal. He seems to vacillate between (*i*) the narrow view that coercion 'implies the deliberate interference of other human beings',[16] (*ii*) the more inclusive idea that coercion refers to the part 'played by other human beings, directly or indirectly, with or without the intention of doing so, in frustrating my wishes',[17] and (*iii*) the broad definition in his 'Introduction' (written later) that the criterion of coercion is its resulting from alterable

---

[12] Ibid., p. 131.   [13] Ibid., p. xliii.

[14] J. Gray, 'On Negative and Positive Liberty', *Political Studies*, 28 (1980), 510.

[15] Berlin, *Four Essays on Liberty*, p. 166.

[16] Ibid., p. 122.   [17] Ibid., p. 123.

or remediable human practices.[18] Nevertheless, (*i*) is the view commonly attributed to Berlin. As can be seen from these interpretive questions, the value of Berlin's contribution, influential as it has been, lies more in raising questions and stimulating discussion than in supplying decisive answers.

So far, we have found little guidance as to which of the two proposed notions of social freedom is more appropriate. Berlin is inclined to emphasise negative liberty, if only because history has taught us that the positive notion lends itself more easily to political abuse. It is no secret that my sympathies are also with negative liberty, although it would take us too far afield to explain at this early point the reasons why. Let it suffice to say for the moment that, of the two, the negative notion seems to have more intuitive appeal, at least for non-philosophers. Perhaps the reason is etymological. In Icelandic, for example, 'frjáls', meaning 'free', is derived directly from the word 'frí-hals' which means literally 'having a free neck', i.e., not being chained like a slave. According to C. S. Lewis' *Studies in Words*, much the same applies to the English equivalent.[19] These etymological facts could be taken to indicate that 'freedom' is by nature what Austin calls a 'trouser word', taking its meaning from something that could have been present (here restrictions) but is not. Austin in fact claims that ' "free" is only used to rule out the suggestion of some or all of its recognised antitheses'.[20] But if 'freedom' is categorised as a 'trouser word', whose meaning is negative by definition, it becomes almost too easy to reject out of hand the positive notion of freedom which has been held in high esteem by many distinguished philosophers.

In recent years, those of us who favour a 'negative' account of freedom have come under heavy attack from two directions. First, there are those who insist that the distinction between negative and positive liberty is merely verbal. Surely, they maintain, if you are free *from* certain restraints, then you are free *to* direct your own life; and conversely, you cannot be in control

[18] Ibid., p. xxix.
[19] Cf. J. Feinberg, *Social Philosophy* (Englewood Cliffs: Prentice-Hall, 1973), p. 4.
[20] J. L. Austin, 'A Plea for Excuses', in V. C. Chappell, (ed.), *Ordinary Language* (Englewood Cliffs: Prentice-Hall, 1964), p. 45.

of your own destiny unless you have been relieved of various restrictions. Hence, there can be no 'pure' negative account of freedom – nor for that matter any 'pure' positive one. Let us call this objection the thesis of *conceptual equivalence*. Second, positive libertarians argue that the negative concept of freedom fails to account for certain paradigmatic cases of constraint. Negative accounts, we are told, concentrate on minimising restraint and coercion while overlooking the numerous ways in which lack of capacities and opportunities can curtail our liberty. Poverty serves here as the standard example. The poor person may not be the victim of direct restraint or coercion by an identifiable individual, but if we deny that he is unfree to enjoy many of the things life has to offer, we are employing a crude and impoverished notion of freedom. This objection underlies the positive libertarian's thesis of the *conceptual superiority* of his own notion.

Before proceeding further, let me make it quite clear that I believe negative libertarians have at their disposal the critical ammunition to counter both the above theses. For our present purposes it suffices to indicate briefly what I take to be the most cogent line of defence against the first one, while discussion of the conceptual-superiority thesis will be shelved until chapter 5.

Joel Feinberg proposes in his *Social Philosophy* a definition of freedom which, while grounded in the negative notion, is also supposed to include the essential elements of the positive one. A constraint on freedom, he says, 'is something – anything – that prevents one from doing something. Therefore, if nothing prevents me *from* doing X, I am free *to* do X; conversely, if I am free *to* do X, then nothing prevents me *from* doing X'. On this account Feinberg claims that 'freedom to' and 'freedom from' are logically linked, and that there can be 'no special "positive" freedom to which is not also a freedom from'. But *what* prevents me from doing X? Feinberg answers that question by invoking four categories of constraints: internal positive constraints such as headaches, obsessive thoughts, and compulsive desires; internal negative constraints such as ignorance, weakness, and deficiencies in talent and skill; external positive constraints such as barred windows and locked doors; and finally external negative constraints such as lack of money, transportation, and weapons.[21]

The major fault with Feinberg's account is that it fails to do justice to his own reference to Helvétius, who remarked that 'not to fly like an eagle or swim like a whale' does not constitute lack of freedom.[22] That is, Feinberg's account is too permissive, for his categories obliterate the distinction between constraints and mere inabilities. A patient suffering from multiple sclerosis who is confined to a wheelchair after an attack of it but then recovers and can walk again – as is common in the course of that disease – has not regained his *freedom* to walk but his *ability* to do so. There is every reason to honour this distinction, both for the sake of ordinary usage (where it is often made) and that of conceptual clarity (sec. 5.5). We are not necessarily able to do everything we have the freedom to do, nor vice versa. Incidentally, being free to do what one cannot do is usually not of much value to the agent but, as Oppenheim points out, 'having a freedom is not the same as valuing a freedom one has'.[23]

Much the same may be said about an earlier attempt by G. MacCallum to challenge the view that we can usefully distinguish between two kinds of social freedom. Admittedly, MacCallum's basic insight, that freedom is a *relation*, not a *property*, was of great importance. Although 'I am free' may look like 'I am alive', it is surely more akin to 'I am tall' – and since Frege we have a clear sense of relational predicates which Plato, for instance, lacked when he tried to understand tallness as a property. Freedom is not something that one happens to possess or stumble across like a chest of gold, it is a relation between agents. MacCallum further insisted that the freedom relation is *triadic*: freedom is always *of* something (an agent or agents (x)), *from* something

---

[21] Feinberg, *Social Philosophy*, p. 13.

[22] Cf. ibid., p. 8.

[23] F. Oppenheim, *Political Concepts: A Reconstruction* (University of Chicago Press, 1981), p. 67. Note, however, that having freedom without ability may in some cases be of value to the agent, *pace* Oppenheim and especially W. J. Norman ('Taking "Free Action" Too Seriously', *Ethics*, 101 (1991)) who emphatically claims that 'the only occasions on which it is valuable for one to be free to do A are those on which one is (or will be) able to do A' (p. 514). We can imagine a person paralysed from the waist downwards finding it valuable to live in a society where he is free to various things which, as a matter of fact, he cannot do, for he realises how it would add insult to injury if he were not only unable, but also unfree, to do them.

(y), *to* do, or not to do, to become, or not become something (z), where y 'ranges over such "preventing conditions" as constraints, restrictions, interferences and barriers'.[24]

Berlin has claimed that the third variable in the definition may be unnecessary, as a man struggling against his chains or a people against enslavement 'need not consciously aim at any definite further state;'[25] and for him this seems to indicate that freedom be better understood as a *dyadic* relation than a triadic one. But I believe Berlin's point here to be mistaken. The freedom of the parties involved *to* do whatever they might have been able to do had they not been chained or enslaved is at least being restricted; whether or not they are aiming consciously at any particular 'further state' now (or even whether or not they are aware of their own enslavement) is not at issue.

More detrimental to the value of MacCallum's proposal is the point made by Oppenheim that MacCallum allows 'y' to cover the agent's own disabilities, or impersonal (physical) conditions, which leads to the conclusion, deemed unacceptable above, that one is necessarily unfree to do what one cannot do.[26] Oppenheim himself suggests a triadic definition somewhat similar in form to MacCallum's: with respect to P, R is unfree to do x;[27] but the vital difference is that Oppenheim's 'P' only ranges over (other) *persons*.

MacCallum was correct in seeing freedom as a triadic relation. However, as we have already noticed, the ranges of the term variables must be defined with adequate specificity if the proposed relation is to be that of *social* freedom. For instance, the examples above suggest that the preventing condition (MacCallum's 'y') must be confined to *agents* or, more precisely, to *obstacles attributable to agents*. The simple logical point that freedom happens to be a triadic, not a dyadic relation, hardly suffices to show that the negative and positive notions are variants of one and the same concept. It may still be that the term variables of one (or both) of them cannot be specified in a way that accords with the proper concept of social freedom. Indeed, I will argue in

[24] G. C. MacCallum, 'Negative and Positive Freedom', *The Philosophical Review*, 76 (1967), 314.   [25] Berlin, *Four Essays on Liberty*, p. xliii.
[26] Oppenheim, *Political Concepts: A Reconstruction*, p. 84.
[27] Ibid., p. 53.

chapter 5 that all proper positive-liberty accounts counter-intuitively and unreasonably violate two central features of social freedom: (*a*) its irreflexivity, i.e., that a person cannot constrain his own freedom, and (*b*) the fact that freedom is an opportunity concept, not an exercise concept, which means that as long as we have the unrestricted option to do *x*, we are free to do *x*, even though we may never care to utilise this option. If this is true, MacCallum's schema could only be rescued by incorporating these central features in the specification of his variables – which would then, of course, exclude the positive accounts from reckoning as putative accounts of social freedom.

This criticism of MacCallum might seem to be misplaced, since he explicitly realised that one who upholds a negative account will insist that the relevant variables must be specified in one way, while an advocate of a positive account will insist on another set of specifications. So, is it not unfair to criticise MacCallum's schema for failing to select uniquely my favoured, negative, account, when this was indeed precisely what he was trying to point out by invoking it? Far be it from me to detract from the merit of MacCallum's observation that translatability into a triadic schema is a *necessary* condition of the intelligibility of any claim about freedom, social or otherwise. I am only concerned to make the point here that, contrary to the conceptual-equivalence thesis, such translatability may not, in the end, prove to be a *sufficient* condition of the intelligibility of a claim about social freedom; there must not necessarily exist some core specification of that particular concept which makes sense of both negative and positive liberty.

One of the points established so far is that only certain kinds of hindrances are to be regarded as infringements of a person's liberty. *B* is not unfree to do *x* merely because he is unable to do so; I am not unfree to visit my friend merely because I am trapped by a landslide and cannot go. Thus, it seems prima facie to be an unavoidable premise of any plausible account of social freedom that the restriction of *B*'s actions be attributable to some agency (human or otherwise), i.e., that it can be traced back to an agent, *A*, who has imposed the restriction. For instance, a criminal, caught on the run by a police dog, would not be considered 'unfree with respect to the dog' (to use Oppenheim's somewhat cumbersome terminology), but to the policeman who controlled the dog. Why? Simply because the dog is, rightly or wrongly, thought to lack agency – or at least the kind of agency required.

Let us try to bring out more clearly what this connection between the constraining-agent and the constrainee must amount to by considering a further example. Suppose a runner B is overtaking his competitor A on the last metres of a long-distance run in an international competition. A, who is from B's enemy country, has been ordered by his president to prevent any runner from B's country from winning a race. To carry out this order, A deliberately pushes B with his elbow so that B falls. In that case, there is no denying the fact that A has constrained B's freedom to finish the run – at least as the victor. But let us now suppose that A, losing his balance for a while, pushes B accidentally. As previously, B falls, but would we say now that he is unfree to win the race? I think not. His chance of finishing the race as the victor is ruled out, not because his freedom has been undermined; it is rather his ability to do so which has suffered, just as if he had been hit by lightning. If true, this is a very important conclusion since the direct material cause is exactly the same as in the first example (A's elbow), and even the most accurate slow-motion playback of the events would not bring to light any difference.

What does it then mean that the infringement must be attributable to an agent? Why is B unfree in the first case but not in the second? Could the reason be that while A is *causally responsible* for B's fall in both cases, he is only *morally responsible* for it in the first? This answer is argued for by Benn and Weinstein in a paper published in 1971. There, they also claim that we are not simply purporting to describe a state of affairs when we say that someone is not free, we are also typically advancing a charge or making an accusation that we expect those against whom we advance it to deny, rebut, or accept.[28]

A great deal will be said in the following chapters about Benn

---

[28] Benn and Weinstein, 'Being Free to Act, and Being a Free Man', 198–9.

and Weinstein's suggestions and about the ideas of some of the philosophers who have followed in their footsteps in arguing for a 'responsibility view' of freedom: the view claiming that only those impediments for which A is morally responsible can constrain B's freedom. In the end, the success of the present study depends on the possibility of formulating such a view in a plausible, coherent way; something which I believe no one has accomplished so far. As a starting-point, in chapter 2 let us examine the relationship between this responsibility view and other, more traditional, accounts of negative liberty.

CHAPTER 2

Negative freedom: the nature of constraints

Although all negative accounts concur in defining freedom as
the absence of constraints, it is common knowledge that they
differ substantially among themselves. The basic question to ask
about each of them is what counts as a *constraint* on freedom.
Thus, we are often told, it is possible to distinguish between
narrower and *broader* accounts of negative liberty. While that is
true, this distinction is itself not as unproblematic as we are
sometimes given to believe. There is a certain elasticity in the
terms 'narrow' and 'broad' as they are used in this context. For
instance, it cannot be assumed that the stronger or more specific
demands a given account makes about the *nature* of the proposed
constraints, the narrower it is. At least one other question has to
be asked, namely, interpretive question (*c*) from chapter 1 (p. 8)
about the necessary *weight* or efficacy of the obstacles described.
For instance, Hobbes' famous *corporeal-freedom account* of liberty,
which I shall examine shortly, is commonly considered narrow
not because of the strict conditions it sets upon the nature of
constraints (in fact, it does anything but that), but because it
requires the weight of constraints to be such as to make a
proposed action literally *impossible*. By contrast, while another
traditional negative-liberty account, the *intentionality view* commonly ascribed, *inter alia*, to Berlin, sets stricter conditions on the
nature of putative constraints by requiring that they be
deliberately imposed by another agent, this conception is
typically more permissive on the weight-question, requiring
only that the constraint render a given course of action *ineligible*
to a normal (reasonable, prudent) person. For this reason, the
intentionality view tends to be considered 'broader' than the

Hobbesian account, although both could be termed 'narrow' in comparison with a responsibility view.

The present chapter investigates what different theories of negative liberty have to say about the nature of constraints, while discussion of their required weight will be postponed until chapter 3. In 2.1, Hobbes', Nozick's, and Berlin's accounts are examined and found to be flawed. The purpose of freedom-talk is examined in 2.2. As an outcome of those considerations, a responsibility view of freedom emerges in 2.3; and, subsequently, the most carefully argued version of it, that of David Miller, is explained and defended against certain objections. In general, this chapter aims to prepare the ground, and then to advance the case, for such a responsibility view; only later shall we see that all versions of it so far presented, including Miller's, have shortcomings which need to be ameliorated.

2.1. VARIETIES OF NEGATIVE FREEDOM

It is often said that philosophical theories are prized in proportion to their incomprehensibility. Not so with Hobbes' celebrated account of liberty, its clarity is beyond compare: 'Liberty, or Freedome, signifieth (properly) the absence of Opposition' – and nothing more.[1] The underlying idea is of a self-activated agent moving through space. If nothing obstructs his path, he is free. If, however, he comes up against external, physical obstacles that restrict his movements, he is unfree. What we have here is a definition of liberty as unimpeded movement, or *corporeal freedom* – some would say of negative freedom pure and simple. It sets no requirements as to the *source* of the obstacle, only its *location* in space, and yields in that respect a most permissive definition of a constraint on freedom.

A basic problem about Hobbes' account lies in the fact that what freedom-talk is meant to be about is arguably not free *movement* but free *action*. For instance, while I might be either free or unfree to enter my neighbour's garden, rabbits never act, only behave; hence, they simply can or cannot enter it.

---

[1] T. Hobbes, *Leviathan* (Harmondsworth: Penguin, 1968), p. 261.

Moreover, even if in a hurricane I were blown up against the
fence surrounding the garden, my situation would not be
usefully described as that of being *unfree to move* further. This
indicates that a constraint on freedom must restrict an *agent*
(with the required kind of agency) from *acting*, not merely any
self-activated *being* from *moving*. Another problem is that Hobbes
does not respect the important distinction between freedom and
ability (secs. 1.1; 5.5). The mere presence of a particular tree in a
forest, which makes me *unable* to walk in a straight line, does not
curtail my *freedom* to do so. Also, suppose *C* has been tethered by
A to a location through which *B* is to pass. *C*'s body there makes
B unable to move on, but we would definitely want to say that it
is *A*, not *C*, who constrains *B*'s freedom.[2] So, it seems that the
location of the obstacle (be it human or non-human) in space is
not so important after all – that what we are hunting for is rather
its source or origin.

Oppenheim's theory of causal responsibility might be brought
to bear here in saving Hobbes' account.[3] Perhaps *C* is not the
constraining agent in the above example because he is not
causally responsible for *B*'s unfreedom although he plays, in a
straightforward sense, *a causal role* in impeding *B*'s action. This is
what Oppenheim would be disposed to say – but his theory is
based on a strict distinction between acts and omissions, the
claim being that a person can only be held causally responsible
for the results of his *acts*. Unfortunately, such a 'causal theory' is
bound to be beset with the same difficulties as the act–omission
distinction in general, and it does not yield plausible results
when applied to particular cases where a person's options are
restricted, as will become apparent later in the chapter. Besides,
since Oppenheim's theory is concerned with action, not
movement, it has departed to such a significant extent from
Hobbes' account that it is hardly correct to speak of it in the
same breath.

---

[2] This example is taken from R. E. Flathman, *The Philosophy and Politics of Freedom*
(University of Chicago Press, 1987), p. 202.
[3] The theory is best exemplified in F. Oppenheim, '"Constraints on Freedom" as a
Descriptive Concept', *Ethics*, 95 (1985).

The house of delusion may be easy to build, but it is draughty to live in. Hobbes' 'pure' negative-liberty account would apply to the movements of any self-activated being, that of automatons as well as that of men. It does not acknowledge certain fundamental distinctions that should form the basis of all freedom-talk: between freedom and ability and between behaviour and action. More generally, it presupposes a deterministic, mechanical universe instead of 'taking free will for granted'. So, if we give any credence at all to what people think and say about morality, we are bound to consign Hobbes' account to the philosophical scrapheap.

It is always debatable what is to count as an 'extreme' view in philosophy. However, if Hobbes' account is extreme, a second account of negative freedom, now to be considered, is at least equally so, while being as different from Hobbes' as chalk from cheese. Some writers, disillusioned with a mechanical, *descriptive* model of freedom, have been driven to view freedom as a *moralised* concept, directly linked to moral rights and justice. Maybe Rousseau's well-known suggestion, that only 'ill will' but not 'the nature of things' maddens us,[4] has some bearing on questions of freedom; maybe nothing counts as a constraint unless it involves a moral offence.

It has long been the view of the law that our freedom to do *x* is only restrained if *x* is something which we have a *right* to do. I do not take my neighbour to court because he forbids me to use his property or sleep with his wife. In law, such obstacles would not count as restrictions of my freedom. However, the question is whether the sort of freedom to which we have a right on the basis of laws or a constitution is of the same sort as the freedom in which we are interested here, i.e., whether *legal* and *social* freedom can be equated.

The most notable attempt to define freedom as non-interference with (absolute) legal or moral rights is that of Robert Nozick. For him, an obstacle counts as a constraint on freedom if and only if it is a violation of legal or moral rights for which an agent can be held *culpable*. Placing limits on other people's opportunities,

---

[4] Cf. I. Berlin, *Four Essays on Liberty* (Oxford University Press, 1969), p. 123.

or not providing them with palatable alternatives, is not a constraint on their freedom, as long as we are acting within our rights.[5] Not surprisingly, Nozick's idea of rights hinges on his general theory of justice; the rights in question are the unconditional rights to which men are entitled in a just society. The political message is then simple and elegant: creating constraints is blameworthy, not doing so is praiseworthy.

If a *moralised definition* of freedom were correct, interference with a person's rights would always constitute an infringement of his liberty, and vice versa. However, this is obviously not so. A jailor may or may not be violating a moral right of the convict he is locking up in his cell. For instance, if the prisoner is jailed by virtue of a just conviction, we would undoubtedly want to say that his moral rights are not being violated; yet, his liberty is obviously infringed. Hence, a moralised definition of negative freedom is wrong. This simple counter-example, which has been invoked by various authors,[6] seems here to constitute a decisive refutation. It might perhaps be objected that it circumscribes the sense of freedom relevant to the *political* questions in which Nozick is interested. But that would not be a strong objection, for what sort of freedom is relevant to political question if not *social* freedom – and what sort of freedom is being restricted when a man is locked up in jail if it is not social? Still, however decisive this refutation is, it only suffices to undermine a *moralised* definition of the kind that Nozick has suggested, not necessarily a *moral* definition of any kind. More will be said about that later in the chapter.

Although the simple Hobbesian account has held strong fascination for some liberal thinkers, the traditional liberal view, to which I now turn, is that an obstacle presents a constraint on freedom if and only if it has been *deliberately* imposed by human

---

[5] R. Nozick, *Anarchy, State, and Utopia* (Oxford: Basil Blackwell, 1971), pp. 262–4. Another moralised definition is suggested by P. Morriss, *Power: A Philosophical Analysis* (Manchester University Press, 1987), pp. 118–22, but his is, as opposed to Nozick's, a relativistic one.

[6] See, e.g., G. A. Cohen, 'Illusions about Private Property and Freedom', in J. Mepham and D. H. Ruben (eds.), *Issues in Marxist Philosophy*, IV (Brighton: Harvester Press, 1981), p. 228, and Oppenheim, '"Constraints on Freedom" as a Descriptive Concept', 305–6.

action. As explained before, this is the position commonly attributed to Berlin. Initially, this definition seems to avoid the extremes of the two accounts examined hitherto: it is action, not movement or mere behaviour, with which we are concerned; and what matters are not the moral rights of the constrained persons but the intentions of the constraining agents.[7]

It is no coincidence that this is the traditional liberal view of freedom. For example, it enables us to distinguish, as Berlin does, between liberty itself and the conditions for it.[8] If a person is not deliberately prevented from voting in an election, for example by laws that deprive certain segments of the population of the right to vote, then he is free to do so, irrespective of whether he has the educational background necessary to make a rational choice between candidates, the economic means to travel to the polling-station, or is healthy enough to go there. These are, according to Berlin, the *conditions* for liberty, not liberty itself. Moreover, inadvertently preventing a person from doing *x* does not make him unfree; neither do institutional arrangements, such as the laws of property, as long as they are not deliberately contrived to impede particular individuals. A man who has acquired great wealth through good fortune or hard work has not necessarily constrained the freedom of his fellow-men, although as an indirect result some of them might be worse off than they would have been had he not been around. He has only constrained them if he has deliberately put obstacles in their path. That he might have *foreseen* the indirect consequences of his actions is not enough as long as these consequences were not *intended*. So, the liberal account of negative freedom fits together well with liberal political philosophy in general.

It should be observed that, unlike Oppenheim's causal responsibility theory, this liberal conception of freedom does not depend on an act–omission distinction. In the former, omissions can never give rise to unfreedom. In the latter, it is possible that *A* refrains from doing *x* (which he might easily have done),

[7] Apart from Berlin, the writer who has argued most diligently for this liberal conception is J. P. Day, 'Is the Concept of Freedom Essentially Contestable?', *Philosophy*, 61 (1986).
[8] Berlin, *Four Essays on Liberty*, p. liii.

thereby allowing an obstacle to be placed in *B*'s path, and if such an omission is intentional, it will count as a constraint on *B*'s freedom. However, this omission must be part of the causal chain leading to the obstacle's creation; the liberal conception does not allow that *A*'s intentional non-removal of an already existing obstacle constitutes a restriction of *B*'s freedom. Even so, the difference from Oppenheim's theory is one more point in favour of the liberal conception, again making it easy to see why it has gained its reputation as a plausible middle-ground proposal. It undoubtedly captures many of our intuitions about the nature of unfreedom. Yet, I believe that it retains aspects of the 'pure' negative account which ought to have been omitted and omits aspects of a moralised view which ought to have been retained.

What is so appealing about the view that only intentionally imposed obstacles constitute constraints on freedom? Perhaps that it accords with the insight illustrated at the end of chapter 1 by the stories of the runners. We saw that an accident, inadvertently brought about by a human being, does not count as a constraint on freedom any more than a natural disaster. Thus, we were led to ask whether moral responsibility had to be located for us to want to describe *B*'s fall as a case of unfreedom. Maybe that is true and maybe intention holds the key to moral responsibility. How could it? One reason could be the difference between consequences which are (*a*) foreseeable and intentional and (*b*) foreseeable and unintentional – witness the well-known doctrine of double effect. Now, this distinction has been *thought* by many to be of great moral import, but I tend to doubt its value and, consequently, to be sceptical of the double-effect doctrine (see also sec. 4.3). This is not simply for reasons of personal prejudice, but because of what I would call the *moral arbitrariness* of the distinction as applied to specific cases.

There are some striking stories from Miller, discussed later in this chapter, that will illustrate my point, but for the moment we can envisage the following scenario. Two adventurers are looking for precious stones in a cave. One of them (*B*) goes deep inside the cave, while the other (*A*) starts digging a hole at the mouth of it. *A* knows, or ought to know, that this might loosen a big rock which would trap B inside, but he does not intend that this should happen (directly or obliquely); he simply does not pay any attention to this possibility. Suppose the rock falls. B, who is trapped, shouts to A in anger, demanding an explanation why A took away his freedom. A answers: 'I didn't take away your freedom, you are just unable to leave. I had no intention to bring about your entrapment, although admittedly I should have seen that my digging this hole could cause the rock to fall'. Now, is B going to be satisfied with this answer – or more importantly, are we going to be satisfied with it? Obviously not. A tries to cash in on a distinction which is arbitrary with regard to moral responsibility. Suppose also the rock falls by accident, without A's contribution. If, following that, A fails to make a reasonable attempt to extricate B, he is clearly responsible for B's condition. The difference between the three cases of (a) A's deliberately trapping B inside, (b) its happening as a foreseeable but unintended consequence of A's action, and (c) A's failing to help B after he has been trapped by accident, does not seem to be of any importance as far as moral responsibility is concerned; and therefore we may wonder why it should give rise to varying judgements about B's (un)freedom.

Here it might be objected, however, that I have systematically misconstrued the liberal argument in order to give myself a handle against it. I have spoken as if the significance and appeal of the liberal conception must lie in its doing justice to the link between unfreedom and moral responsibility. By showing that the spheres of intention and responsibility do not coincide, I claim to have scored a major point. But an objector might maintain that what I have been doing all the time is to saddle the liberal thinker with an additional view; his claim was *not* that constraints on freedom are to be explained in terms of moral responsibility, but simply that a restriction must be brought about intentionally for it to present such a constraint. Responsibility is therefore a red herring in the discussion. Because the necessary intention is missing in case (b) above, it does not involve unfreedom; neither does case (c) since the entrapment there was not *brought about* by A's acts or omissions in the first place.

If this is what is argued, however, we are entitled to ask: what is so important about *intention* in this context if it is neither its relation to acts (as opposed to omissions) nor its link with moral responsibility? One answer might be that it is simply a fact of ordinary language that intention is understood to be a necessary condition of unfreedom. But then cases (*b*) and (*c*) continue to pose a problem for the liberal thinker; for there (doubtless in (*b*) and most likely also in (*c*)) ordinary language would require that we judge *A* to have constrained *B*'s freedom – which contradicts the liberal conception. Besides, even if that conception always happened to accord with ordinary language, we could still ask for a rationale of the concept of social freedom, and such a rationale might undermine common usage (see ch. 7). The examples of the runners seemed to indicate that this rationale is of a moral kind, a point which will be elaborated once we start to examine the views of those who base their definition of freedom directly on moral responsibility. However, it should already be clear why I suggested that the liberal theory of freedom retains too much of the 'pure' non-moral account. It grounds its fundamental tenet on a distinction that is arbitrary from the point of view of moral responsibility, without suggesting any other rationale for freedom-talk, and without even having ordinary language unambiguously in its favour. Berlin may have realised these faults, witness his proposals (*ii*) and (*iii*) above (p. 8) which go much further than a traditional liberal conception allows. It is not clear, however, from other parts of his work that Berlin thought through all the implications of this realisation.

2.2. FREEDOM AS A PRINCIPLE

Before turning to an unmitigated responsibility view of negative liberty, it may be useful to delve further into the purpose and nature of freedom-talk. It has been suggested by writers such as Benn and Weinstein, Miller, and W. Connolly that our language embodies a presumption against impairing the choices of others or obstructing their activity. We are interested in deciding when obstacles are properly seen as constraints on freedom because our understanding that people should be regarded and treated as agents teaches us that a person's freedom should not be constrained, other things being equal. Thus, a question about the restriction of freedom comes to be closely linked with a question about justification. Saying that *A* restrained *B*'s freedom is placing the onus of justification on *A*; it is making a claim that stands in need of a rebuttal. This is why Benn talks about freedom as a *principle*, upholding the importance of non-interference and of respect for persons.[9] Connolly defines 'principle' in this sense as 'a general rule that places, for its adherents, the onus of justification on those who would break it; to accept a principle is to acknowledge at least a prima facie obligation to abide by it'. He adds that most people in our society accept the principle of freedom, namely, that every person should be allowed to do as he chooses unless overriding reasons can be found that justify limiting him in certain respects.[10]

On this account, a constraint on freedom fits J. Kovesi's definition of an *open* or *incomplete* moral term. It refers to something that is considered wrong prima facie and challenges us to bring forth some relevant justificatory considerations. 'Lying' is Kovesi's own example. We might want to say: 'This is an act of lying, but go ahead and do it', but only if we can give some good reasons which override its prima facie wrongness.[11] When Oppenheim claims that it is not the case that everyone or even most people within the same culture adopt the same moral point of view with respect to such concepts, he misses Kovesi's point completely. According to Oppenheim, there might well be people who think that stealing is acceptable, admiring Robin Hood for stealing from the rich to help the poor.[12] The obvious reply is that if anybody thinks stealing is acceptable *in general*, then that person has misunderstood the rationale behind the concept of stealing. He would be better advised to say that there is no such thing as stealing; you simply take things from one person and give them to another. More likely, however, what

[9] S. I. Benn, 'Freedom, Autonomy and the Concept of a Person', *Proceedings of the Aristotelian Society*, 76 (1975–6).

[10] W. E. Connolly, *The Terms of Political Discourse*, 2nd edn (Oxford: Martin Robertson & Co., 1983), pp. 151–2.

[11] J. Kovesi, *Moral Notions* (London: Routledge and Kegan Paul, 1971), pp. 127–8.

[12] F. Oppenheim, *Political Concepts: A Reconstruction* (University of Chicago Press, 1981), p. 151.

such a person wants to say is simply that stealing is justified in many cases, perhaps in more cases than others will grant, and there is nothing in that statement which goes against Kovesi's definition of an open moral term. So, even if freedom is a principle in the above-described sense, the presumption against impairing the choices of others may be successfully rebutted in many cases. Interference with a person's freedom may always be an evil, but it is surely sometimes a necessary evil.

The strongest challenge to the claim that there is a philosophically relevant 'presumption of freedom' embodied in our language has been mounted by D. N. Husak.[13] He draws a parallel to legal practice and points out that there are two kinds of presumptions common in law: *procedural* and *substantive*. Presumptions of the former kind allocate the *burden of proof*; in that case a litigant has either the duty of going forward with evidence for a proposition p or the risk of non-persuasion with respect to p. If the litigant fails to convince the judge/jury of the validity of p, judgement is rendered against him. Presumptions of the latter kind create *rules of inference*, in which case p is regarded as a proof of q in the absence of credible evidence against q, or if the evidence for and against q is of equal weight. For example, p could be 'A has been missing for three years' and q 'A is dead.' Thus, procedural presumptions simply tell us who must do what in court, whereas the substantive ones can in some cases tip the scales of argumentation.

Now, the problem that Husak sees is this. A judge or a jury must arrive at a verdict. Their purpose is to decide what to *do* in a given case. On the other hand, the aim of philosophy is to arrive at the truth about what to *believe*. There is not a need for procedural presumptions in philosophy as there is in law; in philosophy we are not required to pass judgement here and now, we can suspend it until the relevant evidence has been obtained. Hence, the 'presumption of freedom' cannot be of the procedural kind. Suppose, then, that it is substantive. Arguments for the presumption tend to suggest that the mere fact that a given act is a deprivation of freedom is a reason for viewing it as objectionable.

---

[13] See D. N. Husak, 'The Presumption of Freedom', *Nous*, 17 (1983).

Although that reason can be outweighed in certain cases, it still remains a reason against the deprivation. But then, Husak points out, the presumption of freedom functions unlike a substantive presumption in law which plays no role as evidence once (credible) contrary evidence is introduced. Also, the presumption may lead to 'double-counting': interfering with *B*'s plan being considered wrong *both* because it disrespects his agency and because there is a presumption against unfreedom. In general, Husak claims that once a substantive presumption of freedom has been created, the likelihood increases of performing the required balancing of reasons incorrectly. Hence, there is a reason not to create it.[14]

The fault in Husak's argumentation lies in his insistence on modelling the presumption of freedom on legal practice. His position implies that if we know nothing of the effect of *A*'s action on *B* except that it constrains his freedom, then we are not to pass a judgement, as a court of law would be required to, but rather to suspend judgement until more details of the case have been revealed to us. This is like saying: if you know nothing about the statement *A* made to you except that it was a lie, then you ought not to consider his action wrong, even prima facie, nor ought you to impugn his motives in any way until you know more about the relevant facts. But this evidently forbids us to define a lie as a lie (prima facie wrong) until we know why it was made. Thus, Husak's position uses words we know ('constraint on freedom', 'lie') in the way we use them, and then tells us that we are not to use them in this way. What Husak fails to see is that the alleged presumption of freedom is not something we decide to *create* or adopt, like a particular piece of legislation. It is embedded in our language as essential to the purpose of the concepts we use. Moreover, this presumption is not substantive in the sense of serving as a distinct piece of argument: 'Constraining *B*'s action was beneficial in such-and-such a way, the negative elements weigh about the same – the presumption then tips the scales in favour of a negative judgement'. That is not how we think or argue at all. The presumption against the restriction of

---

[14] Ibid., pp. 350–9.

freedom is not something over and above the particular reasons against it; it represents the general case against interference constituted by these reasons, a case that may simply rest upon evidence accumulated during the long course of human existence.

This is also why Benn is wrong in thinking that the presumption/ principle of freedom must be understood in *deontological* terms, as part of a non-'value-centered' obligation to show respect for persons.[15] In *On Liberty*, Mill expounds his substantive, political principle of liberty about the 'fitting adjustment between individual independence and social control',[16] and he does so on *consequentialist* lines, with 'utility as the ultimate appeal on all ethical questions'.[17] When he starts to argue that certain reasons for intervention (paternalistic, moralistic, and emotional) should be ruled out in advance as irrelevant, he is simply making the empirical judgement that the utility promoted by acting on these reasons is, as a matter of fact, always outweighed by their baneful effects on individuality and, hence, real happiness. There is nothing deontological about this *specific* principle as formulated by Mill. If it should be followed unconditionally, it is only because accepting it as such would have the best consequences. I do not see any reason why a more *general* 'principle' of freedom in our language could not (*contra* Benn) have similar roots – the accumulated experience of countless generations that constraining people's activity is usually bad.[18] In the end, however, my understanding of what this general principle amounts to will turn out to be slightly different from that of previous responsibility theorists (sec. 4.3).

---

[15] S. I. Benn, *A Theory of Freedom* (Cambridge University Press, 1988), ch. 1.

[16] J. S. Mill, *Utilitarianism, Liberty, Representative Government* (London: J. M. Dent & Sons, 1931), pp. 68–9.

[17] Ibid., p. 74. These, of course, are Mill's own words. Nevertheless, one of the sharpest points of disagreement among Mill scholars is whether his principle of liberty is genuinely consequentialist, or whether it is somehow independent of his utilitarianism. As I have argued elsewhere, e.g. in my book *Þroskakostir* (*Ways to Maturity*; in Icelandic) (Reykjavík: Rannsóknarstofnun í siðfræði, 1992), I firmly believe Mill should be taken on trust here. This issue is briefly brought up again on p. 202.

[18] For a detailed attempt to show that Benn's principle of freedom can be given a consequentialist grounding, see P. Pettit, 'Consequentialism and Respect for Persons', *Ethics*, 100 (1989).

2.3. A RESPONSIBILITY VIEW OF NEGATIVE FREEDOM

Dissatisfaction with the traditional liberal conception, and the realisation that freedom is a principle, a presumption against the violation of which is embodied in our language, seem to have been the main spurs to Benn and Weinstein's pioneering paper 'Being Free to Act and Being a Free Man', published in 1971. There, most of the basic ideas underlying a responsibility view of freedom are adumbrated, ideas later taken up and expanded upon in many ways by writers such as Connolly and Miller. Earlier, Benn may have favoured the view that only intentionally imposed obstacles curtail freedom.[19] However, in this and subsequent papers he observes that people can be constrained by 'unreasonable social and economic conditions maintained by people with the power to change them':[20] by people who do not necessarily intend to tread on their fellow-men's toes, but do so through their negligence or avoidable omissions.

In Benn and Weinstein's basic conception, freedom amounts to the *non-restriction of options*. They agree with MacCallum that freedom is a triadic relation. The free agent is free to do something relative to some possible frustrating condition. Talk of freedom presupposes an agent in a standard choice-situation where different options are open to him. If an option is closed or made ineligible to him by the acts/omissions of a rational being who can be held responsible for the restriction, then the person interfered with is unfree (in that respect).

Benn and Weinstein undoubtedly managed to clear up many issues that their predecessors had left dark, but their account is not a very systematic one, nor is it illustrated with detailed examples. For a fuller version one may turn to the responsibility view formulated in David Miller's 1983 paper, 'Constraints on Freedom'. Miller's analysis is, I think, the most impressive which has been published so far, although, as we shall later see, it is not completely on target. Let us start by introducing the six examples he uses throughout the paper to illustrate his arguments

---

[19] At any rate, he held such a view of power, see S. I. Benn, 'Power', in P. Edwards (ed.), *The Encyclopedia of Philosophy* (London/New York: Macmillan, 1967), VI.

[20] Benn, 'Freedom, Autonomy and the Concept of a Person', p. 111.

and which are also taken up by Oppenheim in an interesting reply. One way of appreciating the difference between two kinds of obstacles – constraints and non-constraints – is to imagine situations involving the same obstacle, but differing in the details of its history. This particular series of thought experiments concerns an unfortunate person, *B*, who possesses a room with a door which can only be opened from the outside and who repeatedly becomes trapped in it; in most of the examples, *A*, a janitor in the same house, also plays a role.[21]

1. *B* is working in his room. *A*, knowing that *B* is inside and wishing to confine him, pushes the door shut.
2. *A* walks along the corridor and, without checking to see whether anybody is inside, closes the door.
3. The wind blows the door shut. It is *A*'s job to check the rooms at 7 p.m. each evening, but he is engaged on a private errand, and this evening he fails to do so.
4. The wind blows the door shut. At 6.30 p.m. *B* calls to a passer-by to unlock the door, but the passer-by, who knows about *A*'s duties, is busy and pays no attention.
5. *A* comes to *B*'s room and looks round it. *B* has concealed himself in a cupboard and *A* closes the door without having seen him.
6. The wind blows the door shut. There is no one assigned to check rooms, and no passer-by within earshot.

To be sure, all will agree that in case 1 *B* is rendered unfree to leave his room by the deliberate action of another human being, whereas in 6 the cause of the imprisonment is entirely natural and we would say that *B* is free but unable to leave. The intermediate cases are clearly more complex and bring out the pith of Miller's position. In 2 and 5 *A*'s action is the main cause of the confinement, but in Miller's analysis only 2 constitutes an infringement of freedom. There, *A* behaves in a negligent fashion. He ought to know, being a janitor, that shutting doors without checking first if anybody is behind them is likely to lead to disaster. In case 5, by contrast, *A* does everything that could

[21] These examples are slightly changed from D. Miller, 'Constraints on Freedom', *Ethics*, 94 (1983), 70–1.

reasonably be expected of a janitor. *B*'s imprisonment results from his own unforeseeable eccentric behaviour, notwithstanding the fact that *A*'s action is its direct cause. In both cases *A* is causally responsible for *B*'s confinement, but I think we have to agree with Miller that *B*'s claim that *A* had restricted his freedom would sound much less convincing in 5 than in 2. The reason for this could be that we are, in fact, not interested in *causal* responsibility when considering obstacles to freedom but *moral* responsibility. That would then also confirm the original insight gained at the end of chapter 1 where the story of the two runners was discussed.

Let us look, finally, at cases 3 and 4. Notwithstanding that in case 3 the main cause of *B*'s imprisonment is a natural event, a contributory cause is the janitor's omission, his failure to check the room at the appropriate time. Similarly, the failure of the passer-by to answer to the call is a contributory cause of *B*'s confinement in 4. Still, Miller sees a world of difference between the two cases. The janitor has an obligation to check rooms; the passer-by has no obligation to fulfil another man's duties, and can hardly be held responsible for the outcome. Hence, Miller concludes that whereas *B* has been rendered unfree to leave in case 3, in 4 he is free to leave although he cannot do so.

In sum, then, Miller's answer to the question of what causal history an obstacle to action must have in order for it to count as a constraint on freedom, and at the same time the upshot of his theory, is that the origin of the obstacle must be attributable to an agent who can be held morally accountable for its existence, i.e.:

$$(x) ((Ox \ \& \ Cx) \leftrightarrow (\exists y) \ (Ay \ \& \ Ryx)),$$

where $O = (1)$ is an obstacle, $C = (1)$ is a constraint on freedom, $A = (1)$ is an agent, and $R = (1)$ is responsible/accountable for (2).[22] This brings out the outstanding characteristic of a responsibility view of freedom.

As we have already seen, when *A* is morally accountable for *O*, he can be called upon to justify its existence and if he cannot do so, he is liable to being considered culpable for *O*. The

---

[22] For this formulation of Miller's theory, I am indebted to W. J. Norman, 'Obstacles and Constraints', unpublished seminar paper (London School of Economics, 1985), p. 3.

examples are supposed to show (and this is in part specific to Miller's version) that A can be called upon to justify the existence of O if and only if (a) he imposes O intentionally, having a prima facie obligation not to create it, (b) he imposes O negligently, having a prima facie obligation not to let it be created, or (c) fails to remove O despite having a prima facie obligation to do so. The inclusion of (b) and (c) may be somewhat unexpected at first sight, especially to those used to the liberal conception, but Miller's point is that they are necessary to enable us to capture some of the most subtle ways in which the omissions of one can contribute to the obstacles faced by others.

It is vital at this juncture to be quite clear on the difference (a) between a *moral* and a *moralised* account of freedom, and (b) between *moral* and *causal responsibility*. A moralised account (such as Nozick's) links constraints on freedom with moral wrongness or culpability; a moral account (such as Miller's) links them with moral responsibility. It must be re-emphasised that holding A morally responsible for a state of affairs is not saying that he is blameworthy: 'Responsibility . . . opens the door to questions of praise and blame without deciding them'.[23] Perhaps the janitor's errand in case 3 was of such vital significance that he cannot by any means be blamed for failing to do his professional duty; he could, for example, have been taking his critically ill wife to hospital. But that does not change the original conclusion about his being morally responsible for B's unfreedom. A failure to grasp this difference leads Oppenheim badly astray in his reply. He adduces as critical ammunition against Miller the story I used earlier: of the prison guard who locks up a justly convicted criminal in his cell. Oppenheim claims that in Miller's account the prisoner is free to leave in such a case since the guard is not morally responsible for his confinement.[24] This is, of course, misconstruing the very point of Miller's definition. The guard may well be morally responsible for the imprisonment, by locking the door of the cell, but this does not mean that he is blameworthy for it, that he is doing the *wrong* thing. Responsibility

[23] D. Miller, 'Reply to Oppenheim', *Ethics*, 95 (1985), 313.
[24] Oppenheim, '"Constraints on Freedom" as a Descriptive Concept', 305–6.

is not the same as culpability. Oppenheim's example, as we saw, is telling against a *moralised* definition, but not against a *moral* definition.

To illustrate more clearly the difference between *moral* and *causal* responsibility, the best we can do is to recount Oppenheim's analysis of Miller's examples, since he holds that any obstacle for which human agents are *causally* responsible should be counted as a constraint.[25] Oppenheim, who is a non-cognitivist, is working with an operationalist model of freedom (see sec. 7.1). To accept the moral dimension of what he takes to be a non-moral concept would be to wreck the point of his whole enterprise. The following schema summarises the conclusions Miller and Oppenheim reach on the six cases: (Who shut the door? J = Janitor, W = Wind. Constraint on freedom? Y = Yes, N = No.)

			Miller	Oppenheim
J	(1)	Deliberate wish to confine	Y	Y
J	(2)	Closes door without checking	Y	Y
W	(3)	Omission despite obligation	Y	N
W	(4)	Passer-by turns a deaf ear	N	N
J	(5)	*B* in the cupboard	N	Y
W	(6)	No janitor or passer-by	N	N

As seen from this schema, their difference of opinion leads to discrepancies in the interpretations of cases 3 and 5 (and, as can be imagined, the arguments behind the conclusions in the other examples are also different although the final verdicts happen to be the same). For Oppenheim, 5 is a relationship of unfreedom such as that between the guard and the prisoner. *A* is the cause of *B*'s imprisonment, and whether he is blameworthy, responsible or not is beside the point. In connection with case 3, Oppenheim claims that on Miller's account *B* will be counted unfree to leave with respect to everyone who does not unlock his door, including those unaware of his predicament – and that this account thereby shrinks the scope of mere inability (as opposed to lack of freedom) almost to vanishing point.[26] Thus, Oppenheim does

---

[25] Ibid., 306. [26] Ibid.

not take seriously Miller's contention that only those who are violating a (prima facie) obligation towards *B* render him unfree in this case.

As an operationalist, Oppenheim rejects all talk of 'moral concepts': concepts incorporating a moral dimension. It would take me too far afield here to try to wreck the point of such a general objection; that will be the aim of sections 7.2–7.3. However, a more subtle objection to Miller's treatment of freedom as a moral concept is conceivable, and should be mentioned at this point. Could it not be that, although such concepts exist, for instance *justice*, which arguably presupposes morality, freedom is not among them? Consider the following argument, with an honourable place in political philosophy: 'Suppose that we are in a totally amoral condition, the state of nature. In such a condition each person would find that others interfered with his liberty. Because these interferences would be serious, people would agree to construct a morality, demanding that basic liberties be respected.' Now, on Miller's view, this argument would be conceptually impossible to make; not just wrong but unintelligible. But such a claim is counter-intuitive in a significant way since it tells us that something which has long been accepted as meaningful is senseless.

Miller's response might be that the above argument would sound more convincing if we replaced 'liberty' with 'ability'. The argument would then claim that morality had been constructed to extend the scope of people's abilities: their powers to do various things, which were for various reasons restricted in the state of nature. I find this way of speaking less counter-intuitive, but I am not sure all readers will agree. At any rate, the viability of a responsibility view of freedom cannot in the end rest on such thin intuitions. To be sure, I would not have spent so much time explicating Miller's account if I did not think that its insights were more or less correct. His responsibility view overcomes many of the problems we have seen facing other accounts of negative liberty: the *corporeal-freedom* one, the *moralised* definition, and the *liberal* conception. Moreover, it is at least less at variance with common usage and intuitions than Oppenheim's theory, as shown by their respective answers above. A responsibility view has the additional advantage of enabling us to include under our concept of constraint certain features of modern society, notably economic inequalities, which are for various reasons excluded by other negative-liberty theories (sec. 4.4). However, even a detailed account such as Miller's leaves many questions unanswered, and some of the answers it gives may prove to be inadequate or wrong. Many such problems will be addressed in the following chapters, and it is not until after reading those that the reader should be expected to pass a final judgement on whether the general case made out for the moral dimension of freedom holds good.

Meanwhile, let me end this chapter with an observation which is often taken to be a cause of some embarrassment for negative theories in general, which would include responsibility views of freedom. The observation is that the language of constraint is wholly inappropriate for actions that a person is *forced* to perform. For instance, an election cannot be considered 'free' if people are forced to vote; yet they are not *constrained from* voting.

The conclusion of one of G. Cohen's favourite arguments is that 'one is in general free to do anything which one is forced to do'. The two premises which are supposed to support this conclusion are that (*i*) if one is unable to do something, one cannot be forced to do it, and (*ii*) if one is unfree to do something, one is unable to do it.[27] The conclusion follows from these premises, i.e., the argument is valid, but the second premise is wrong since we have seen that there is no necessary connection between inability and unfreedom. This will be further demonstrated in the next chapter when I discuss the 'impossibility view' of unfreedom. However, what is true is this: if a person is not constrained from doing *x*, he is free to do *x*; when he is forced to do *x*, he is not constrained from doing *x*; hence, he is free to do *x* when he is forced to do it. This argument is both valid and sound – but should it be of great concern to negative theorists?

Oppenheim obviously thinks so, and to solve the problem he

[27] Cohen, 'Illusions about Private Property and Freedom', p. 223.

draws one of his operationalist distinctions: between *being unfree* and *not free* to do something. A person is 'unfree' to do x if he is restrained from doing x; a person is 'not free' to do x if he is either unfree to do x or unfree to abstain from doing x. Hence, everybody who is unfree to do something is not free to do it, but not vice versa since Belgians are, for example, not unfree to vote – but they are not free with regard to voting as voting is mandatory in Belgium: they are *forced* to vote.[28]

I do not think this distinction is helpful; it has no foundation in our language and simply confuses the issue at hand. (The former may not worry the operationalist but the latter should.) What would a Belgian person say if we asked him the simple question 'Are you free to vote?' He might well say 'Yes', or even 'It's not only that I'm free to vote; I am forced to do it!' He would not answer 'No' unless he understood the question to mean something like 'Are you free with regard to voting?' or 'Do you vote freely?' which could be taken to imply both 'Are you free to vote?' and 'Are you free to abstain from voting?'

In general, discussions of this 'problem' seem to be making much ado about a trivial verbal point. Acknowledging that I am free to do x when I am forced to do it is not a *concession* for the negative theorist; he would simply add 'But then you are of course not free *not* to do x'. In other words, I am free under the description 'to do x' but unfree under the description 'not to do x'. What the objector is trying to cash in on is the fact that the freedom to do x is usually not of much *value* to us if we are not also free to abstain from x-ing. Moreover, it is true that in most cases when we ask if B is free to do x, what we are really interested in is whether he does x *freely* in the above sense, i.e., whether he is free with regard to x-ing under both the above descriptions. But clearly neither fact supports the claim that 'the language of constraint' has been shown to be inappropriate in a number of cases.

Here it should also be noticed that if B is forced to do x, he is no less unfree *not* to do x although his desire happens to coincide with the only course of action open to him, namely, to do x.

[28] F. Oppenheim, *Dimensions of Freedom: An Analysis* (New York: St. Martin's Press, 1961), p. 111.

Otherwise, the successfully manipulated slave would be the freest person in the world. In general, as Berlin has pointed out, there is no connection between freedom and desire; *B* does not become freer just by curtailing or changing his desires.[29] For whether or not an actual wish is violated in forcing *B* to do *x*, his range of possible options has still been abridged.

[29] Berlin, *Four Essays on Liberty*, p. xxxviii.

CHAPTER 3

Obstacles and their weight

In the preceding chapter, the problem of what is to count as a constraint on freedom in the negative model led to the conclusion that a necessary condition of a constraint is that an agent is morally responsible for its existence.[1] Thus, *a* responsibility view of freedom emerged as the most promising version of negative liberty. As yet, I hesitate to say *the* responsibility view, since we shall see in the sequel that the ideas expressed by different responsibility theorists sometimes conflict in important respects.

For any such view to be viable, many pressing questions about the nature of moral responsibility need to be answered. How far does it extend? How uncontroversial can it be? For the most part, these problems will be left to subsequent chapters. Here in chapter 3, I shall focus on a question that may not be as profound, but still demands an answer. Somebody might say: a definition of a constraint requires *two* necessary conditions of which you have furnished *one* – regarding its *nature*. But the remaining question is how *weighty* or serious must an obstacle be to count as a constraint? Might there not, for instance, be obstacles which satisfy the responsibility condition but are simply too small or trivial to count as constraints?

In order to pursue this point, I examine in 3.1 five accounts of the necessary *weight* of a constraint, none of which is deemed to be completely watertight. Of particular note will be their failure to accommodate the common-sense view that, whereas threats can restrict freedom, offers or requests cannot. Hence, some

---

[1] Hereafter, 'responsible' shall be taken to mean 'morally responsible', unless otherwise stated.

space is devoted in 3.2 to a discussion of the different kinds of proposals and to the notion of an *obstacle*, since that is found to hold the key to many of the problems posed. It will be argued that a number of writers, some of whom are responsibility theorists, have put the cart before the horse by trying to define a *constraint* on freedom without first giving due weight to the question: what is, more generally, to count as an *obstacle* to choice or action? Finally, in 3.3 my conclusions are used to show the inadequacy of some current views about the threat–offer distinction.

3.1. FIVE VIEWS ON WEIGHT

The first account I shall consider is (*a*) the *impossibility view*, according to which a constraint must be weighty enough to render the proposed action literally *impossible*. Thus, it is supposed to be illogical to say that a person was not free to do something which he in fact did. If prisoners manage to escape from jail by climbing down the drain-pipe, then they were free to escape, however great a risk they took in doing so, or however unlikely such a feat appeared beforehand. This view is usually advanced by thinkers who are stuck in the grooves of the behaviouristic model of negative liberty as corporeal freedom of movement (sec. 2.1), thinkers such as Hobbes, W. A. Parent, and H. Steiner, but they have found some unlikely allies, witness the Marxist G. Cohen (p. 35). No writer inclined to a responsibility account of freedom has, to the best of my knowledge, supplemented it by the 'impossibility view'. However, there would be no logical inconsistency involved in doing so, i.e., holding that the two necessary conditions of a constraint on freedom are that (*i*) an agent is responsible for it and (*ii*) it renders the proposed action impossible.

The main point in favour of the 'impossibility view' is its simplicity, a grace not easily matched in philosophical analysis, but its major drawback is that it sets ordinary language and intuitions utterly at naught. According to this view, threats do not constrain freedom, however severe the threatened sanction is, since it is 'possible' to turn a deaf ear to them if we are willing to sacrifice enough. But could we say (or imagine) that a man imprisoned in a ten-foot-square cage is unfree to leave (as he cannot possibly do so), whereas a man placed inside a square of the same size marked out on the ground, and told that moments after he steps out of it he will be shot, is free to leave his confinement?[2] The mere asking of this question should be enough to show the true state of the case. Surely, a man behind prison bars (although possibly able to escape) and a man who will be instantly killed if he performs some action, are both paradigmatic cases of unfreedom. The 'impossibility view' forfeits this fact – and that is too high a price to pay for simplicity. Perhaps we might, as Crocker has suggested, call the unfreedom under which B's being unfree to do x entails that B does not do x, a 'decisive unfreedom',[3] but the fact remains that other, less 'decisive', unfreedoms are in no way less real. Just as there are many circumstances in which we cannot do what we are free to do, so there are many in which we are unfree to do what we can do. Or are we really willing to hold that laws, for instance, do not restrict our freedom since it is generally 'possible' to violate them?[4]

   To rebut these objections, one of the things that an advocate of the 'impossibility view' must do is to produce arguments for the counter-intuitive claim that threats cannot constrain our freedom. Steiner does so in his paper 'Individual Liberty'. There, the point is that all types of 'interventions', as Steiner calls offers and threats collectively, affect the individual's practical deliberation in the same way: changing his desire to do x into a desire not to do x. But as desires are irrelevant to freedom, neither threats nor offers curtail liberty.[5] J. P. Day has challenged Steiner's argument, claiming that its first premise is wrong. For example, when a highwayman points a gun at a traveller and says to him 'Your money or your life', he does not change the traveller's desire, which is, both before and after the

---

[2] This example is taken from D. Miller, 'Constraints on Freedom', *Ethics*, 94 (1983), 76.
[3] L. Crocker, *Positive Liberty* (The Hague: Martinus Nijhoff Publisher, 1980), p. 27.
[4] Most laws are of this nature, though admittedly not all. For example, a law forbidding divorce in society S makes divorcing in that society impossible. Hence, such a law could count as a constraint on freedom in the 'impossibility view'.
[5] See H. Steiner, 'Individual Liberty', *Proceedings of the Aristotelian Society*, 75 (1974–5).

threat, to keep the money *and* his life. However, the threat makes him realise that he will not be able to do what he wants to, namely, to keep both.[6] Day's point about the desire is right, but he may be too concerned about satisfying Steiner's necessary condition, that one cannot do what one is unfree to do, and his own analysis of the highwayman case invites problems (p. 44).

I believe there is no need to concede as much to Steiner's insight as Day does. The reason why the highwayman's threat counts as a constraint is that it affects a possible choice: an option that was eligible for the traveller is not so any more. If Steiner insists that no option has been completely *closed*, on the grounds that the traveller could still say no, he is presupposing the 'impossibility view' which his argument was meant to support, and is thus begging the question. If, however, he claims I am begging the question against him by assuming that making an option ineligible is a constraint on freedom, the answer is that I am simply upholding the common-sense view that his argument above was meant – but failed – to undermine. This leaves us with little more than an articulation of Steiner's own belief that the 'impossibility view' must somehow be right. Now, Weber's dictum, that academic men feel as proprietary of their preferred vocabularies as of their toothbrushes, may be true. But claiming that a person cannot be considered unfree to act unless the action is rendered *impossible*, seems as unreasonable as employing a wire brush to clean one's teeth.

So much for the 'impossibility view'. Next we turn to a view that looks like a natural outgrowth of the objections to (*a*) and is, besides, invested with more importance for this study since it is the alternative suggested by Benn and Weinstein, and Connolly. Thus, in (*b*) the *ineligibility view*, a person is constrained when the proposed course of action is rendered impossible for him – or made *ineligible*, i.e., such that it would be inappropriate for the normal (reasonable, prudent) man to choose it. Nevertheless, a person might in certain contexts opt to perform the action; he could be a hero, saint, or martyr, but that does not change the fact that he is, for ordinary, practical purposes, rightly considered

---

[6] J. P. Day, 'Threats, Offers, Law, Opinion and Liberty', *American Philosophical Quarterly*, 14 (1977), 258.

unfree to do so.[7] This view handles pretty well the cases that left
(a) stranded: of the prisoners, the man in the 'imaginary' cage,
and the traveller. All of them could try to defy their constraints,
but none of them would, as normal adults, be expected even to
try to, let alone succeed in doing so; hence they are unfree.

The virtues of this view are striking; but so, unfortunately, are
its vices. One difficulty concerns ignorance. Suppose a terrorist
announces that he has chosen one particular citizen of New
York to be killed in revenge for some governmental intervention
abroad. John Smith happens to be this person, but as he does not
know it, this threat does not make it unreasonable for him to
walk the streets (where hundreds of people are mugged and
killed anyway); yet, surely it is a constraint on his freedom. It
does not help to say that Smith is here constrained in a sense that
differs from the ordinary; if A locks B in a room, B seems to be
(socially) unfree to leave in exactly the 'same sense' whether or
not he knows that the room is locked. The severity of this
objection can be lessened by the modification that an obstacle,
for which an agent is responsible, counts as a constraint if the
(normal) subject, *were* he to know of its existence, would find it
ineligible in consequence to perform certain actions.

Another problem is, however, that on the 'ineligibility view'
weak threats do not curtail freedom. I am not here thinking of silly
threats, such as 'If you don't buy me candy, I will tell the sun not
to shine on you', but real ones such as 'If you do x, I'll prick you
with a drawing pin.' If x is something that the subject really
cherishes, such a threat will hardly debar him from doing it. In
this sense, many laws constitute weak threats since experience
tells us that ignoring them is a live option for normal persons.[8]
The problem for the 'ineligibility view' is that it seems more
plausible to say in such cases that the intended threat or legal
sanction does not constitute a *serious* constraint on people's
freedom, than to say that it does not restrict their freedom at all.

[7] S. I. Benn, *A Theory of Freedom* (Cambridge University Press, 1988), pp. 146–8.
[8] I would not be understood here as claiming that all laws (and regulations, etc.) are
potentially freedom-constraining, by imposing weighty enough obstacles, for obviously
some laws are not backed by sanctions (that is, do not create obstacles) at all but rather
constitute offers (see sec. 3.2), e.g., by promising certain rewards to those reporting on
crime.

Moreover, some threats are of the nature that a normal person is not expected to find it eligible to comply with them, however strong the threatened sanction is. On Aristotle's view, for example, matricide should never be a live option for a normal person, not even for a person threatened with severe sufferings if he did not perform it.[9] But surely, such a threat would be a constraint on his liberty.

There is also a question concerning the invocation of the 'normal' or 'average person' criterion. If my enemy lights a fire in front of my door, am I still free to leave the house if the average person would find it 'eligible' to jump over the fire? What if I happen to be endowed with less-than-average physical ability – am I then unfree? The answer could either be 'No, you are free but unable to cross it' or 'Yes, since what matters is the normality of your reasoning, not the normality of your athletic ability.' But neither answer seems satisfactory for they both imply, counter-intuitively, that we need to know a great deal about the individual characteristics of person *B* before we can tell whether an obstacle, for which *A* is responsible, is a constraint on *B*'s freedom.

Finally, in taking the 'ineligibility view', Benn and Weinstein, who want to insist that in general threats, but not offers, restrict freedom, are forced to concede that certain offers do, namely, those which make it ineligible to reject them.[10] If I am offered such a high sum of money for my house that it would be absolutely unreasonable of me to decline, then that offer satisfies both the proposed criteria for a constraint: an agent (the bidder) is accountable for it, and resisting it is ineligible for me. Hence, I am unfree to say no. The question of 'irresistible offers' will be raised again in 3.2, but here it suffices to say that this and the other problems discussed above go some distance toward undermining the plausibility of the 'ineligibility view'.

[9] Aristotle, *Nicomachean Ethics* (translated by T. Irwin, Indianapolis: Hackett Publishing Co., 1985), p. 55 [1110a]. It is not always clear whether the considerations which are supposed to convince the normal person of the ineligibility of doing *x*, in the view under discussion here, can merely be of a prudential, or also of a moral, kind. In this latest counter-example I assume the latter.

[10] S. I. Benn and W. L. Weinstein, 'Being Free to Act, and Being a Free Man', *Mind*, 80 (1971), 202–3.

Day has proposed a third alternative: (*c*) the *conjunctive impossibility view*.[11] For him, (*b*) involves a paradox since it entails that a person can do a thing which he is unfree to do. In this, Day concurs with the presupposition of the 'impossibility view': a constraint on freedom must make a proposed action impossible. However, Day's point is that we should not look at any one simple action but at the complex (i.e., *conjunctive*) action which is, in the highwayman case, that of having *both* one's money and one's life. The highwayman makes that complex action impossible for the traveller; before the threat he could unconditionally have both, but after the threat he cannot. Thus, the traveller's freedom is constrained. Day claims that this view explains why threats, but not requests or offers, can restrict freedom; the latter do not make the recipient unable to do anything which he could unconditionally do beforehand. However, I am not sure that Day is right in this. If I propose to a girl, it is impossible for her conjunctively to avoid disappointing a suitor and to remain unmarried – which she could beforehand. Consequently, my proposal, ruling out a conjunctive action, will on Day's criterion count as a constraint on her freedom. Taken at face value, the 'conjunctive impossibility view' entails, as Miller notes, that any disadvantageous change in the environment curtails a person's freedom.[12] That is surely much too permissive. However, if we add to it a responsibility view of the *nature* of constraints, the similarity to Miller's own account ((*e*), below) becomes striking.

G. Dworkin and H. Frankfurt's so-called 'second-order preference theory', which has attracted wide attention in connection with the free-will controversy, could also be seen to provide a solution to the weight/efficacy problem. I shall call this solution (*d*) the *identification view*. In the context of a responsibility view of freedom, it could be spelled out as follows. Since an agent is responsible for any request, offer, or threat he makes, all may seem to restrict a recipient's freedom. However, what must be noticed in these cases is, as always, not only *A*'s responsibility, but also the attitude *B* takes toward the reasons for which he acts; whether or not he identifies himself with these

[11] Day, 'Threats, Offers, Law, Opinion and Liberty', 259.
[12] Miller, 'Constraints on Freedom', 77.

reasons – assimilates them to himself. A man asked by a relative for a loan might be glad to hand over some money to him, and is thus not unfree to refuse, whereas the victim of a highwayman does so grudgingly and with pain. He does not identify himself with the desire to hand over the money and, hence, does so unfreely.[13] Generally speaking, in this view, having an effect on B's choices only counts as freedom-constraining when there is disharmony between B's current 'first-order desire' to accept the effect and his more fundamental 'second-order desire' to evade it.

The problem about this solution is that it again invokes a reference to the subject's desires. Only if B feels that the effect A is having upon him is undesirable, is A constraining B's freedom. Furthermore, the 'identification view' (at least as formulated by Frankfurt) turns a blind eye to manipulation; the most serious, if most subtle, form of unfreedom which, as Rousseau put it, 'penetrates into a man's inmost being'.[14] If B's fundamental desires cohere with his current first-order desires, it does not matter how the former were originally acquired. Consequently, the successfully manipulated slave, who has been led to believe by his master that all the obstacles he faces are for his own good, is free. Later, the Dworkin/Frankfurt model will be re-examined in connection with questions about free will and autonomy (sec. 5.5), and there attention will be called to a correlative defect.

After having seen the various weaknesses of the views surveyed so far, we may start to wonder whether the notion of weight (seriousness, efficacy, significance, etc.) is really of any value in discussions of social freedom – or if it is simply a red herring. Here, the fifth and final view which I shall consider may come to our aid. Thus, (*e*) Miller's *irrelevance-of-size view* is not so much a new thesis as the claim that a separate account of the weight of an obstacle is superfluous. For Miller, the moral responsibility condition is not only a *necessary*, but also a *sufficient*, condition for constraints – we need look no further. The weight of an imposed obstacle turns out to be of no intrinsic importance; at most there will be a contingent connection, Miller says, between the

[13] G. Dworkin, 'Acting Freely', *Nous*, 4 (1970), 371–3.
[14] Cf. Day, 'Threats, Offers, Law, Opinion and Liberty', 263.

obstacle's 'size' and its counting as a constraint, based on the fact
that we are more likely to be responsible for not removing large
obstacles than small. But 'any obstacle, however small, may
potentially be regarded as a constraint on freedom'.[15]

Strangely enough, some of the things Oppenheim has to say
about obstacles to freedom accord well with Miller's 'irrelevance-
of-size view'. While adhering in general to a version of the
'impossibility view' (*B* is unfree to do *x* if *A prevents* him
beforehand from doing *x*), Oppenheim supplements it with a
punishability condition. Thus, *B* is also unfree to do *x* if *A* will
punish him afterwards if he does *x*. Even a small penalty
attached to an action restricts *B*'s freedom in this way; however
small it is does not matter. But, as always, Oppenheim carries
this view to its operationalist extreme by assigning a degree of
unfreedom to any given action in strict proportion to the actual
probability of a penalty being applied. Thus, he claims that if 40
per cent of all drivers who exceed the speed limit in a certain
state are fined, then drivers there are unfree to a degree of 0.4 to
speed.[16] This way of speaking would, generally, be most bizarre,
and even more so in the case of an action such as speeding which
is prohibited by law. As a matter of fact, if all obstacles were on a
par with legal prohibitions, the 'weight'-problem would hardly
have arisen, for it seems obvious that a law against doing *x* makes
us unfree to do *x*, however 'weak' the threatened sanction is, or
however unlikely it is that we will be caught.[17]

---

[15] Miller, 'Constraints on Freedom', p. 80. Miller may be thought to have changed his
position, for in his *Market, State, and Community* (Oxford University Press, 1989) he
emphasises that we 'surely do not want to say that any feature of a proposed course of
action that makes it less attractive to us thereby also makes us less free to undertake it'
(p. 39). However, although these words occur in the context of a discussion of the
necessary weight of obstacles, I take Miller here to be referring back to the
responsibility condition: that some 'small' obstacles are exempted from counting as
constraints on freedom, not because of their 'size' *as such*, but rather because no one
can possibly be held responsible for removing them (e.g., satisfying those craving for
champagne or caviar! (ibid., p. 42)).

[16] F. Oppenheim, *Political Concepts: A Reconstruction* (University of Chicago Press, 1981),
p. 72.

[17] However, superannuated laws or laws which have fallen into desuetude might
constitute an exception here. A forgotten, but still formally valid, law from the
nineteenth century, prohibiting kissing horses in public, with a maximum fine of 25
cents, on grounds of which no one has been prosecuted for 95 years, would scarcely
count as a constraint on our freedom to kiss horses.

Miller and Oppenheim seem to be right in that the tiniest obstacle can sometimes count as a constraint on freedom, but the latter is wrong in claiming that in such cases, we do not consider ourselves constrained, period, but constrained to a degree of 0.1, 0.4, etc., according to the above criteria. The correct view here is clear and in accordance with common usage: if there are no constraints upon my performing x, I am free to do x, and then my *freedom* to do x cannot be increased, although I might be made more *able* to do it. On the other hand, if I am constrained, I am not free to do x, however 'small' the constraint is. The cases examined earlier when dealing with the 'ineligibility view' should have convinced us of this fact; even a weak threat can restrict freedom, and a fire lit by an enemy in front of my door to prevent me from stepping outside is a restriction of my freedom, however likely or unlikely, reasonable or unreasonable it is that I shall cross it. Also, if there is a ban on speeding in two states, X and Y, then I am not free to speed in either, however likely or unlikely it is that this regulation will be enforced and however reasonable or unreasonable it is for me to ignore it. To be sure, someone might be inclined to say, knowing the efficiency of the police in state X, that he is 'less free' to speed there than in state Y, but, if pressed, what he would probably want to say is that while he is not free to speed in either X or Y, the constraints are more effective (and the regulation thus a better deterrent) in X than in Y.

A possible cause of confusion on what it means to be constrained (not free) is the technical word 'unfree' which is, notably, never used in ordinary language, and in this book only intermittently as short for 'not free'. Once philosophers start invoking this term, people get the impression that 'being unfree' must be something much more serious than 'not being free', and thus a crucial question is begged in favour of the 'impossibility' or 'ineligibility views'.

Before finishing the discussion of the 'irrelevance-of-size view', let us look at two more possible objections to it. Charles Taylor tries to cash in on the fact that some goals are seen as highly significant for human behaviour while others are considered less so. Thus, Taylor claims there is a world of difference between the authority's decision (*a*) to put up new traffic-lights at an intersection close to my home, and (*b*) to forbid me to worship according to the form I believe in. Whereas the latter would be a serious blow to my liberty, the former is so trivial that it could not be called a restriction of freedom, at least not in a 'serious political debate'.[18] It has already been pointed out that the desires people happen to have are not crucial to ascriptions of unfreedom; for instance, even if I am an atheist, a ban on a form of worship would still restrict my liberty. So what Taylor must show in the case of the traffic-lights is something much more radical, namely, that altering our rhythm of movement through the city is such an insignificant obstacle that no one could possibly be concerned about the installation of new traffic-lights in his neighbourhood – that no one could possibly consider that a constraint on his freedom. This is, however, much too strong a claim to make, since most of us know people who would be more upset with a one-minute delay at an intersection on their way to work than at a ban on some (outlandish) type of worship. There is simply nothing in the nature of a restriction imposed by traffic-lights which can exclude it from reckoning as a possible constraint on freedom. But could not Taylor's general thesis about significance hold good although his particular example fails? I have yet to be convinced that it does, unless it is simply taken to mean that some restrictions are too insignificant to count as *serious* limitations of freedom – a point that is true but trivial.

Benn and Weinstein pursue a somewhat more palpable line of reasoning about the non-triviality of alleged constraints by introducing a second eligibility clause into their theory. They claim that while we can say that a person is free or unfree to do something without his having an actual interest in doing so, it is only apposite to use these terms if the proposed action is 'a possible object of reasonable choice', i.e., if it is possible to see some point in performing it. The presumption against impairing choices does not arise unless such a point can be discerned. For instance, we are told that a man's *wanting* to torture his cat is not

---

[18] C. Taylor, 'What's Wrong with Negative Liberty', in A. Ryan (ed.), *The Idea of Freedom: Essays in Honour of Isaiah Berlin* (Oxford University Press, 1979), p. 182.

a reason for letting him do it; nor is cutting off one's ears a suitable object of choice in this sense.[19]

Now, as we shall see later (sec. 5.5), there is a sense in which a person must be 'autarchic' for us to hold him freedom-evaluable in the first place. It may be that animal molesters or 'Van Goghs' are often insane and, hence, not autarchic. However, it is apparently not this specific point about insanity that Benn and Weinstein are making, but a more general one, along Anscombean lines, about the concept of wanting. For us to call an obstacle to a possible choice a constraint on freedom, the choice must relate to something *wantable*. As Anscombe puts it, 'to say "I *merely* want this" without any characterisation is to deprive the word of sense'. But, as she notes, almost anything can count as 'wantable', given the appropriate context, even 'a saucer of mud'.[20] In the examples above, the torture of the cat might be part of a performance in the Museum of Modern Art and the man cutting off his ear part of a religious ritual; then there would be a *point* in performing these actions. A natural first step to find out if such a point exists is to ask the person to give us a reason why he should want x (x being prohibited). However, that procedure has a flaw for, as Benn rightly says, the burden of justification lies with the person interfering, not the one interfered with: 'unless Ian can supply some reason why Alf should be stopped, Alf is free to go ahead. He doesn't have to have a reason.'[21] So, on the one hand, Alf does not need to have a reason for doing x before we can call obstacles to x constraints; on the other hand it is 'incongruous to talk of unfreedom to do things that there could be no point in doing' – and wanting to do them is not enough.[22] There is no logical contradiction here, but the two claims are *practically* at such odds with one another as to deprive this second eligibility condition of any importance in locating constraints.[23]

[19] Benn and Weinstein, 'Being Free to Act, and Being a Free Man', 195; S. I. Benn, 'Freedom, Autonomy and the Concept of a Person', *Proceedings of the Aristotelian Society*, 76 (1975-6), p. 109.

[20] G. E. M. Anscombe, *Intention* (Oxford: Basil Blackwell, 1976), p. 71.

[21] Benn, 'Freedom, Autonomy and the Concept of a Person', p. 109.

[22] Benn, *A Theory of Freedom*, p. 128.

[23] See also criticisms of this 'rationalist' condition in C. Swanton, *Freedom: A Coherence Theory* (Indianapolis: Hackett Publishing Co., 1992), pp. 50ff.

None of the objections considered so far poses a serious threat to the 'irrelevance-of-size view'. Moreover, it seems to be the natural standpoint for those who favour a responsibility view of freedom. Thus, responsibility and weight are on a par in that both are all-or-nothing affairs. For the responsibility condition to be satisfied, it is enough to establish that an agent bears some degree of responsibility for the obstacle's existence,[24] and for the weight condition to be satisfied, it is enough to establish that an obstacle has been created by A, irrespective of its 'size' – although it does not follow that A is responsible for the existence of an obstacle, however small, simply in virtue of his having created it.

To conclude this section, a word might be said for the fascination that the 'ineligibility view' holds for a number of responsibility theorists. Perhaps the reason lies in a conflation of the ideas of *constraint* and *coercion*. While some writers (such as Berlin) use them interchangeably, the latter concept is more at home in *legal* contexts where it has a specific function to perform. That function is to exculpate a person from moral *blame* and, consequently, from legal sanctions. The rapidly growing mountain of literature on moral and legal coercion cannot be dug into here.[25] Let it suffice to say that a man claiming to have signed a document under *duress*, because he had been threatened with a pinprick, would be laughed out of court,[26] and that another man, extenuating his decision not to save a drowning child in a pond outside his office, because he had been warned by his employer not to leave his desk, would not get a very positive response there either. This does not mean that a threatened pinprick or a strict order from your boss cannot constitute constraints on your freedom (in both these cases they do), but it means that neither of them will count as coercive.

Coercion is best understood as a subclass of constraints on freedom, and a brief glance at traditional legal procedures indicates that the criterion most commonly used in picking out instances of coercion is none other than the 'ineligibility view'.

---

[24] See Miller, 'Constraints on Freedom', 75 (footnote 15).
[25] See, e.g., A. Wertheimer, *Coercion* (Princeton University Press, 1987).
[26] Benn, *A Theory of Freedom*, p. 142.

In general, a suspect can successfully defend his case if he can prove that the constraint on his freedom was of such grave a nature that it coerced him, i.e., made any other course of action ineligible for him as a reasonable, normal person. If, however, the constraint (such as the pinprick) is not deemed coercive, the fountain of pity soon dries up. Stressing the importance of the 'ineligibility view' in such contexts is fine, but, precisely because of its use there, it is inadequate as an account of the much wider notion of a constraint on freedom.

3.2. THREATS, OFFERS, AND OBSTACLES

The discussion in the preceding section seemed to indicate that the basic insight of Miller's 'irrelevance-of-size view' is right: *A*'s moral responsibility for an obstacle to *B*'s action is a *sufficient*, as well as a *necessary*, condition for the obstacle's counting as a constraint on *B*'s freedom. However, there is one problem with Miller's position which we need to consider. Does it not yield a definition of a constraint on freedom that is too permissive? I began this chapter by noting that many such definitions violate common sense by implying that offers and requests can restrict freedom. Unfortunately, Miller's view can easily be seen to carry this same implication. A bidder is surely in general responsible for his offers to me; sometimes his offer (or request) may affect me adversely, by presenting me with a difficult choice, one which I find it hard to refuse, etc. So, it seems to follow that offers and requests can restrict my freedom – along with almost any disadvantageous effect on me for which another person is responsible. It is true that sometimes our intuitions or common-sense views may have to be discarded if good reasons are found for their inadequacy. Here I shall argue, however, that this is not the case; there is no ground for abandoning our common-sense view that offers (as opposed to threats) are not freedom-restricting.

The resolution of this issue may lie in the notion of an *obstacle*, one which is conceptually prior to that of a constraint: for something to count as a constraint, it must first be an obstacle. The 'impossibility' and 'ineligibility' views disagree among

themselves as to how serious an obstacle must be in order for it to count as a constraint – without, however, defining 'obstacle'. Miller rightly dismisses the weight question as irrelevant *per se* to the definit
other philosophers, pay careful attention to the notion of an obstacle. I believe that by attending to this notion the 'irrelevance-of-size view' can be made even more plausible than it is in Miller's formulation.

My aim here is not to give some new, fancy definition of 'obstacle' which narrows its ordinary meaning. Anything which impairs our possibility to choose or do *x* rightly counts as an obstacle, whether it is a natural or a man-made impediment. Even not being sent to the moon or not being able to fly like a bird can constitute obstacles to our choices. The class of obstacles is thus very broad, much broader than that of constraints on freedom (for which agents must be accountable).[27] But not everything which *affects* someone is an obstacle; obstacles must impair, must narrow down possibilities or close options. Can offers do this? The simple answer is no, for the very nature of offers is to open new possibilities and extend the range of options, not to narrow this range. Typically, an offer is a proposal of the form 'If you do *x*, I'll let *y* happen to you' where *y* is something which creates a new option for us (which we can choose or refrain from choosing) or makes an old one more eligible. Similarly, a request does not as such close any options. Thus, in the case of real offers or requests, the question whether someone is responsible for them, in connection with talk of a possible constraint, need never so much as arise since they do not present obstacles to our actions in the first place.

This is not to say that offers and requests do not sometimes carry implications which make life more difficult for the recipient. But that does not have to mean that they constitute, *qua* offers, obstacles to his choices or actions. To begin with a parallel example, I may hand you a written exposition of my

---

[27] Thus, W. J. Norman ('Taking "Free Action" Too Seriously', *Ethics*, 101 (1991)) is right in pointing out the non-moral, naturalistic nature of 'obstacle'. Advocates of different conceptions of unfreedom can use this concept uncontroversially without ceding any ground to their opponents (p. 512, footnote 14).

theory of freedom. You read it and say 'I hate this!' I ask 'Why?' You answer 'Because there are so many typing errors in it!' If that is your answer, I may be relieved to find out that what you hate is not my exposition *qua* theory of freedom but *qua* paper with too many typos. At most, we could say that my theory of freedom carries implications or has side-effects which you hate, although even that would not be fully accurate.

As will be further explained in chapter 7, to understand the nature of concepts, we must consider the point or rationale for inventing them and then for employing them in one way rather than another. The 'same' exposition can be described in various ways, brought under various concepts, depending on our purpose in the given case: on the point of view from which we look at it. The crucial question to ask in each case will be what our purpose is in collocating certain aspects and qualities and drawing attention to features of a certain sort. Likewise, in describing something as an 'offer', we collocate certain elements in order to draw attention to a particular fact: the fact that an option has been opened or made more eligible. This 'something' could be described from a different point of view as erecting an obstacle – but not *qua* offer. Whether an obstacle has been erected or not is thus relative to our descriptions. Let us clarify this point by looking at examples.

Suppose *A* writes a letter of proposal to a woman, *B*. Now, *B* might not appreciate receiving this proposal. First, she might not want to receive letters at all. If *A* knows of this idiosyncrasy and sends the letter to annoy her, he is constraining her freedom in a certain respect; but the obstacle he creates does not lie in his letter *qua* request but *qua* nuisance to *B*. More specifically, it does not lie in *the proposal* that he makes but in *his making* the proposal. Similarly, *A* might know that *B* is allergic to the kind of ink he chooses to use in the letter, but here again it is not the proposal as such which narrows her options (on the contrary, *as such* it increases them) but rather the ink with which it is written.

It should also be noticed that in certain cases a *reward offered* may, although the *offer* itself does not, constitute a constraint on freedom. We can imagine an advertisement: 'Relive the past, spend a day in the castle prison, chained to a wall.' If we care to be constrained in this way, just for the experience, we will accept the offer, but that does not mean that the offer itself imposes any constraint. On the contrary, it extends our scope of options instead of creating an obstacle to them. This shows that advertisements cannot be said to curtail freedom merely on the ground that what is advertised is potentially harmful (drugs, etc.). Also, it should be clear why silly threats, such as 'If you don't buy me candy, I'll tell the sun not to shine on you', do not restrict freedom. For though the person making them may be responsible for doing so, they do not constitute real obstacles. In this, *silly* threats are distinguishable from *weak* threats (sec. 3.1) which are potentially freedom-restricting since they create real obstacles, although these may not be considered very serious.

Since Miller does not have a clear notion of an obstacle to work with, my counter-example to Day's 'conjunctive impossibility view' (of the girl who received a marriage proposal) would evidently also cut against his 'irrelevance-of-size view'. Given that the responsibility condition is satisfied, Miller would have to construe this proposal as a constraint on the girl's freedom, for she might possibly neither want to get married nor to disappoint a suitor. This is why his 'irrelevance-of-size view' is liable to produce counter-intuitive results. My amendment, as explained above, is to say that the proposal is not *qua* request a constraint on B's freedom, for a request cannot *ex hypothesi* create an obstacle, but of course it could be such a constraint *qua* nuisance to the girl – or *qua* something else.

Probably not everyone will be convinced that the argumentation so far is sufficient to show that offers cannot constrain freedom. Let us look at two contentions which go against my view. In the first place, many philosophers insist that there are *irresistible offers* which can curtail our freedom. Thus, Benn claims that a special feature of character or situation can, in some cases, make declining an offer a course of action that we would not expect a reasonable man to take. Hence, the person has a good reason to say 'I cannot refuse' or 'I have no option but to accept.'[28] What Benn may have in mind is a case such as

---

[28] Benn, *A Theory of Freedom*, p. 138.

the following. Suppose an American billionaire offers me a million dollars if I run stark naked down High Street during the rush hour. (Running naked in public is not a thing that appeals more to me than to most people.) In this case, I would have to do a thing that is highly distasteful to me to receive my reward. I might have to ponder a lot in order to reach a decision – which would probably be to run. As I might explain, the prospect of receiving this enormous sum of money, even if accompanied by some embarrassment, would simply be 'irresistible' to me. In the second place, there are philosophers who insist that some offers not only constrain our freedom, but do so in the strong sense of *coercing* us to accept. Feinberg takes an example of a woman who is badly off financially. She receives an offer from her employer to pay for expensive surgery that alone can save her child – if she becomes his mistress for a period. This case satisfies Feinberg's criteria for a *coercive offer*: it offers a prospect that is not simply much preferred but one which is an exclusive alternative to an intolerable evil.[29]

Perhaps, though, 'irresistible' offers are merely those which are so good that it would be stupid to reject them. If I am offered twice the market price for my rusty, old car, I would probably be a fool to refuse. This reading of 'irresistible' is quite innocuous and does not entail any constraint on freedom. It seems adequate to the case of the naked runner above: the billionaire's offer is simply *too good* to refuse for most people. But if I happen to value my dignity more than the normal person would, I can simply reject the offer, and my freedom has not been constrained. We would hardly say, however, that the employer's offer is too 'good' for the woman to refuse; on the contrary, we would consider it a *terrible* offer, but still one which she somehow seems forced to accept. To deepen our understanding of these cases, some conceptual clarifications are called for.

Let us distinguish between two kinds of proposals: (*a*) 'If you do *x*, I'll let *y* happen to you' and (*b*) 'If and only if you do *x*, will I let *y* happen to you'. I shall call the former *tentative proposals* and the latter *final proposals*. These are not the only possible kinds of

[29] J. Feinberg, *The Moral Limits of the Criminal Law*, III: Harm to Self (New York: Oxford University Press, 1986), pp. 229–33.

proposal, but for our present purposes this distinction will suffice.

Tentative proposals, which do not create obstacles to our choices, are offers. The reason why they do not impair any choice is partly a logical one: 'If you fetch the paper for me, you'll get a candy' does not entail 'If you don't fetch the paper, you won't get a candy', for the person might get the candy whether or not he fetches the paper, for instance, by doing something else. Further, this tentative proposal does not exclude the possibility of the person fetching the paper but declining the reward, i.e., it does not imply that if he fetches the paper, he cannot fail to get a candy whether he wants it or not. What the proposal really means is that *if* he wants a candy, he will get one if he runs this errand for the bidder. A tentative proposal of this sort is a pure offer, for it obviously closes no option.[30] Perhaps it does not propose to remove some obstacle which the recipient would like to have removed, or it proposes to remove such an obstacle in the wrong way – or maybe to an extent not deemed sufficient by the recipient. But being offered half a loaf cannot be more restrictive than being offered no bread at all, since a tentative proposal does not exclude the possibility that the recipient will get the whole loaf anyway.

Someone might object, however, that such tentative proposals are virtually non-existent: 'If you fetch the paper, you'll get a candy' always implies (conversationally, not logically): 'Unless you fetch the paper, you won't get a candy.' Thus, the objector might say, even if a shopkeeper tells you that you can get a particular thing *if* you pay a specific amount for it, what he really means is that you will get it *if and only if* you pay this amount. Hence, the so-called tentative proposals are of no real importance in daily life. It is true that final proposals are often formulated as tentative ones, but it is not true that the latter play

---

[30] Of course there are proposals with the same grammatical form as 'If you fetch the paper for me, you'll get a candy' that *do* close options and no one will mistake for offers, e.g., 'If you lift a finger, I'll shoot you'. Why the former conversationally imply the condition 'if you want', but not the latter, is an interesting question that cannot be pursued here. J. P. Day ('On Häyry and Airaksinen's "Hard and Soft Offers as Constraints"', *Philosophia* (Israel), 20 (1990)) suggests a plausible answer to it, emphasising the speech-agent's *intentions*. My aim in the sequel, however, is merely to examine the difference between proposals of the former kind and 'if and only if'-proposals.

no part in our daily lives. Tentative proposals are, for instance, used in common bargaining situations, especially in trade. As a matter of fact, in some parts of the world most business proposals are of the tentative kind; even if you see a price-tag on an item you would like to buy, it does not mean that you will not get it for anything less than the price offered there. On the contrary, it is still up to you to bargain with the seller for the final price to be paid for the item.[31]

As noted above, tentative proposals which do not close any options constitute offers. Plainly, these cannot constrain anyone's freedom. Let us now turn to the second kind. *Final proposals* have the form 'If and only if you do x, will I let y happen to you': 'I'll give you a candy if and only if you fetch the paper'. This obviously entails that the person will not get a candy from the bidder unless he fetches the paper. Final proposals combine an offer and a threat; they are what we may call 'throffers'. The 'if'-part of the proposal signifies the offer, the 'only-if'-part the threat. The latter creates an obstacle by precluding the possibility that the person will get a candy without fetching the paper. However, the question still remains whether the threat (that is, the obstacle created by the threat) is a constraint on freedom. To find that out we must, according to a responsibility view of freedom, ask if the bidder can be held morally responsible for the obstacle – if, for example, he can be held responsible for not giving the person a candy without his fetching the paper first.

The task of deciding whether a proposal constitutes a constraint on freedom thus involves *two* separate steps. First, we must distinguish between proposals that create obstacles (threats) and those which do not (offers, requests, etc.). Then we must apply a test of moral responsibility to the former to decide whether the obstacle imposed is a constraint on freedom. We already have some idea from chapter 2 what such a test involves, and a fuller description of it awaits us in chapter 4. However, we

---

[31] However, of course, even the most flexible business offers usually have a limit: you will not get the item *gratis*. In that sense, it could be said that offers in trade are tentative only up to a point. There is nothing murky about this: the property rights of others certainly do erect obstacles to our choices. However, it does not follow that they necessarily limit our freedom (see below).

do know that for a threat to fail the test of a constraint on freedom it is not enough that it be *weak*; it must be such that an agent cannot be held morally responsible for the threatened sanction *qua* obstacle to our choices.

Let us now apply this two-step analysis to the cases of the billionaire's and the employer's proposals. The first question to be asked is whether they were meant as tentative or final proposals. If the former was the case, both were offers and thus not even possible candidates for constraints on freedom. However, let us assume that they were both *final* proposals, i.e., that I had been promised the money if and only if I ran naked, and the child would be saved by the employer if and only if its mother became his mistress. In that case, both proposals are 'throffers', creating obstacles *qua* threats (through the 'only-if'-parts). Given this, the next question to ask is whether the billionaire could be held responsible for not supplying me with a million dollars in case I do not run, and the employer for not helping the child without the sacrifice by its mother. Here, the difference between the two cases becomes apparent. We hardly need to wait for a detailed test of moral responsibility to assert that whereas the billionaire cannot be morally responsible for my failing to earn a million dollars in this way, the employer can be held responsible for refusing to help the child unless its mother sleeps with him. So, Feinberg does not succeed in undermining the view that offers cannot constrain freedom. His *coercive offers* are not pure offers but 'throffers' which can easily constrain (and even coerce) *qua* threats.

3.3. IMPLICATIONS FOR SOME VIEWS ABOUT THREATS AND OFFERS

A great deal has been written in recent years about the threat–offer distinction. The discussion above can be used to expose some perennial misunderstandings.

One assumption often made is that a person faced with an offer will not be worse off than he was before whether he decides to accept or decline, whereas in the case of a threat, whatever he decides will bring about consequences that leave him worse off than he would otherwise have been. Here 'worse off' is taken to mean worse off relative to a *baseline* involving the present situation and the expected future course of events. Lately, the exact nature of this baseline has become an embattled issue, for instance in the writings of Nozick, Wertheimer, and Feinberg. Philosophers tend to provide grist for their mills by concocting fanciful stories. I shall start the discussion by recounting some cases contrived by Nozick and Wertheimer, a number of which are also discussed by Feinberg.

> *Drug Case I. A* is *B*'s normal supplier of drugs. Today, however, when *B* comes to *A*, *A* says that he will not sell drugs to him, as he normally does, for $20, but will rather give them to *B* iff *B* beats up a certain person.
> *Drug Case II. A* is a stranger who knows that *B* is a drug addict. Both know that *B*'s usual supplier of drugs has been arrested and that *A* had nothing to do with the arrest. *A* approaches *B* and says that he will give him drugs iff *B* beats up a certain person.
> *Drowning Case. A* who is sailing in his boat comes upon *B* who is drowning. *A* proposes to rescue him iff *B* agrees to pay $10,000. Both know that there are no other potential rescuers around.
> *Slave Case. A* beats *B*, his slave, each morning for reasons unconnected with *B*'s behaviour. *A* now proposes not to beat *B* the next morning iff *B* does *x*.

The crux of the current debate is whether the baseline is a *statistical* or a *moralised* one, i.e., whether the 'expected' course of events is the *predicted* or the *morally required* course. Those, like Feinberg, who favour a statistical test see the normal course in the *Drug Case I* as one in which *A* continues to supply *B* with drugs for money; hence his proposal there is a threat. In *II*, however, *A*'s proposal comes unexpectedly upon *B* and is an offer – whether *B* cares to accept it or not. In the *Drowning Case* there is some controversy about how the statistical test should be interpreted. Nozick sees the expected course of events as one in which *B* drowns and *A*'s intervention is an offer. Feinberg thinks this analysis is mistaken; the statistical test should not be applied to what B might have expected had A not appeared on the scene, but to what generally happens when a drowning swimmer encounters a boat whose occupants have the ability to rescue him. In such a case, the swimmer has an 'epistemic right' to rescue, irrespective of all moral claims.[32] Finally, the predictable course in the *Slave Case* is one in which the slaveholder continues to beat B up; hence the new suggestion is an offer.

Wertheimer is a notable advocate of a moralised test for distinguishing between threats and offers. For him, neither *Drug Case I* nor *II* involves a threat, since A is not morally required to supply drugs at all. However, both the other cases do: A is morally required to save B in the *Drowning Case*, and beating up your slave (or perhaps slavery in general) is morally prohibited.[33]

I am not the only one to find the result of the statistical test bizarre in the *Slave Case* and that of the moralised test equally so in the *Drug Case I*. Nozick has suggested a combined test which mends matters here: if the two tests yield conflicting results, the one to be used is that which the recipient of the proposal prefers.[34] Thus, the *Slave Case* involves a threat because the slave presumably prefers the result of the moralised test, and in the *Drug Case I* we also have a threat, given the fact that the addict would opt for the statistically predicted course there.

Notice that all the writers seem to overlook the possibility of what I have called *tentative* proposals (pure offers). All the cases above are of the 'if and only if'-kind ('iff'), i.e., they all constitute *final* proposals or 'throffers'. The swimmer will be saved *iff* he pays $10,000, etc. Then the question is asked whether these 'throffers' are to be understood as threats or offers, when it is obvious from my analysis that they are to be understood as both at the same time. The writers mentioned above disagree on whether the test to decide if the proposals are threats or offers should be a statistical, moralised, or a combined one. In reality, what such a test might do is to decide which of the threats constitute constraints on freedom. In other words, when these

[32] Feinberg, *The Moral Limits of the Criminal Law*, III: Harm to Self, pp. 220–6.
[33] Wertheimer, *Coercion*, pp. 208–9.
[34] R. Nozick, 'Coercion', in P. Laslett, W. G. Runciman, and Q. Skinner (eds.), *Philosophy, Politics and Society*, IV (Oxford: Basil Blackwell, 1972), pp. 112–16.

writers think they are answering the question which of the proposals are threats and which are offers, they are really trying to ascertain when the threat-part of a 'throffer' is a constraint on freedom. From my point of view, they conflate the *two tasks* of distinguishing (*a*) between obstacles (threats) and non-obstacles (offers), and (*b*) between those obstacles/threats which are, and those which are not, freedom-restricting. Even if the word 'threat' is reserved for those proposals which constrain freedom, their tests would be mistaken, for then a proposal such as 'I won't give you a million dollars unless you run naked down High Street' would fail the test of a threat – but surely it is not an offer!

In my analysis, owing to the 'only-if'-part of the proposals, the drug addict is being threatened in both *Drug Cases I* and *II* with not getting what he wants, the swimmer in the *Drowning Case* with not being rescued unless he pays the set amount, the slave in the *Slave Case* with not being treated more humanely unless he does *x*, etc. It seems strange how anyone could mistake this part of the proposals for an offer. However, I have claimed that in accordance with a responsibility view of freedom, a test of moral responsibility is required to decide whether the threatened sanctions constitute an encroachment of freedom. Can the dope peddlers be held morally responsible for not supplying the addict with drugs, the sailor for not rescuing the swimmer, the slaveholder for continuing to beat up his slave, etc.? Now, could one of the three tests discussed above, even if they are inadequate for deciding whether or not something is an *obstacle*, help us with the second step, namely, that of deciding whether an agent is responsible for the creation/non-removal of the obstacle, and thus whether it constitutes a *constraint* on freedom? Unfortunately not.

The *moralised* test employs the notions of moral requirement and moral prohibition. However, that for which we can hold our fellow-men morally responsible is surely more extensive than that which they are, strictly speaking, morally required to do. To return to the *Drug Case I*, it seems clear that a correct test of moral responsibility would ascribe responsibility to the dope peddler for failing to supply *B* with drugs, although he does not have a moral *duty* to do so. In general, previous arguments against a moralised test apply here (sec. 2.1).

The *statistical* test is hardly more plausible. It seems plain that the slaveholder can be held responsible for his threat to the slave although he might be 'statistically expected' to continue beating him up. Also, it is hard to see what kind of an 'epistemic right' the swimmer would have to expect rescue on Feinberg's test if it so happened that in the area in which he finds himself, sailors were not in the habit of rescuing drowning strangers. It should already be clear that whatever the exact boundaries of moral responsibility are, they do not coincide with that which we can statistically expect people to do at a given time in a given society.

In effect, Nozick himself produces a telling counter-example to his *combined* test as a possible test of unfreedom.[35] A person tells me that he will not turn the information he has about my crime over to the police if and only if I pay him $10,000. The morally required thing is to turn the information over, and we can suppose that the story is set in a context where this would be the statistically expected course, as well. However, I think we would be inclined to say that the man is threatening me *and* constraining my freedom (to escape punishment).

In short, the three tests suggested by Feinberg, Wertheimer, and Nozick fail both as tests to distinguish between threats and offers and as tests to distinguish freedom-restricting from non-freedom-restricting threats. For the latter purpose, I have claimed that a precise test of moral responsibility is needed.

In this chapter I have been arguing that the moral concept of a constraint, based on responsibility, presupposes a non-moral concept of an obstacle, of which constraints are a subclass. This insight first helped us to see the controversy about the necessary 'weight' of an obstacle in a better perspective, and later also enabled us to discern certain shortcomings in the literature about threats and offers. It is now time to turn to more fundamental questions about the concept of moral responsibility.

[35] Ibid., p. 118.

CHAPTER 4

The test of moral responsibility

In chapter 2 I threw in my support for a responsibility view of negative freedom, possibly creating the impression that previous advocates of it had left little in this department for others to do. By contrast, much of chapter 3 was taken up by direct or indirect criticisms of their views: Benn and Weinstein's 'ineligibility view' of the necessary weight of obstacles was rejected, and, although Miller's analysis was deemed more acceptable, it also was found wanting in its appreciation of the concept of an obstacle. The present chapter will critically examine the accounts of *moral responsibility*, given by these same writers, for that notion is obviously the cornerstone of any responsibility view of freedom.

To recap, a *responsibility view* of freedom is the view according to which an obstacle counts as a constraint on an agent's freedom if and only if there is another agent who can be held *morally* responsible for the existence of the obstacle. The latter agent may be responsible because he imposed the obstacle himself (deliberately or negligently), refrained from preventing its imposition by someone else, or failed to remove the obstacle after it had been created. (To avoid unnecessary repetition, I have coined the term 'to suppress an obstacle' for use in the sequel. Saying that an agent *A suppresses* an obstacle *O* shall be taken to mean that he refrains from imposing *O*, or prevents its imposition by others, or removes *O* if it has already been imposed.)

In 4.1 the perils of overly narrow and overly broad definitions of responsibility become apparent, and among the proposals which do not stand up to scrutiny is Benn and Weinstein's 'standard choice-situation model'. In 4.2 I examine the link drawn by Miller between responsibility and obligation; this, in the end, gives rise to a strange apostasy from his earlier insights. I attempt to show why and where his analysis goes awry. As a result, a revised definition of moral responsibility, applicable to cases of unfreedom, is proposed in 4.3 and defended against charges of relativity. My conclusions are then used in 4.4 to answer the question of under what circumstances poverty can be seen as a constraint upon freedom. Finally, in 4.5 some attention is given to the problem of attributing moral responsibility to collectivities. After reading chapters 3 and 4, a sceptic might ask whether the quest for a moral test of unfreedom does not import ten times as many difficulties as it removes. My answer is no. I shall continue to hold that the main insight of the responsibility view is correct, although previous accounts of it need to be modified.

4.1. OVERLY NARROW AND OVERLY BROAD RESPONSIBILITY

Benn and Weinstein are, as we recall, the original proponents of the responsibility view. Let us call their conception of responsibility the 'standard choice-situation model'. They insist that what is to count as a restriction of freedom depends on the range of options that would, under standard conditions, be available and eligible to the normal person. Thus, when attributing moral responsibility, we must be aware of various contextual conditions, in particular what is taken to be a standard expectation.[1] For example, a shopkeeper who offers eggs at the reasonable price of 62 cents a dozen cannot be said to interfere with our freedom. Given the laws of property, which in this case define the normal conditions of action and therefore the alternatives available, we cannot complain that we are being deprived of free eggs, even if we happen to be too poor to buy them.[2]

This model may find support in an idea which one frequently encounters when discussing moral responsibility, especially with

[1] S. I. Benn and W. L. Weinstein, 'Freedom as the Non-Restriction of Options: A Rejoinder', *Mind*, 83 (1974), 436.
[2] S. I. Benn and W. L. Weinstein, 'Being Free to Act, and Being a Free Man', *Mind*, 80 (1971), 201–2.

non-philosophers. The idea is that each individual has a 'quota' of responsibilities that he can be expected to fulfil. As long as he is doing that, for example by helping persons *A* and *B*, he cannot be held responsible for neglecting those needs or wants of other people (*C*, *D*, etc.) to which he might just as well have chosen to attend; for his time and energy do not allow him to serve these needs while he is doing his part somewhere else.

However, this idea arguably rests upon a confusion between responsibility and culpability. To show that it does, we can make use of Kant's well-known distinction between perfect and imperfect duties toward others. We have, in Kant's view, an unexceptional duty not to harm others, but we are only loosely bound to help others; since we cannot help everybody, we are to a large extent entitled to decide for ourselves which needy persons we will favour with our attention.[3] It is important to note that on this view, devoting our assistance to *A* and *B* does not exempt us from our imperfect duty to help *C* and *D*, but we only violate that duty if we are not filling our 'quota' elsewhere. There is a lot to be said for Kant's insight here. By invoking a quasi-Kantian terminology, we could talk of *perfect* and *imperfect responsibilities*. For instance, we could say that the Icelandic government, which has decided to concentrate its developmental help on the Cape Verde Islands, has only an imperfect responsibility toward the starving masses in Ethiopia; one that it is not violating by its non-action there as long as it is spending all it can reasonably be expected to on Cape Verde. Such an analysis seems more plausible than the verdict of the 'quota view', according to which the Icelandic government would have *no* responsibility toward the starving people in Ethiopia. This view could help us to dismiss a charge of culpability but not of responsibility; it seems apt to say that the government is not *culpable* for failing to relieve the plight of the Ethiopians, but that it is still (imperfectly) *responsible* for its decision not to assist them.

To return to Benn and Weinstein's model, the difference between culpability and responsibility is again of vital importance. The problem is that the 'normal conditions of action' can

---

[3] H. J. Paton, *The Moral Law: Kant's Groundwork of the Metaphysics of Morals* (London: Hutchinson & Co., 1976), pp. 30–1, 84–6.

themselves often be put into question. Recall why we refused to accept the conclusion of Feinberg's statistical test that the slaveholder's proposal could not be considered a constraint on the slave's liberty (sec. 3.3). The reason was that we refused to accept the presupposition that the slaveholder could not be held responsible for the (continuation of) the 'normal' relationship between him and his slave. Now, there is undoubtedly, as Cohen points out, a tendency 'to take as part of the structure of human existence in general, and therefore as no "social or legal constraint" on freedom, any structure around which, *merely as things are*, much of our activity is organised'.[4] In capitalist society, the institution of private property happens to be such a structure; and Cohen seems to assume that we are collectively responsible for it since we could change it for something better if we wanted to. That is a fairly radical thesis, for we may be inclined to doubt that some of society's most deeply ingrained institutions can be changed through individual or collective action. Could we, for example, decide one day to abolish the family? Social structures do change with time, but it does not necessarily follow that some individual or some uniquely definable group of persons can change them. This brings up questions about the nature of social entities and processes which will be briefly addressed in the final section of this chapter.

Fortunately, however, I do not need a radical individualist thesis about social change to undermine the 'standard choice-situation model'. Once we get down to the level of everyday situations and individual action, we ascribe responsibility to persons without worrying too much about the nature of social processes. Even presupposing that a person cannot change the rules of the 'game' in which he is taking part, it does not follow that he cannot be held responsible for obeying them, i.e., for playing the game. It may well be that the shopkeeper who offers eggs at 62 cents a dozen cannot be blamed for not selling them cheaper, if his price is 'reasonable', but this does not mean that he can automatically be absolved of all responsibility for offering them at this price, say to a starving person. We must

---

[4] G. A. Cohen, 'Illusions about Private Property and Freedom', in J. Mepham and D. H. Ruben, (eds.), *Issues in Marxist Philosophy*, IV (Brighton: Harvester Press, 1981), p. 227.

remember that there is even a sense in which we want to hold people who act under duress *responsible* for the outcomes of their actions although showing that B was coerced by A into doing x may be sufficient to exculpate B from moral *blame*.[5]

So, absolving people from responsibility for the results of their action simply because that action happens to be the standard practice in a given society seems to involve a mistake. In fact, Benn and Weinstein themselves concede, in a rejoinder to a critique of their original paper, that 'if we see the poor man's indigence as the consequence of arrangements that do deny him options that would be available to him in some possible and better ordered society, we may indeed be disposed to say that his inability to buy eggs is a case of his being unfree to buy them'.[6] In the face of this concession, little remains of the 'standard choice-situation model' which is shown to be much too restrictive.

The inadequacies of this view should remind us of one thing. A correct view of moral responsibility must be able to account for a distinction that is subtle, but nevertheless real, between (*a*) cases of responsibility which is 'imperfect' or easily overridden, such as that of the Icelandic government toward Ethiopians, and (*b*) cases where there is no responsibility at all.

If Benn and Weinstein's conception of responsibility (and hence of constraints upon freedom) is too narrow, why not simply embrace the broad proposal that we are morally responsible for all the *foreseeable* consequences of our action – here, for the existence of all obstacles that we could *possibly* suppress? This is, for instance, the answer that would be given to us by the so-called *strong doctrine of responsibility* (one that is often imputed to utilitarians) and, curiously enough, also by Berlin in his most permissive mood (pp. 8–9). There, however, we venture onto a field mined with counter-examples. A father might plainly be held responsible for constraining his child's freedom to take part in a ball game if he neglected to tie the laces of the child's shoes,

---

[5] This, of course, is one of the main ideas behind Aristotle's discussion of 'mixed actions' in book 3 of the *Nicomachean Ethics* (translated by T. Irwin, Indianapolis: Hackett Publishing Co., 1985).

[6] Benn and Weinstein, 'Freedom as the Non-Restriction of Options: A Rejoinder', 437.

without which it could not compete. The reason lies in his special role as the child's father. However, he would not be held responsible for failing to tie the loose laces of all the children in the city, although he could foresee that each of them who had loose laces would be ineligible for the game. Here, the strong doctrine seems to go badly wrong since it would hold the father responsible for all the loose laces which he could possibly have tied. Miller also enters the lists against this doctrine. His own counter-example is that because all those who wish to fly to the moon might be able to do so if human resources were devoted entirely to this end, we would have to say that those people are now unfree to fly there. This, he contends, is not a 'helpful extension'.[7] It is simply wrong that we are morally responsible for not granting these people their wishes.

Miller undoubtedly hits the point; it is wrong that just *any* humanly removable, remediable, or preventable obstacle renders me unfree. Were that so, the subclass of constraints on freedom would take up most of the class of obstacles, since the great majority of everyday obstacles could *possibly* be overcome by concerted human effort; the domain of mere inability would shrink down to that of physical and logical impossibilities. It is odd how Berlin could turn a blind eye to this fact in suddenly giving up the liberal conception for the view that the freedom of social arrangements is determined by their alterability or remediability.[8] Following Berlin, however, this overly broad view has been embraced by many negative theorists, some of whom think, incidentally, that they are upholding the values of positive liberty (see sec. 5.3).

Connolly is the responsibility theorist who comes nearest to subscribing to this overly broad view. He claims that the notion of a constraint 'involves the idea of a normal range of conduct people can be expected to undertake or forgo when doing so restricts the options of others'. This might at first seem little more than an echo of the already discarded 'standard choice-situation model'; but Connolly's view turns out to be much broader than that. His point is that moral responsibility for the

[7] D. Miller, 'Constraints on Freedom', *Ethics*, 94 (1983), 74.
[8] I. Berlin, *Four Essays on Liberty* (Oxford University Press, 1969), p. xxix.

non-suppression of an obstacle can be established 'if agents are limited with respect to important actions or goals by circumstances potentially alterable at less than *prohibitive* cost by agents that stand in a strategic position to do so'. Thus, poor people can be counted unfree with respect to certain individuals (politicians, etc.) who stand in a particularly strategic position to enable the poor to escape poverty, providing there are means available which would not impoverish the entire society.[9]

We could call Connolly's suggestion the 'feasibility view' of moral responsibility, with *feasibility* being placed somewhere between *possibility* and *normality*. We are not responsible for the non-suppression of all obstacles that we could possibly suppress, nor only of those which we would normally be expected to suppress in a standard choice-situation, but rather of those which it is feasible for us to suppress, namely, those which we are in a strategic position to suppress at less than prohibitive cost. Connolly's ideas seem initially more plausible than those discussed so far, but they turn out to establish a test of moral responsibility that is unsatisfactory because it is too broad.

Consider once again *Drug Case II* (sec. 3.3) where *B*'s usual supplier had been arrested and *B* got an unacceptable offer from another dope peddler (*A*). Now, on Connolly's view, *A* would there stand in a strategic position to supply *B* with drugs at a 'reasonable' price; it is presumably both possible and *feasible* (in the above sense) for *A* to do so. But there is no way in which we can hold *A* responsible for not offering *B* a better deal (and thus claim that he is constraining *B*'s freedom to obtain drugs). If we did that, we would have to hold every person for whom it would be 'feasible' to offer us good deals at less than prohibitive cost for himself responsible for not doing so; and that would include most people in our own country, if not the whole world.

In sum, not all obstacles to a person's choices, although possibly or feasibly suppressible, constitute constraints on his freedom since people cannot always be held responsible for not suppressing them. On the other hand, the attempt by Benn and Weinstein, discussed earlier, to narrow the sphere of moral

[9] W. E. Connolly, *The Terms of Political Discourse*, 2nd edn (Oxford: Martin Robertson & Co., 1983), pp. 165–7.

responsibility seemed to undermine the vital distinction between a test of responsibility and a test of culpability.

4.2. RESPONSIBILITY AND PRIMA FACIE OBLIGATIONS

In the final part of 'Constraints on Freedom', where Miller argues for his responsibility view (sec. 2.3), he aims to apply his account to the ongoing debate between libertarians and socialists.[10] That debate tends to focus on the distribution of wealth in the world, and a question which often crops up is whether such distribution is relevant to an assessment of people's freedom. Miller's basic observation is that nothing in the nature of *financial* obstacles disqualifies them from featuring in a discussion of freedom. Like any other obstacles, they count as constraints if there are agents who can be held morally responsible for not suppressing them. So, to decide whether a certain distribution of wealth is freedom-restricting, more than a conceptual analysis is needed; the moral responsibility in question must be established. According to Miller's analysis, this 'requires in turn a theory of moral obligation'.[11] Thus, in order to clarify the socialist point of view, Miller finds it necessary to invoke two general obligations: that of ensuring that the needs of others are met, and that of dealing fairly with people placed in dependent positions. However, for Miller the existence of these obligations is irreducibly controversial. Generally, his claim is that because libertarians and socialists hold conflicting theories of interpersonal moral obligations, *ultimate disagreements* between them are inevitable. Often what the former call freedom, the latter would call unfreedom – and there is no rational way to decide who is right.[12]

I am not the only reader of Miller's paper to wonder if, in making these apparent concessions, he is not cutting off the branch from which his own theory hangs. Any attentive reader will be somewhat taken aback by the sudden change of tone

[10] Miller, 'Constraints on Freedom', 81–6.
[11] Ibid., 86.
[12] At the very end of Miller's paper, however, he claims a kind of a victory on points for the socialists. For though their case rests 'on a view of obligation that is in principle contestable', it 'derives persuasive force from the fact that the obligations it invokes must be invoked even by the libertarian to handle cases of monopoly satisfactorily' (ibid.).

toward the end of his piece. Up to that point, the whole exposition has a very optimistic air. What Miller seemed to be showing by his 'office-stories' was this: once we realise how the notion of a constraint on freedom is tied up with that of responsibility, we can decide when an obstacle is freedom-restricting. Thus, Miller's aim appeared to be that of providing us with a decision procedure for locating and defining constraints on freedom; a procedure that somehow claimed the acceptance of every perspicuous thinker. The reader may be excused for believing that here we had finally reached the conceptual common ground on which meaningful, substantive controversies about the value of particular freedoms could be staged.

Maybe this was never Miller's point; at least he ultimately backs away from this conclusion. But, once the assumption of a firm common ground has been abandoned or relaxed, the whole edifice of his theory begins to crumble. Obviously, we cannot understand Miller to be claiming, on the one hand, that there is a consensus on responsibility and, on the other hand, that moral obligations are a matter of irresolvable dispute, without imputing to him a glaring inconsistency. It is therefore of vital importance to find out where exactly Miller goes wrong in his analysis.

The cause of Miller's apparent about-face must lie somewhere in the links he supposes to obtain between responsibility, justification, and the (prima facie) obligation to suppress a given obstacle. Since the last of these three is, for Miller, prior in the order of explanation, it is the concept of obligation, or more precisely of *prima facie* obligation, that turns out to be the logical foundation of his analysis. His eventual claim is that having a prima facie obligation to suppress an obstacle is a necessary and a sufficient condition of an agent's moral responsibility for that obstacle and, hence, for its counting as a constraint on freedom.

It is reasonable to suppose that Miller understands 'prima facie obligation' in a deontological or a quasi-deontological sense. Typically for the deontologist, prima facie obligations are obligations which are *real* but not *absolute*. That is, they exist unless overridden – usually by other obligations but perhaps sometimes by other things: I have an obligation to meet you for dinner tomorrow if I have promised to do so, but if I should have to save someone's life tomorrow, my obligation to dine with you is overridden. Hence, it is not an absolute but a prima facie obligation. Consequentialists may well use the notion of 'prima facie obligation' to serve some purpose in their theories, but the notion is not as naturally at home there as in the deontological ones since consequentialists consider one and only one obligation as overriding: that of promoting the best state of affairs. Anyway, we shall see in the sequel that Miller's interest is in deontological prima facie obligations.

There, however, a fundamental problem confronts us. It is well known that deontologists disagree on what obligations we have and, also, which of those obligations (if any) are absolute. However, most of them define 'obligation' rather tightly; it would be difficult to imagine the usefulness of invoking the term if we had, for instance, an obligation (even prima facie) to promote whatever another person happens to want. In the context of a responsibility view of freedom, it seems implausible to hold that the only time we are morally responsible for the non-suppression of an obstacle is when we have a prima facie obligation to suppress it. Would it not be stretching the concept of obligation beyond the breaking point to claim that the reason why a jailer, who locks up a justly convicted criminal in his cell, thereby constrains the prisoner's freedom, is that the jailer has a prima facie obligation not to lock him up? Or, to take another example, would we want to say that a fireman rescuing a semi-conscious person from a burning house has, *qua* fireman, a prima facie obligation to leave him in there, if he knows that the person lit the fire himself in order to commit suicide? I take it that we would probably not want to say that, although we would grant that the fireman is restricting the person's freedom to commit suicide.

These cases seem to indicate that there is an extensional difference between being morally responsible for not suppressing an obstacle, on the one hand, and violating a prima facie obligation to suppress it, on the other. The jailer and the fireman would easily fall under the former description, but scarcely under the latter. If Miller insists that they do fall under the latter also, he is using the term 'prima facie obligation' in a more

permissive way than most deontologists would allow. Not that I
have anything against such deviant usage; deontological theories
contain in general much baggage that I do not want to carry.
But this creates problems for Miller's own view. *First*, it means
that he can no longer use prima facie obligations to *explain* the
onus of justification and thus moral responsibility; the former
are no longer prior in the order of explanation. For on this
permissive reading, 'having a prima facie obligation to suppress
an obstacle' simply turns out to mean the same as 'being obliged
to justify the non-suppression of the obstacle', that is, 'having the
onus of justification for its non-suppression placed on you'. Now,
it is clear what would be meant by saying that the jailer and the
fireman are morally responsible for the non-suppression of the
relevant obstacles because they are obliged to justify their
action/inaction (in the above sense of having the onus of
justification placed on them), although we could still ask *why*
they are obliged to do so. But it would not add anything to say
that they are so obliged *because* they have a prima facie
obligation to suppress the obstacles, if they are *ex hypothesi*
deemed to have such a prima facie obligation whenever they are
obliged to justify their non-suppression.

So, to explain the two apparently clear-cut cases of unfreedom
above, Miller would have to adopt a very permissive definition
of 'prima facie obligation' that is at best synonymous with, and
at worst less clear than, the notion it was supposed to explain. I
am not denying that we would understand what Miller was
saying if he claimed that the jailer had *qua* human being a
general prima facie obligation not to lock anyone up (see p. 76).
There is even a sense in which it is true to say that my account of
constraints of freedom presupposes a theory of moral obligation
(p. 78). However – and here we come to the *second* problem –
when Miller starts to discuss different moral claims of 'socialism'
and 'libertarianism', it is not this permissive sense that he has in
mind at all, but the more traditional and narrow one; he
imagines different deontological systems with conflicting views
of prima facie obligations. In the light of that, he considers it a
matter of controversy whether we have even a prima facie
obligation to help people in need; such an obligation must, he

thinks, be 'invoked' by the socialist in a way that the libertarian is not forced to accept. In other words, Miller would need the permissive definition to account for many common cases of unfreedom, but he uses the narrow definition to show that judgements about freedom are bound to be the object of an irresolvable disagreement. However, he has not produced any convincing arguments for the claim that there is a link between moral responsibility and prima facie obligations on the narrow reading. In fact, the cases above indicate that there is no such link. Whether one is a socialist or a libertarian, a deontologist or a non-deontologist, the jailer is restricting the prisoner's freedom to leave his cell.

Perhaps obstructing a person by violating such prima facie obligations toward him as are recognised within a certain deontological system – say, a libertarian system – is a *sufficient* condition of a constraint on freedom; but there is no reason to believe that it is a *necessary* one. So, there could well be an uncontroversial sense in which we are morally responsible for the non-suppression of obstacles despite its being controversial when we are morally obliged to suppress them; it is not true that because deontological views of prima facie obligations differ, judgements about freedom will necessarily differ, too.

In sum, Miller's claims about the link between moral responsibility and the onus of justification, on the one hand, and prima facie obligations, on the other, are either *trivial* or *wrong*. They are trivial on the permissive definition of 'prima facie obligation' and wrong on the narrow one.

4.3. RESPONSIBILITY AND REASONS

Instead of criticising further attempts to define the moral responsibility in question, I shall now suggest and argue for the following view: An agent A is morally responsible for the non-suppression of an obstacle O to B's choices/action when it is appropriate to request from A a justification of his non-suppression of O, and that in turn is when there is an objective *reason*, satisfying a minimal criterion of plausibility, why A, given that he is a normal, reasonable person, could have been expected (morally or factually) to suppress O – however easily overridable this reason is.

When I talk about there being an objective reason for the suppression of *O*, I am emphasising that *objective*, not *subjective*, standards of appropriate requests are being referred to. In general, if we ask whether *C* has a good reason to request a justification from *A* of his actions, the answer will depend on many factors having to do with *C*'s position. For example, if *C* sees a child, *B*, being forced to opt out of a ball-game because its shoelaces have become untied while *A*, whom *C* takes to be *B*'s father, sits immobile on a bench nearby, it seems appropriate for *C* to ask *A* for a justification of his inaction. Meanwhile, another observer (*D*) knows that *A* is totally paralysed and/or that *A* is in fact not *B*'s father; hence, it does not seem appropriate for *D* to make the same request. But surely, *A*'s responsibility cannot depend on what *C* and *D* happen to know about him. To overcome this problem, my definition implies that a rational agent, *C*, can be mistaken about *A*'s responsibility, because of his lack of knowledge, and that he may have to admit after becoming aware of the facts: 'I thought there was a reason to ask for a justification, but now I know there wasn't; that's why I mistakenly believed *A* was constraining *B*'s freedom.' Note that this 'adequate knowledge condition' does not mean that *C* must be omniscient or able to read *A*'s mind; it is only meant to rule out the possibility that the reason for *C*'s requesting a justification from *A* merely lies in his ignorance of the basic details of the situation, such as who *A* is, whether *A* would be able to do something about the relevant obstacle, etc.

One advantage of the proposed definition is that it honours the subtle distinction between *imperfect* responsibility and *no* responsibility, mentioned earlier. It is incumbent on the Icelandic government to justify why it does not help the starving Ethiopians, because there must always be at least a minimally good reason why people in a life-threatening situation should be helped, if possible (p. 87). However, the justification for not doing so may be easy to find since the responsibility in this case is imperfect. On the other hand, there is no reason why the father could be expected to tie the loose laces of all the children in the city (barring the unlikely possibility that he has been employed especially to perform that function). The responsibility here is not imperfect; it is non-existent. For if we held that, even in this case, there was a reason of the above kind, we would have robbed that notion of any significance in our language. There would no longer be any difference between a reason for doing x and the possibility of doing x.

The case of the jailer and the prisoner may be a little thornier. However, I think it is fair to say there that we have a grip on a reason, satisfying a minimal criterion of plausibility, why the jailer should not lock up the prisoner. He is preventing another person from doing something that happens to be of paramount importance to people in general. We would understand the point of the claim that there was a reason for not locking up people at all, although we might find this reason outweighed by other considerations – or at least put no blame on the jailer for doing his job.[13] On the other hand, we would not understand the point of the claim that we have a reason for walking around the city all day, looking for any loose shoelaces we could possibly tie. That claim may be *intelligible* but it is *unreasonable* or foolish. As these examples show, we must look at each case on its own merits and check whether an appropriate reason presents itself there.

My proposed account of A's responsibility for the non-suppression of O also supplies us, I believe, with the correct moral test for which we were looking at the end of chapter 3, a test which can determine when threats do constitute constraints on freedom. For instance, in the *Drug Case I*, it is surely appropriate to ask B's normal supplier for a justification of his threat not to sell B more dope unless B kills a certain person. However, in the *Drug Case II*, the question is inappropriate, for there is no sense (moral, factual or otherwise) in which B could reasonably expect the stranger to offer him dope anyway. Furthermore, in the *Slave Case*, the slaveholder's threat 'Unless you do x, I'll continue to beat you up tomorrow', does constitute

---

[13] This also solves the problem, which at first might seem a daunting one for the responsibility theorist, how a law against, say, child-abuse curbs the freedom of the potential malefactors. For what objective reason (factual or moral) could there be for expecting the law-giver to permit such atrocities? The answer would be that the sanctions imposed by the law (extended imprisonment, etc.) are such that we could reasonably question their moral legitimacy.

a constraint on *B*'s freedom (*contra* Feinberg), for, although the slaveholder could be *statistically* expected to continue the beating, it is surely possible to give a good reason of another kind (here a moral one) why he should be expected to stop the beating and, hence, it is not inappropriate to ask him for a justification.

It is now time to consider charges of *relativity* that could be brought against my test of moral responsibility. An objector may complain that I have eliminated various *material* ways of specifying what a person's moral responsibilities are and replaced them with a merely *formal* criterion that leaves it all up to intuitions. To be sure, he might say, there must be a reason why *A* could have been expected to suppress *O*, but the point of substance at issue between the rejected accounts above is exactly this: *when* is there such a reason? In reply, there is no denying the fact that all conceptual studies are partly dependent on our intuitions (see ch. 7). However, the main line of argument I have tried to indicate is this: the rejected accounts suggest various tests of responsibility which fail to account for paradigmatic cases of freedom or constraints on freedom. These shortcomings can be ameliorated if we introduce the notion of a minimally plausible reason for suppressing an obstacle, a notion I have tried to explicate by means of examples. It is not true that this notion merely supplies us with a formal test of responsibility, for anyone who understands what constitutes such a reason will readily accept that:

1. There may be a minimally plausible reason why *A* can be expected to suppress *O* even though such a suppression is not the standard convention – which leads to the rejection of Benn and Weinstein's 'standard choice-situation model'.
2. There is not a minimally plausible reason for expecting *A* to suppress all possibly- or feasibly-suppressible obstacles – which leads to a rejection of the 'strong doctrine' of responsibility and Connolly's 'feasibility view'.
3. There may be a minimally plausible reason why *A* can be expected to suppress *O* although he has no prima facie obligation to do so within a given deontological system – which leads to the rejection of Miller in his restrictive mood.

However, there may be little to choose between my analysis and that of Miller in the first part of his paper, where he tacitly invokes a more permissive notion of 'prima facie obligation'. So, why not simply tighten up the account of such obligations rather than jettisoning it in favour of a talk of minimally plausible reasons, which in the end may come down to more or less the same thing? My answer here is much the same as my earlier response to Miller. I think it is desirable in a moral inquiry to retain Miller's narrow definition of 'prima facie obligation', which allows for disagreement among different moral systems over the prima facie obligations we have. Recall that on Miller's view, an agent is responsible for the non-suppression of an obstacle when he is obliged to justify its non-suppression, and that in turn is when he has a prima facie obligation to suppress it. Note that my account explains what the onus of justification (being obliged to justify the non-suppression) really amounts to, without recourse to a prima facie obligation to suppress, a recourse which proved either to be wrong (on the narrow definition) or trivial (on the permissive one). In other words, my account allows for there being a good reason to expect A to suppress O without A's necessarily having a prima facie obligation to suppress it. A libertarian could, for example, justify his non-suppression of obstacles in certain cases by pointing out that he had no obligation, not even a prima facie one, to suppress them: 'To be sure, I constrained this person's freedom but I had no obligation not to do so.' This seems much more plausible than insisting that since he had no prima facie obligation to suppress the obstacle to B's choices, he could not have constrained his freedom. Thus, although there is a sense in which my account, like Miller's, presupposes a theory of moral obligation, namely, the obligation to *justify* a given non-suppression, this sense is quite distinct from that of Miller's.

To clarify further the point about justification, we can ask what exactly is true in the claim, commonly made by proponents of the responsibility view, that there is a 'principle of freedom' embodied in our language. It cannot be right that this principle amounts to a general presumption against restricting the choices of others or obstructing their activity, for we are doing so all the time without there being any reason for us not to; the father is, for instance, restricting the possible choices of those children whose loose laces he does not tie. What is true, on the other hand, is that there is a presumption against constraining other people's freedom. When there is some minimally plausible reason why A could have been expected to suppress O, we expect him to come up with a justification for his non-suppression. Thus, freedom is a 'principle' in the sense that when the onus of justification can be placed on us for the non-suppression of an obstacle, to avoid blame we must be able to explain satisfactorily our non-suppression. This means that the connection between the principle of freedom and the onus of justification is more intimate than previous writers may have realised. It is not, as Connolly suggests, that once we have decided that a description of unfreedom correctly applies, there is a presumption against that relationship.[14] We do not *first* locate instances of unfreedom and *then* place the onus of justification on the constraining agents; this onus is a defining characteristic of what constitutes unfreedom in the first place. When it can be placed on a specific person, A, that person is responsible for the given obstacle to B's choice and, hence, A has constrained B's freedom.

I think I have satisfactorily rebutted the objection that my test of responsibility is merely of a formal kind and that it sets in motion a vertiginous slide into a relativism based upon varying intuitions. Still, an objector might urge that, once I start to flesh out this suggestion and apply it to specific cases, the results are influenced by my consequentialist commitments. Unfortunately for you, the objector would say, rational agents do not agree on when it is appropriate to ask for a justification. Some utilitarians,

---

[14] Connolly, *The Terms of Political Discourse*, pp. 151–2. J. Raz, *The Morality of Freedom* (Oxford: Clarendon Press, 1986), who expands on insights from D. Husak's ('The Presumption of Freedom', *Nous*, 17 (1983)) arguments (sketched in sec. 2.2 of this book) in refusing to accept the presumption of freedom, is simply expecting too much of this presumption when he complains that it tells us nothing 'about which freedoms are important, which are not, and why' (p. 11). The presumption of freedom allocates responsibility (here liability to blame) for an obstacle's non-suppression, although it does not allocate the blame itself. By comparison, it would scarcely undermine the presumption against *lying* embodied in our language to point out that by characterising a speech-act as a lie, we have not yet ascertained whether the liar is blameworthy or whether the lie is perhaps a justifiable one, given the context.

for example, find it appropriate to ask such questions about all the foreseeable effects of our acts/omissions, whereas many deontologists have a much narrower conception of what is appropriate, some of them so much so that they find it inappropriate to ask for a justification of anything but intended effects. Thus, the objector would continue, your general moral perspective determines what reasons you are willing to accept as appropriate, and the results of your test of moral responsibility will always be relative to such a perspective. In reply, I shall argue that, from the vantage-point of their own moral perspectives, the utilitarians and deontologists referred to by the objector would be mistaken in holding the views ascribed to them.

It is true that the strong doctrine of responsibility is often imputed to utilitarians, but I see no reason why any coherent utilitarians should embrace it. For instance, if they claimed that a father could appropriately be asked to justify his not tying the shoelaces of all the children in the neighbourhood, this would require them to give us a reason, satisfying a minimal criterion of plausibility, why he could have been expected to do so. What kind of a reason might these (imaginary) utilitarians produce? The only one I can think of is that the father could *possibly* have tied all the laces, by devoting all his time and energy to it, but that reason happens to be counter-productive from the utilitarian standpoint itself by making unrealistic demands of people. Thus, there are sound utilitarian reasons for *not* holding the strong doctrine of responsibility.

To examine the objector's claim about deontologists, it is worth looking at what Antony Duff has to say about the way 'absolutists' may view responsibility. Generally speaking, Duff holds that ascribing responsibility to an agent for the effect of his action is claiming that he *should* (not *does*) see it as relevant – as providing a reason against the action – and that he should be answerable for it. Duff then thinks of a possible absolutist analysis of a scenario where a person (Albert) could save five lives by killing, with intent, one innocent. The absolutist believes that killing with intent is absolutely prohibited. He also believes that this absolute prohibition limits his responsibility by requiring him to ignore as irrelevant effects which would otherwise have been relevant. Here, he sees the fate of the five as irrelevant to his decision, as something which he should not regard as a reason against refusing to kill the innocent. In this way, the absolutist can understand the doctrine of double effect as absolving him of responsibility for those of his acts which are not directly intended.[15]

Duff realises that the obvious objection to this is that an effect such as five deaths must always be significant for an agent's actions and that he must be able to justify these deaths by reference to reasons which carry more weight in the particular cases or in every case. Duff's answer to this objection is that it 'fails because it distorts the status and the meaning of the absolute prohibition on killing the innocent which informs Albert's thought and action'. It ascribes to Albert the belief that not intending to kill the one innocent is better or more important than saving the other five, but fails to see that the absolute prohibition excludes precisely such considerations of good or bad consequences.[16]

The problem about Duff's answer is that the objection does not purport to describe the considerations which *do* inform Albert's actions but those which *should* do so, and this is in full accordance with Duff's own view of how responsibility is to be ascribed. Furthermore, as Duff himself explains, the principle of double effect – which distinguishes an agent's relationship to the intended results of his actions from his relationship to the effects he foresees but does not intend – can be understood in different ways. I have already stated that I am generally suspicious of the moral fruitfulness of this principle (p. 22). However, if it is taken to mean that it may be *morally right* to do a good act in the knowledge that bad consequences will ensue, it is at least an intellectually respectable principle which can be argued for or against on substantive grounds. If, on the other hand, as Duff holds, it can be taken to mean that when you intentionally do a good act in the knowledge that bad consequences ensue, you are not *morally responsible* for those consequences, it begins to sound

[15] A. Duff, 'Intention, Responsibility and Double Effect', *The Philosophical Quarterly*, 32 (1982), 6ff.
[16] Ibid., 14–15.

too morally bizarre to be taken seriously and is thus inimical to the absolutist's own cause.

There is a lively ongoing debate about *intention* which is largely outside the purview of this study. What I can say in brief compass is that I agree with Kenny that 'it is not usually natural to speak of someone as intending foreseen consequences of his actions when these are unwanted or when he is merely indifferent to them'.[17] I also agree with George Graham's taxonomy, according to which something can be done (*a*) with the intention of doing it, (*b*) intentionally but without the intention of doing it (things brought about as foreseen avoidable consequences of intended doings), and (*c*) non-intentionally.[18] A principle of double effect may perhaps be invoked to distinguish between (*a*) and (*b*) on the one hand and (*c*) on the other, or between (*a*) on the one hand, (*b*) and (*c*) on the other, with the aim of making some point in a moral debate. But neither distinction has any bearing on the definition of moral responsibility, for we can obviously be held responsible for many acts which fall under (*c*) (as well as (*a*) and (*b*)), for instance, acts of negligence.[19]

Interestingly enough, as far as responsibility for the non-suppression of obstacles is concerned, it is not only that intention (direct or oblique) is not a *necessary* condition; it is not even *sufficient*. Let us return once again to the case of the loose shoelaces: even though the father went for a walk through the city with the sole intention of refraining from tying any loose shoelaces he came across, and rejoiced each time that this happened, he would still not be morally responsible for the obstacles he failed to remove by not tying the laces, since it would still be inappropriate to ask him to justify these particular omissions.

This observation sheds light on an important point. There is no such thing as moral responsibility *simpliciter*; we are always morally responsible *for our actions* with regard to some *effect*, and

---

[17] A. Kenny, *Freewill and Responsibility* (London: Routledge and Kegan Paul, 1978), p. 50.
[18] G. Graham, 'Doing Something Intentionally and Moral Responsibility', *Canadian Journal of Philosophy*, 11 (1981), 668–72.
[19] See ibid., 668.

how this effect is described is determined by our purpose in ascribing responsibility in the given context.[20] For example, what I have been saying so far concerns exclusively our responsibility for the non-suppression *of obstacles* to people's choices. Establishing such responsibility is placing the onus of justification on the constraining-agent; he is liable to blame unless he can supply us with a morally acceptable reason why he did not suppress the obstacle.

Meanwhile, we must remember that there is another sense in which we ought to be prepared to justify our actions generally, i.e., show that they are rational or even reasonable. I agree with J. R. Lucas that the 'central core of the concept of responsibility is that I can be asked the question, "Why did you do it?" and be obliged to give an answer'.[21] So, in that sense a person (*A*) would be morally responsible for taking his car out of the garage in the morning and driving to work, if only because he supposedly has a free will and does this as a result of a voluntary *decision* (or an Aristotelian *habit,* which is also voluntary). Hence, I could appropriately ask him to explain or 'justify' what he is doing to see if it is a rational course of action – and in this sense, intention is surely sufficient for responsibility. However, even if I am delayed for a minute at an intersection because *A* happens to be driving in front of me, it would not be appropriate to ask him to justify his having created an obstacle to my choices (by altering my preferred rhythm of movement through the city). In other words, *A* could not be held morally responsible *for creating that obstacle*; or, to be more exact, if I asked a question like that, implying that he is responsible for constraining my freedom, I would have to give a minimally good reason for asking that question, a reason which other people could acknowledge, for instance, my reasonable suspicion that *A* has a motive for holding me up when I am on my way to work. Then I could at least say that I *thought* he was constraining my freedom.

---

[20] H. L. A. Hart (*Punishment and Responsibility* (Oxford University Press, 1968), pp. 211–30), has some interesting things to say about the different ideas expressed by the word 'responsibility' which might be brought to bear on my claim. Note especially what he says about 'role-responsibility'.

[21] J. R. Lucas, *Responsibility* (Oxford: Clarendon Press, 1993), p. 5.

But is this not the same as taking the standard choice-situation (here the ordinary traffic conditions) as given, and as beyond the scope of responsibility, as Benn and Weinstein do? No, since that very choice-situation might still be questioned in many ways. I could, for example, appropriately ask the relevant authorities why they put up traffic-lights at this intersection where they were not needed, delaying the traffic considerably instead of expediting it, and as I have already touched upon (p. 48), there is nothing in the nature of traffic-lights or other standard conditions of traffic that excludes them a priori from counting as possible constraints on freedom. We simply have to find an agent who is morally responsible for such obstacles to our choices.

Recall that this observation about the different purposes behind ascribing moral responsibility is an offshoot of my answer to the objection which proposed that what we deem appropriate in asking for a justification is relative to our general moral perspectives. The drift of my answer was that the views imputed to the utilitarian and the absolutist would work against the plausibility of their own substantive moral beliefs. Arguably, these views also suggest that what we can appropriately be asked to justify is something quite different from what the man in the street would think. His understanding would, I believe, be that we can appropriately ask people to justify the non-suppression of those obstacles which we have some minimally plausible reason for expecting them to suppress – and it is this simple understanding that I have been trying to capture by my account of our moral responsibility for the non-suppression of obstacles.

However, once we start to appeal to the intuitions or beliefs of the ordinary man, a new threat of relativism emerges, this time not with regard to divergent philosophical standpoints, but rather to the varying customs and intuitions of ordinary people in different societies. Since I believe that, in general, relativism is the most serious threat facing any conceptual or substantive moral thesis, this is also an objection that we must not overlook.

Let us start by considering a *Dating Case*[22] in which a man has dated a woman for three months without any sexual intimacy

---

[22] The Dating Case is taken from A. Wertheimer, *Coercion* (Princeton University Press, 1987), p. 211.

and then suddenly tells her that he will not take her out again unless she sleeps with him. Now, someone might ask whether he is constraining her freedom by his implicit threat. This, in my analysis, would be the same question as 'Is it appropriate to ask him for a justification of it in this context?', i.e., 'Is there no minimally good (moral or factual) reason why the man could have been expected to continue his pursuing the woman without demanding these sexual favours?' The point of the objection, which the story is meant to highlight, is that you do not really know what is the normal moral or socially expected course of events until you know quite a lot about the context (time, place, etc.) – and, until you know about the expected course, you cannot answer the question whether the man can appropriately be called upon to justify his ultimatum. Is the story set in Mormon Utah or promiscuous Hollywood? What are the views of the parties involved on pre-marital sex? So, no judgements about freedom in society or community S can be passed by people who do not know the norms and values of S inside out. What counts as an instance of unfreedom in your community may not count as one in the community on the other side of the track, or not even in your own community in a couple of years' time. Consequently, we are left with an account of freedom which is at least as radically relativised as that of Miller.

My response to this objection would be to start by accepting some of its insights. There is no denying the fact that the outcome of the test of moral responsibility will, to a certain extent, be relative to time and place. For instance, there is a reason in the 1990s why a doctor can be expected to provide his patient with the necessary medication to cure his tuberculosis, although such a reason did not exist in the 1930s. But such 'factual relativism' is of an innocuous kind, for the *nature* of the reasons we are looking for would basically be the same at any time and anywhere. (Confessedly, as far as the *Dating Case* itself is concerned, I find it hard to imagine a context where it would be inappropriate for rational agents to ask the man for a justification, namely, a society where there is no good factual or moral reason for expecting a man to date a woman without demanding that she sleep with him!) Recall that my understanding of a reason here is quite flexible; it only requires that it satisfies a minimal criterion of plausibility. What is more, in borderline cases I can always recommend that we err on the side of responsibility, for in a responsibility view of freedom a person has not scored a very big point by persuading us that a restriction of freedom is taking place. To be sure, a justification of any such restriction is called for, but that may be easy to find (imperfect responsibility, etc.). Still, however flexible my definition is, there is no reason to think that it is apt to collapse into the 'strong doctrine of responsibility', since I have already given examples of obstacles which are suppressible but which we have no reason to expect anyone to suppress in any real society or under any plausible circumstances.

I conclude from all of this that the charge of factual relativism does not seriously threaten to undermine my view. The kind of relativism that would undermine it is of a more intrinsic kind, not relating to varying judgements about particular cases but to essential controversies about the criterion of a good reason itself. The problem, the thoroughgoing relativist might say, does not lie in petty arguments about whether it is appropriate here or there to ask A for a justification of his action, or in people from different societies giving different reasons to explain why a question is appropriate, but rather in the fact that there is no common standard of a good reason available between societies; people with different social backgrounds are bound to be working with irreconcilable notions of reasonableness. This, of course, is an objection that not only challenges my views of responsibility and freedom but which challenges, more generally, any rational philosophical doctrine. It assumes that we not only differ over whether a given case constitutes good reasons for saying such-and-such, but also on what it means for something to constitute good reasons.

It may be little more than an articulation of faith to state that I find this radical relativism with respect to human rationality unconvincing. I would even question whether a population who did not (roughly) share our idea of what a good reason is could be said to constitute a human society. At least, the potential threat of such relativism should no more debar us from trying to establish a sound responsibility view of freedom than from arguing for any other rational doctrine.

4.4. POVERTY AS A CONSTRAINT ON FREEDOM

A question often asked in political debate is under what conditions poverty can be considered a constraint upon the liberty of the poor. An answer can be easily read out of the analysis of the preceding section: poverty is such a constraint when there are agents who may appropriately be asked to justify its existence, i.e., when there is a good reason why the agents could be expected to alleviate the poverty *qua* obstacle. There is little doubt that we can appropriately be asked to justify not helping a person (B) in serious need when the following minimal conditions are fulfilled: (a) B is faced by serious (life-threatening) difficulties and requires assistance by somebody; (b) A is able to be of assistance; (c) B is unable to assist himself; and (d) A is reasonably sure that B desires assistance of the sort he proposes to give.[23] It is difficult to suppose that the moral responsibility here could be relative to a particular world-view or political outlook. It is, indeed, difficult to envisage any morality where A could not, in this case, be held responsible for failing to assist B. However, this does not mean that he *should* necessarily do so. People have many responsibilities which may at times conflict. Perhaps A can only remove B's unfreedom at the expense of somebody else's freedom which is deemed more important, or A believes in the value of desert, claiming that B's afflictions serve him right since he has only himself to blame for them. But it is one thing to say that B should not be helped here because he is not unfree (which is a conceptual mistake); another to hold that despite B's unfreedom there are overriding reasons for non-assistance (which is a substantive, political thesis that will not be argued for or against here).

[23] See G. Elfstrom, 'Dilemmas of Intervention', *Ethics*, 93 (1983), 720. However, as D. Miller (*Market, State, and Community* (Oxford University Press, 1989)) correctly points out, being responsible for ensuring that, as far as lies within our power, others enjoy a decent standard of living, does not mean that we are responsible for ensuring that they enjoy any particular items, unless these items turn out to be indispensable (p. 42).

Moreover, since lack of time and resources prevents us from helping everybody in need, the responsibility in question can often be seen as an *imperfect* one, i.e., as one we are not culpable for ignoring as long as we are doing as much as might be expected of us in removing constraints of a similar sort. However, in such cases blame seems to be ascribed differently to governments and public bodies, on the one hand, which in their domestic duties are supposed to follow a rule of non-discrimination among the citizens, and individuals and relief organisations, on the other hand, that can choose their clientele more arbitrarily.

When I say that it is difficult to envisage any morality where A could not be held responsible for failing to assist B in the above context, it might be objected that there is a whole school of libertarian thinkers which holds the opposite view. My response is that I am not sure they really do; however, if they insist that this is their view, they are wrong in holding it. The important libertarian point ought to be that people have, in general, no obligation, even prima facie, to help others in need: helping in such cases is a supererogatory good. But as I have tried to show (sec. 4.2), a person could appropriately be asked to justify his non-suppression of an obstacle without his having a (prima facie) obligation in a given deontological system to suppress it. So, libertarians and socialists may differ on the obligations people have to suppress obstacles without necessarily disagreeing about what people can appropriately be asked to justify. They may also differ on the extent to which people's freedom should be weighed against claims of other values (justice, deserts, etc.). But again, that is a political dispute, not a conceptual one, and does not warrant Miller's conclusion that the concept of responsibility (and hence of freedom) is bound to be the subject of an endless, irresolvable conflict between these two schools of thought.

We should now be able to see where various writers on freedom have missed the mark when dealing with poverty. For example, Berlin claims that it is 'only because I believe my inability to get a given thing is due to the fact that other human beings have made arrangements whereby I am . . . prevented from having enough money to pay for it' that I think of myself as a victim of unfreedom.[24] The use of the term, then, depends on a particular social or economic theory about the causes of my poverty, since it is a logically prior question whether a causal relation can be presumed at all between human arrangements and my situation. Oppenheim makes more or less the same point when claiming that whether poverty under a given economic system such as capitalism constitutes unfreedom depends on the general theory of the causes of poverty one adopts: 'Some tend to explain poverty and unemployment in terms of anonymous causal factors inherent in that . . . economic system; others are inclined to lengthen the causal chain to arrive at specific persons or groups whom they *accuse* of being the cause of what they consider to be instances of unfreedom'.[25]

Even if we grant the claim that there are social and economic processes for the origin and workings of which no individuals can be held morally responsible, Berlin and Oppenheim's conclusion does not follow. For, although the most important sense of responsibility for the non-suppression of obstacles may be that of being accountable for the imposition of one, we have seen that there is also a sense in which we can often be held responsible for not altering a state of affairs, irrespective of its original causes. *A* does not need to be responsible for the causal chain leading up to the creation of *O*, that impedes *B*, for the question 'Why don't you suppress *O*?' to be appropriate. Thus, if the results of an economic system are such that some of us find ourselves in pockets of affluence surrounded by seas of destitution, then it is certain that we, as individuals, can appropriately be asked to justify turning a deaf ear to our fellow-men's call for help. The responsibility established may often be an imperfect one but it is still a responsibility; hence, those left destitute by the system are unfree.

In this section, I have simply applied the conclusions from 4.3 to the question of poverty as a potential constraint on freedom.

[24] Berlin, *Four Essays on Liberty*, p. 123.
[25] F. Oppenheim, *Political Concepts: A Reconstruction* (University of Chicago Press, 1981), p. 56.

The upshot is the same as before: appropriateness in asking for a justification begets responsibility and responsibility is presupposed when ascribing unfreedom.

4.5. THE RESPONSIBILITY OF COLLECTIVITIES

One important objection might still seem to require a more thorough response. Even if everything I have said so far about individual agents being responsible for the non-suppression of obstacles is true, the problem remains of how to move from considerations of such individual relations to those involving collectivities: corporations, organisations, classes, or nations. How are 'impersonal agencies' to be personalised in order that we can hold them responsible? How can we put our grievances to Mr Nobody and ask him to justify his acts or omissions? Answers to these questions have already been hinted at in the previous section and in my reply to Benn and Weinstein's 'standard choice-situation model' (sec. 4.1), but some observations of a more general kind may be in order.

There has been in the social sciences, especially since the early 1960s, an ongoing methodological debate between *structuralists* ('holists', 'institutionalists') and *individualists*. I shall not enter that debate here except in so far as it has bearing on questions of moral responsibility. The basic idea of the structuralists is that in the case of collectivities, no specific entity can be located as the source of the agency and, hence, that all attempts to attribute moral responsibility are apt to break down. The problem here is that we often want to say that B is unfree to do x with respect to A, where A is a collectivity, such as a big corporation. If the structuralists are right in their analysis of such claims, then it seems that, contrary to the view upheld in this book, unfreedom is possible without responsibility.

A typical individualist response to the structuralist view of social entities is to deny the existence of any such entities which cannot, in principle, be reduced to individuals. Thus, Mill stated that 'the laws of the phenomena of society are, and can be, nothing but the actions and passions of human beings'.[26] In this

---

[26] Cf. S. Lukes, 'Methodological Individualism Reconsidered', *The British Journal of Sociology*, 19 (1968), 119.

view, groups are nothing more than the people who belong to them and practices nothing over and beyond the actions in which they are respected. Gray explains the individualist position more grandiloquently as holding that 'it amounts to an error of reification, a mystifying and animalistic superstition, to regard social structures as more than residues of the practical and intellectual activities of human subjects'.[27]

Admittedly, I tend to have some sympathy with the individualist position. Thus, I share Pettit's commitment in *Judging Justice* to the basic individualist claims that the purpose of social institutions is to serve the interests of individuals, and that institutions are 'intrinsically perfectible'.[28] However, while these claims represent an essentially anti-holistic standpoint, I do not agree that they must lead to the kind of radical *methodological individualism* subsequently espoused in Pettit's book.[29] According to the latter view, no purported explanations of social (or individual) phenomena are to count as (rock-bottom) explanations, unless they are couched wholly in terms of facts about individuals.[30]

Fortunately, I do not need this radical thesis, of whose truth we have good reasons to be sceptical, to defend my responsibility view of freedom. My view only requires that *if* a collectivity is held to constrain freedom, it should be possible, in principle, to point to one or more individuals who can appropriately be asked why they did/do not suppress the relevant obstacle. But it is one thing to claim that; another to say that collectivities are nothing but groups of individuals, to whom attributions of responsibility for the collectivities' workings are *always* possible.

However, the request for a justification will clearly be appropriate in more cases in my responsibility view than, for example, in an intentionality view of freedom. To make use of two examples discussed by Lukes in a different context, I would claim that a pharmaceutical company had constrained the freedom of people harmed by the marketing of a dangerous

[27] J. Gray, 'Political Power, Social Theory, and Essential Contestability', in D. Miller and L. Siedentop (eds.), *The Nature of Political Theory* (Oxford: Clarendon Press, 1983), p. 93 (describing what he calls the 'actionist' view).

[28] P. Pettit, *Judging Justice* (London: Routledge and Kegan Paul, 1980), p. 45.

[29] Ibid., ch. 6.

[30] See Lukes, 'Methodological Individualism Reconsidered', 121.

drug, even if its scientists and managers did not intend this to happen, not knowing of the drug's effect, given that they *could have* been expected to take steps to find out but did not. On the other hand, cigarette producers did not restrain the freedom of smokers, by refraining from informing them of the hazards of their habit, *before* anyone could reasonably be expected to think that smoking was harmful.[31] Another reason why followers of an intentionality view of freedom tend to underestimate the number of cases in which the results of a collectivity's workings can be seen to constrain people's freedom, is that they do not allow that *A*'s intentional non-removal of an already existing obstacle constrains *B*'s freedom, as long as *A*'s intention was not part of the causal chain leading to its creation (sec. 2.1).

There is yet another reason why an attribution of responsibility to individuals within a collectivity might be appropriate in more cases than is often thought. Philosophers are prone to commit what Parfit calls the fifth mistake in moral mathematics: the mistake of thinking that 'an act cannot be either right or wrong, *because* of its effects on other people, if these effects are imperceptible'.[32] But, as Parfit points out, the only way to solve many Prisoner's Dilemmas that are relevant to problems of pollution, congestion, unemployment, over-fishing, etc., in the modern world, is to ask ourselves: 'Will my act be one of a set of acts that will *together* harm other people?'[33] Parfit's argument underwrites what I take to be Miller's correct insight: that in many cases when 'I add my straw to the camel's load in circumstances where it can be foreseen that others will do likewise, I bear my share of responsibility for the resulting injury to the camel'.[34]

In this chapter, I have attempted to lay the most important foundation of a responsibility view of freedom, by providing a plausible account of moral responsibility. I have taken serious exception to the views of other responsibility theorists, such as Miller, and Benn and Weinstein; and, in the last two sections,

[31] S. Lukes, *Power: A Radical View* (London: Macmillan, 1974), pp. 51–2.
[32] D. Parfit, *Reasons and Persons* (Oxford: Clarendon Press, 1984), p. 82.
[33] Ibid., p. 86.
[34] Miller, 'Constraints on Freedom', 81.

have argued that my account explains among other things the conditions under which poverty can be seen as freedom-constraining, and under which collectivities can be said to restrict people's liberty. This, I hope, has shown how the responsibility view can provide us with promising solutions to some of the most stubborn puzzles about the nature of social freedom.

CHAPTER 5

Internal bars and positive liberty

In chapter 1, objections were levelled against the thesis of the *conceptual equivalence* of negative and positive liberty. Then, in chapter 2, a 'responsibility view' emerged as the most promising variant of a negative-liberty theory. After developing such a view further in chapters 3–4, it is now time to ask how it stands up to the challenge of positive-liberty accounts, for which *conceptual superiority* is claimed by their advocates. The aim of the present chapter is to answer this question.

It should be recognised at the start that the term 'positive liberty' has often been used in a rather amorphous sense in the literature, covering a wide range of accounts and ideals that divide positive libertarians in many ways from one another as well as from negative libertarians. Berlin argues that the notion of positive liberty has historically assumed two distinct forms, the point of the first being *self-abnegation* (or what he calls the 'return to the inner citadel'), and of the second *self-realisation*.[1] However, it must be said that, notwithstanding Berlin's renowned lucidity of style, he uses a rather disconcerting variety of expressions and metaphors in his exegesis of the essence of positive theories. As I understand him, Berlin takes both these forms to involve a bifurcation of the self: the 'higher' self being, in the self-abnegation model, that which is immune from physical determination and, in the self-realisation model, the rational self that I am supposed to identify with and actualise. Thus, Berlin overlooks the more common variety of self-realisation accounts which simply equate freedom with autonomy

---

[1] I. Berlin, *Four Essays on Liberty* (Oxford University Press, 1969), pp. 131ff.

and make do without a split self. He also fails to recognise, as logically independent of the other two, a historically important form of positive liberty that I shall call 'communal freedom'.

The first two sections of the present chapter, which preface a more systematic investigation of positive liberty in the remaining sections, take as their point of departure a simple observation. According to the responsibility view of negative liberty, *A* constrains *B*'s freedom when he can be held morally responsible for an obstacle that restricts *B*'s options. But what if *A* and *B* are the same person? Are there not cases where we can be held responsible for our own remediable ignorance and self-deception, or other avoidable deficiencies in our awareness of our genuine interests or will? The problem is that if we accept the reality of such *internal bars* to freedom, we seem to have saddled ourselves with a central tenet of the most radical theories of *positive* liberty, a tenet which has been used to justify some repugnant forms of paternalism. For in such cases the traditional (prima facie) objection against paternalism, that it takes away people's freedom, does not seem to apply. On the contrary, your paternalistic intervention in my life can be seen as a way of relieving me of my own unfreedom: of forcing me to be truly free. I purposely approach this problem without providing any exact initial characterisation of positive liberty, simply assuming that most of us share a rough idea of what this notion comprises: an idea indicated, for example, by Berlin's general remarks referred to in chapter 1 (pp. 7–8). The rationale behind this method of deliberate 'conceptual sloppiness' is to let the features which characterise positive accounts and distinguish them from their negative counterparts emerge and manifest themselves gradually in the course of the discussion.

In 5.1, I first look into arguments from Charles Taylor that seem to reinforce the embarrassing implication mentioned above, arguments which aim to show that by granting certain unavoidable claims about internal bars to freedom, we are forced, in two steps, into following the path of positive liberty. In 5.2, some truths about freedom as a social concept are revealed, shedding new light on the connection between internal bars and freedom. The thrust of Taylor's positive-liberty argument is ultimately resisted, although the relation of a correct negative-liberty account to paternalism does not turn out to be the one that some people might have expected. I then pay attention, in 5.3, to certain accounts of freedom which, although often termed 'positive' by their proponents, are actually negative-liberty theories in disguise. After that, in 5.4–5.6, I delineate what I take to be the three most common forms of proper positive-liberty theories: *Promethean freedom*, *freedom as autonomy*, and *communal freedom*. These are seen as relating to distinct and even divergent ideals, though the borderline between them is fuzzy and sometimes straddled by particular writers. Writ large, the conclusion of this chapter, presented in 5.7, is that as important as many of these ideals are, nothing short of a rejection of these three kinds of positive-liberty theories is required, since their ideals are logically distinguishable from, and some even incompatible with, the concept of social freedom.

5.1. BEYOND THE MAGINOT LINE

In his article 'What's Wrong with Negative Liberty' Charles Taylor directs our attention to the somewhat curious fact that while the most 'caricatural' version of positive liberty is pinned on its protagonists by their opponents, negative liberty theorists tend to be eager themselves to embrace the 'crudest version' of their theory. By that he means the extreme Hobbesian view where freedom is understood simply as the absence of physical constraints: 'freedom of movement' (sec. 2.1). The reason for this, according to Taylor, is their fear of the 'Totalitarian Menace;' their suspicion that any modification of the Hobbesian notion will lay itself open to totalitarian manipulation. To thwart that menace, the proponents of negative liberty hold the line around a simple issue of principle, embracing what Taylor calls the 'Maginot Line mentality'. The purpose of the Maginot Line strategy is to nip the opposition in the bud, by holding on stubbornly to the belief that you are free as long as you are able to do what you want, unrestrained by external barriers: 'what you want' being unproblematically understood as what you can identify as your desires.[2]

For Taylor, the journey from the Maginot Line to the fortress of positive freedom is made in two steps. The *first* consists in equating 'doing what you want' with 'doing what you *really* want', truly directing your life; the *second* consists in granting that you cannot achieve this 'outside of a society of a certain canonical form, incorporating true self-government'.[3] It seems that *step 1* typically involves two smaller steps, *1a* and *1b*. In taking *1a*, we accept some qualitative ranking of our desires, conceding that some of them are much less significant than others, even to the point where external bars to them can hardly be called constraints on our freedom at all. Simultaneously, we admit that we do not always carefully weigh up the significance of our various wants prior to acting, and that some of our actions are, in that way, non-rational. These concessions may seem so small that even though they bring in the notion of the unequal significance of desires, we could still grant them without abandoning the Maginot Line.

Is accepting *1a* and stopping there a tenable position? Not according to Taylor, for our position thus far still rules out *second-guessing*; we remain the final arbiters of the authenticity and importance of our own desires and the degree of our freedom/unfreedom. However, Taylor asks us to consider whether our freedom is not also at stake when we find ourselves carried away by a less significant goal at the cost of a highly significant one, or when we are led to act out of a motive which we consider bad or despicable. To bolster his case, Taylor takes as examples a man whose irrational fear of public speaking prevents him from taking up a fulfilling career, and another whose spiteful reactions undermine an important relationship. Is it not, he asks, quite understandable if I consider such emotions and motives as obstacles I would be freer without – as something I could get rid of without any loss to my identity?[4]

What Taylor has in mind is apparent from his examples,

[2] C. Taylor, 'What's Wrong with Negative Liberty', in A. Ryan (ed.), *The Idea of Freedom: Essays in Honour of Isaiah Berlin* (Oxford University Press, 1979), pp. 175–9.
[3] Ibid., p. 181.   [4] Ibid., pp. 185–6.

namely, the familiar cases of false consciousness, repression, weakness of the will and self-deception. At least some of his examples imply that we can be radically wrong about what we really want and that seeing ourselves in the final-arbiter role is an illusion. If we rule out, in principle, that a person can ever be wrong about what he really wants, it must be because there is nothing to be right or wrong about in the matter; that desires are simply incorrigible brute facts.[5]

Taylor goes on to contend that our desires are not incorrigible, referring to Rylean arguments about the necessary logical conditions of certain feelings such as shame and fear. In fact, Taylor claims that our emotional life is largely made up of desires and feelings that we can experience mistakenly. He concludes that we can experience some desires as fetters because we can experience them as not ours. Keeping all this in view, how can we possibly rule out second-guessing of our desires; how can we exclude, in principle, that the agent has for a long time or even permanently a distorted sense of his fundamental purposes, being for example radically self-deceived?

the subject himself can't be the final authority on the question whether he is free; for he cannot be the final authority on the question whether his desires are authentic, whether they do or do not frustrate his purposes.[6]

Step 1b consists in accepting the reality of such permanent internal bars – and if these are not to count as constraints on freedom, how can we possibly apply the notion consistently?

Taylor never really answers the question whether we are also committed to take *step 2*, i.e., to accept that we need a government of a certain canonical form to correct our mistakes and tell us what our real desires and purposes are, but at least he claims that such a conclusion cannot be rejected out of hand by a 'philistine definition of freedom'.[7]

To recapitulate, Taylor tries to move us, as proponents of negative liberty, to make the following series of concessions. First, we are invited to accept that some of our desires are more significant than others (*step 1a*), even if we still cling to the belief

[5] Ibid., pp. 187–91.   [6] Ibid., p. 180.   [7] Ibid., p. 193.

that we can in principle judge their relative significance for ourselves. But we are then forced to concede, in addition, that we can be systematically deceived about our real preferences (*step 1b*). By that concession, we implicitly admit that there are internal bars to our freedom; and since real freedom cannot be achieved without surmounting these bars, there can be good reasons for *forcing* a person to surmount them, although he himself does not recognise the need for it at the time. If we admit this, we have accepted *step 2* and laid ourselves open to the paternalistic thrust of positive theories. Some would even replace 'paternalistic' by 'totalitarian'; for seeing ourselves as 'forcing others to be free' is (as Berlin has pointed out to us) the argument 'used by every dictator, inquisitor, and bully who seeks some moral, or even aesthetic justification for his conduct'.[8]

As Taylor is inclined to direct his animadversions to the proponent of a 'crude' negative-liberty view, it is in order to ask at this point if and how they pose a challenge to a more 'enlightened' account such as the one presented in this book. As far as *step 1a* is concerned, my responsibility view seems safely protected from it – for two reasons. Firstly, I have defined freedom without any recourse to actual *wants* or their significance. A constraint on freedom is something that impairs a possible choice, whether we now (or ever) want to make the particular choice, and irrespective of how important it might seem to us. If James Joyce's works are blacklisted by the authorities, I am banned from reading them and, hence, unfree to do so, although, as a matter of fact, I may find his books so boring that I would never care to open one of them in the first place. Secondly, as will be argued later, the responsibility view can make do with a minimal rationality requirement (sec. 5.5). We are not unfree to try out new ways of living simply because we happen to be too lazy or content with the way things are to give any attention to them, as long as we could make the effort if we wanted to and as long as nobody is responsible for manipulating us to conform.

Although *step 1a* does not pose a threat to a responsibility view of negative liberty, *1b* might do so. If it is true that, owing to our

---

[8] Berlin, *Four Essays on Liberty*, pp. 150–1.

own fault or carelessness, we can be radically wrong or systematically deceived about our real *options*, the positive libertarian seems to have scored an important point. For then there really are internal bars satisfying my proposed criteria for a constraint on freedom: they are real *obstacles* to choice for which an agent, in this case the person himself, is *responsible*. Suddenly, the opponent seems to have the game in his hands while the negative libertarian is defenceless against what would normally seem to him to be the most hideous claptrap: of people not being socially free unless they are in control of their own passions, have 'realised themselves', etc.

We should note that it is the *origin* of the obstacle, but not its *location*, that need concern us. The idea of an internal bar arises from the recognition that I am sometimes thwarted by factors within me, but it is not the location of such a bar ('under the skin') that threatens to undermine a negative account like mine, or to make it collapse into a positive one. If the bar is of a natural origin (mental retardation caused by mongolism, etc.), it restricts the person's ability but not his freedom. If it has its origin in another agent, it is simply on a par with any other externally created bar, although it happens to be internally situated. Thus, there is no morally relevant difference between preventing a man from entering a room by locking it up or by hypnotising him into staying away from it. In both cases, the victim is unfree to enter, on a correct negative view. The problem first arises if the origin of the obstacle can be attributed solely to the agent himself, if he can be held responsible for his own situation. It is only after we concede that internal bars of this sort exist and constrain the agent's own freedom that the positive libertarian will have a field day.

I see three possible rejoinders to Taylor's *step 1b* and his subsequent *step 2*. The *first* is to reject *1b* by denying the existence of the sort of internal bars it describes; hence ruling out what Taylor calls second-guessing of our interests or the options open to us. The *second* rejoinder is to accept *1b* but to deny the implication that these internal bars must be seen as constraints on our freedom. The *third* is to accept *step 1b* and this implication, but to modify the force of *step 2* by some overriding arguments against paternalism.

It seems safest to adopt the first defence strategy. To focus on one clear example, *self-deception* is an act or a state typically seen as a weakness of rational thinking to which the self-deceived person could and should have avoided falling prey, and for which he is *himself* responsible. If this plausible candidate for an internal bar can somehow be explained away, the first defence strategy might be made to work, since other candidates could then easily be considered to be tarred with the same brush.

As a matter of fact, it would be no novelty to claim that there can be no such thing as self-deception. In ordinary deception, *A*, being aware that something is false, intentionally gets *B* to believe it is true: by lying, pretending, or withholding appropriate information. An air of paradox arises, many writers have pointed out, when we try to understand self-deception by modelling it strictly after such interpersonal deception, for how can we simultaneously be the victims/objects and the source of the deception, the deceiver and the deceived? This scepticism is reinforced by the fact that we all know of many instances where self-deception is invoked *ad hoc* as an explanation of morally unacceptable behaviour. Often the reason lies in our disinclination to self-ascribe what we hold to be serious defects of character, unworthy feelings, etc.[9] Thus, most of us seem to suffer from what I have elsewhere called 'the moral myth of the given': the myth of the priority of goodness in the universe and our own nature.[10] We tend to identify ourselves with our most mature state – as opposed to our previous 'childish' ones – as well as with our most rational and critical moments. The nervous student with butterflies in his stomach before the *viva voce* is not the 'real me'; if I could control my nerves, I would probably want to say that not only had I changed into a less nervous person, but that I had found my 'real self'. Similarly, it seems much easier for us to say 'I knew all the time deep down that what I was doing yesterday was wrong but I just deceived myself' than to admit frankly 'What I did yesterday was wrong and I regret it today.' For most of us, moral progress is not a maturation or transform-

---

[9] B. Szabados, 'The Self, Its Passions and Self-Deception', in M. W. Martin (ed.), *Self-Deception and Self-Understanding* (University Press of Kansas, 1985), p. 164.

[10] I elaborated on this point in my B.A. thesis, see K. Kristjánsson, 'Böl og bölsvandi', B.A. dissertation (University of Iceland, 1983), pp. 53–9.

ation, but a return to the original goodness of our nature which
has somehow been temporarily defiled and obfuscated.

Generalising from such examples and pointing to the alleged
inconsistency of a person deceiving himself, the so-called 'heretical
view' of self-deception has in recent years gained many followers
in philosophical circles, notably Mary Haight in her book *A
Study of Self-Deception*. According to this view, what we ordinarily
call self-deception is at best no more than wishful thinking,
gullibility, or misplaced good intentions; at worst simply lying to
other people – and there is no paradox about a lie.[11] This
heretical view is an extreme stance which denies the very
existence of self-deception. Notwithstanding its insights into the
many occasions where the term is metaphorically or wrongly
applied, this stance seems in the end to be as unrealistic as the
view at the other extreme, represented by thinkers such as Freud
and Sartre, according to whom self-deception is a permanent
and perhaps necessary feature of man's consciousness. Between
these two extremes still lurks the position of common sense: that
people sometimes, but not always, deceive themselves. Then,
how can this be accounted for without inconsistency?

R. Demos' paper 'Lying to Oneself' offers a plausible solution.
According to Demos, self-deception entails that a person A
believes both p and not-p at the same time, or believes p and
disbelieves p. But as believing and disbelieving are contraries, 'it
is logically impossible for them to exist at the same time in the
same person in the same respect'.[12] It is this 'same respect' clause
which holds the key to Demos' analysis since he claims that
whereas self-deceivers attend in explicit consciousness to the
belief they are happy with, they manage to keep the contrary
unpleasant belief, which they are unwilling to attend to, latent.
Self-deceivers are in this sense able to retain both beliefs
inasmuch as, not noticing one of them, they do not compare the
two and do not appreciate their incompatibility.

Has the paradox of believing p and not-p at the same time
then been dissolved? I tend to think that Demos' account makes
it very innocuous, to say the least. We only have to think of the
mind as a large building with many storeys and rooms, stacked

---

[11] M. R. Haight, *A Study of Self-Deception* (Sussex: Humanities Press, 1981), p. 120.
[12] R. Demos, 'Lying to Oneself', *Journal of Philosophy*, 57 (1960), 591.

with experiences and beliefs. Why should we not be able to close off certain rooms or even storeys of the building from our consciousness if their contents are incompatible with certain other beliefs that we are strongly disposed to cherish? Sartre's famous answer, that you can in fact wish not to see a certain aspect of your being only if you are acquainted with the aspect you do not wish to see, and in order to take care not to think of it, you must think of it constantly, seems to be tantamount to saying that you cannot close a room from outside without first checking carefully what is inside. That assumption simply flies in the face of all experience, the experience that, as Bishop Butler once put it, 'it is as easy to close the eyes of the mind as those of the body'.[13] To take the decision of closing off a room, it seems quite sufficient to have a hunch that there is something inside you do not want to see. And after a while, even the hunch is not necessary. The room is just closed and you bypass it.

I do not profess to have revealed any new truths by this short detour into the realm of self-deception. I have only tried to show that the common sense view of what self-deception involves may well be sound, and that the logical case against it probably does not hold.

It is worth remembering that my discussion of self-deception started as part of the first defence strategy to rebut Charles Taylor's claims against negative theories of liberty. This particular strategy – denying the existence of internal bars for which the agent himself is responsible – does not hold out much prospect of success. Thus, Taylor's second-guessing cannot be ruled out, and we seem forced to accept the implication that people can constrain their own freedom. But sometimes one must draw back in order to leap further.

5.2. SOCIAL CONCEPTS, IRREFLEXIVITY, AND PATERNALISM

Self-deception debars us from seeing the world aright, and is thus an impediment to our choices. What Charles Taylor held out against the doctrine of negative liberty was its failure to

[13] Cf. P. Gardiner, 'Error, Faith and Self-Deception', in J. Glover (ed.), *The Philosophy of Mind* (Oxford University Press, 1976), p. 36.

accept the reality of such impediments which, although 'less immediately obvious'[14] than the more palpable, externally created ones, are just as real. Now, Taylor might seem to have an easy time cashing in on the concessions we have made to his point, forcing us next to take *step 2* in the direction of positive theories that, if taken to their furthest extreme, would have us kneel before the omniscient Big Brother, and ask him humbly to protect us against our own follies – thus making us truly free.

To resist the drift of Taylor's arguments, one might still try to invoke the second defence strategy, claiming that we have only acknowledged the *existence* of internal obstacles, not that these obstacles constitute *constraints on freedom*. But initially this manoeuvre does not sound very convincing, since we have also conceded that agents (namely ourselves) may be responsible for the origin of these obstacles, and thus seem to have satisfied the previously presented conditions (restricted choices and responsibility) for an obstacle's counting as a constraint on freedom. However, one rather subtle point has so far been overlooked in the presentation of my responsibility view. The point, which I shall try to drive home in this section, is that we cannot in any coherent sense say that an agent constrains his own (social) freedom. If this is true, we would foil Taylor's attack on a rather unexpected battleground. Now, it could seem odd, after granting that the relation *to deceive* may be reflexive, to claim that the schema '*A* constrains *A*'s freedom' yields no significant statements. But this is what I want to contend.

In recent discussions of moral and social theory, freedom and justice are often juxtaposed, so it may prepare the ground for discussion to say a few things first about the irreflexivity of justice. There is a passage in Aristotle's *Nicomachean Ethics* where he tackles the question of whether it is possible to do injustice to oneself. Aristotle invokes various arguments to rule out this possibility: (*a*) that no one suffers injustice willingly, (*b*) that you cannot lose and get the same thing at the same time, (*c*) that you cannot do and suffer the same thing at the same time, and (*d*) that doing injustice involves doing particular acts of injustice;

14 Taylor, 'What's Wrong with Negative Liberty', p. 176.

but, in fact, you cannot commit adultery with your own wife, burgle your own house, and steal your own possessions. Aristotle concludes that 'what is just or unjust must always involve more than one person'.[15] As easy as it would seem to pick holes in some of Aristotle's arguments, his conclusion is intuitively appealing. Although we do not grant Hobbes' famous claim, that the notions 'just' and 'unjust' have no place before the time of covenants and coercive power, it seems fair to say that the idea of Robinson Crusoe being just or unjust to himself on a desert island does not make much sense. Justice seems to be a social term, a term that can only have application in interpersonal relationships.

But how about freedom? Does the same apply there? Consider the possibility of the earth colliding with a comet, as a result of which only one man survives. Plainly, that man would be surrounded with obstacles, and we can suppose that he would not be able to survive very long on his own. But could he do anything that might sensibly be said to infringe upon his own freedom? I am inclined to doubt that. In a rage of despair, he might lock himself up in a cage, but would that not only make him unable, not unfree, to leave? At first glance, I can think of no suitable case where a person could be said to constrain his own freedom. However, we might ask if that is not simply an example of the imperfections of ordinary language – or of a deviant intuition which has to be modified in light of the correct general theory of freedom. I shall argue that this is not the case. There are important logical reasons for upholding the irreflexivity of social freedom and, hence, for adding an *extra* condition to my definition of a constraint: not only has the potential constraint to be a real obstacle for which an agent is responsible; this agent and the victim of the constraint must not be the *same* person.

First, a useful distinction should be drawn. Of course, you can 'make yourself unfree' in the sense of deciding to become unfree to do something with respect to somebody else. You may decide, for example, to rent your house to me and sign a contract to that

[15] Aristotle, *Nicomachean Ethics* (translated by T. Irwin, Indianapolis: Hackett Publishing Co., 1985), pp. 145–6 [1138a].

effect. But then you become unfree to do certain things not with respect to *yourself* but to *me*.[16] So, the correct thing to be said there is not that you have constrained your own freedom, but that you have brought about the restriction of your freedom by somebody else. A famous example of the same sort is Odysseus' request to his shipmates to bind him to the mast so that he could listen to the beautiful singing of the Sirens without being enchanted and trapped by them. If we deny the irreflexivity of freedom-constraining, we are forced to say that Odysseus had somehow plotted against his own future self, constraining its freedom, when the simpler and more reasonable thing is to say that the other sailors constrained his freedom, as he had ordered them to. (On my theory, a person's past, present, or future wants and wishes do not matter in assessing his freedom.) Now, it seems profitable to distinguish cases of this sort from ones where a person deceives himself, or sets an alarm clock before retiring to prevent himself from sleeping in, etc. In the former sort of case, an ordinary constraint of freedom by another agent has taken place (although incidentally with the constrainee's prior assent); in the latter sort the correct thing to say is, I believe, that no constraint of freedom has occurred. The person may not be able to sleep in because of the alarm clock's ringing, but he is surely not unfree to do so.

According to the *Encyclopedia of Philosophy*, in the history of political thought, 'freedom' 'has a specific use as a moral and a social concept – to refer either to circumstances which arise in the relations of *man to man* or to specific conditions of *social* life'.[17] Flathman concurs with this view in his insistence on historical and social 'situatedness' as a condition of freedom.[18] Even more explicitly, Oppenheim's view chimes in with mine when he states that all power relations are irreflexive: that no actor can stand in such a relation to himself.[19] Understanding freedom as

[16] F. Oppenheim, *Dimensions of Freedom: An Analysis* (New York: St. Martin's Press, 1961), p. 102.

[17] P. G. Partridge, 'Freedom', in P. Edwards (ed.), *The Encyclopedia of Philosophy*, III (London/New York: Macmillan, 1967), p. 221 [emphasis added].

[18] R. E. Flathman, *The Philosophy and Politics of Freedom* (University of Chicago Press, 1987), pp. 3, 36–7, 68ff., etc.

[19] Oppenheim, *Dimensions of Freedom: An Analysis*, p. 102.

a *social* as well as a *moral* concept, and 'constraining freedom' as an irreflexive relation, is the only way to grasp a vitally important feature of its nature, historical as well as logical, that is pointed out by these three writers. Precisely as Aristotle claimed for justice, the relation of social freedom must involve more than one person.

If someone insists on the oddity of allowing that a person may deceive himself, while denying that he can restrict his own freedom, I can only answer that the two concepts arise out of radically different situations. The lone survivor of the comet collision could easily deceive himself to varying degrees, since self-deception is concerned with the *intra*personal matter of how a spurious belief can prevent us from seeing the world aright, but he could not constrain his own freedom, for freedom is essentially an *inter*personal relation that arises in the context of social responsibility. If we deny this, we have no way of explaining the soundness of various distinctions, such as that between the Odysseus- and alarm-clock cases explained above, which seem to lie at the heart of all freedom-talk. Needless to say, I am not arguing merely that restricting one's own freedom is not *wrongful*, because done with consent. My definition of a constraint is a moral, not a moralised one, and clearly I could often be appropriately asked to justify the obstacles I create to my own choices. The point I am making is a much stronger one, namely, that the logic of the concept of social freedom is such that it does not allow for the possibility of A's constraining his own freedom, without the intervention of somebody else.

Now, if we grant this point, which will be further scrutinised in sections 5.4–5.7, we see that the second defence strategy does indeed cut against Taylor's arguments. If an agent cannot be said to constrain his own freedom, although his options are restricted by self-deception or other internal bars for which he himself is responsible, we cannot see paternalistic measures as simply relieving people of their *own* (reflexive) unfreedom. An important assumption leading to Taylor's *step 2* would thus have been undermined. Meanwhile, the responsibility view has two other implications which are pertinent to the issue of internal bars and freedom. First, because we can often be held responsible for failing to remove obstacles that restrict other people's choices, *my* self-deception can be considered a constraint on the freedom of *others*, in so far as it has consequences which restrict their options, and in so far as I can be held responsible for not ridding myself of it. Second, a self-deceived man, although not unfree with respect to *himself*, might in some cases be counted unfree with respect to *others*, namely, those who could be held responsible for not relieving him of his self-deception – just as the occupant of the room, locked in by the wind, was unfree to leave with respect to the janitor who did not arrive.

What is apt to seem odd about the second of these implications is that, while we have alleviated the force of Taylor's *step 1b*, we appear to have argued ourselves into taking his *step 2*, thus committing ourselves to some kind of *paternalism*. There is no reason why we could not often be potentially culpable for failing to remove the scales from other people's eyes, just as we are potentially culpable for failing to relieve them of some of their other plights, even if we were not responsible for creating them in the first place.

It may surprise some to see that a sound negative theory of freedom can entail a prima facie reason *for* paternalism. However, there is a world of difference between this reason and the one which follows from Taylor's arguments. For Taylor (and many other positive-liberty theorists), we are not necessarily restricting a person's liberty by 'forcing him to be free', that is, not if we are merely removing self-imposed constraints on his own freedom. Thus, as I noted earlier (p. 99), the main substantive objection against paternalistic intervention, that it constrains the person's freedom, melts away – for allegedly a constraint is only being removed, not imposed. In my responsibility view of negative liberty, however, we *are* constraining a person's freedom in certain respects if we try to set him right by paternalistic measures, since he cannot be said to have restricted his own freedom in the first place. But if we consistently refrain from limiting a person's freedom in this way, we may possibly wind up restricting his freedom in other (and perhaps more significant) ways. So, on balance, a *limited* paternalism may serve, rather than hinder, the interests of freedom; a conclusion that is still far from the potential extremism of Taylor's *step 2*.[20]

At the end of this section some important things stand out. The responsibility view of freedom has been shown to entail a prima facie case for a limited paternalism in situations where we can, for example, be appropriately asked to justify not removing the scales from other people's eyes, and where these people are, hence, unfree with respect to *us*. However, positive-liberty theorists tend to make out a much stronger case for paternalism. The reason for this difference is the latter's insistence on the claim that people may be unfree with respect to *themselves*; a claim which can now serve as the first of our insignia of a positive liberty account. But, as this claim seemed to be incompatible with the nature of freedom as a social concept, doubt has already been cast on the justification of positive liberty in general: a doubt that will be reinforced in the following sections.

5.3. NEGATIVE FREEDOM IN DISGUISE

The previous section revealed the *first* of what I consider to be the two main characteristic elements of positive liberty theories: the supposition that agents can (and frequently do) constrain their own freedom. The *second* element emerges once we start to scrutinise proper positive-liberty theories in sections 5.4–5.7. For convenience of exposition, let me state here without argument the crucial point of the latter also: while negative libertarians see freedom as an *opportunity concept*, which only requires that our capacity to choose whatever we might care to choose is not restricted by others, positive libertarians demand that we actually utilise this capacity. So, for them, freedom is an *exercise concept*; being free means 'doing something with it, not

---

[20] Berlin (*Four Essays on Liberty*) is thinking along the same lines when he remarks: 'It is one thing to say that I may be coerced for my own good which I am too blind to see: this may, on occasion, be for my benefit; indeed it may enlarge the scope of my liberty. It is another to say that if it is my good, then I am not being coerced' (p. 134). It might be argued that by using the term 'limited paternalism' I am conceding too much to the paternalist. Suppose I am faced with two options, *1* which limits another's freedom to degree *x* and *2* which limits it to degree *x + y*. If I choose *1*, it is not clear whether that is even to count as 'limited paternalism', since the reason for intervention is to minimise interferences with liberty, which is not paternalistic.

just sitting pretty on it'.[21] In the ensuing discussion we shall see how these two elements are reflected, to varying degrees, in theories of positive liberty and examine what bearing this has on their potential viability as accounts of social freedom. Before that, however, let me in this section clear up some misunderstandings which have led to an unfortunate conflation of negative and positive liberty.

I have already mentioned some accounts of negative liberty such as Berlin's most permissive one (or a possible responsibility view on the strict-responsibility reading) which, although being faithful to the form of a negative account, yield definitions of a constraint that are too broad to be acceptable. Meanwhile, some of the reasons that tend to lead negative liberty thinkers away from the crude Hobbesian model or the narrow liberal one were shown to be perfectly respectable. Now, many of these same reasons have been invoked by writers who do not claim to be advancing an improved account of negative liberty but one that transcends the distinction between negative and positive liberty – or even a purely positive account. These 'mixed' or 'pure' accounts are then supposed to reveal the indispensability, if not the conceptual superiority, of positive liberty. Shedding some light on the conceptual confusions that lie at the heart of these claims will help us to focus on the real dividing line between negative and positive freedom.

It is fair to say that a common characteristic of these 'aberrant' writers is their disillusionment with the traditional narrow accounts of negative liberty – which leads them to conclude, mistakenly, that what is wrong with these accounts is not that they are too narrow, but that they are negative. This error may be partly vitiated by the fact that the received wisdom about what a negative theory can and cannot involve is often highly distorted. Thus, we may be told that a haemophiliac living in rural Alaska, who cannot afford to see a Park Avenue haematologist, is only socially unfree to do so in a positive model of liberty – or that a negative theory gives a baby, abandoned in a public thoroughfare, only the right to be left

---

[21] B. Crick, 'Freedom as Politics', in P. Laslett and W. G. Runciman (eds.), *Philosophy, Politics and Society*, III (Oxford: Basil Blackwell, 1967), p. 206.

alone.[22] The baby may lack 'enabling conditions' but it is not 'blocked by countervailing forces', to use a common terminology. Providing help in cases like these, education to the uneducated or means of life to the poor is, we are given to believe, something that a negative account cannot possibly explain as ways to remove constraints on freedom. I have already exposed the falsity of these claims, and shown how they apply only if one accepts an overly narrow definition of a constraint, for instance, as an obstacle which has been *deliberately* imposed by another agent. Freedom, on a plausible and coherent negative account, is much more than bare immunity from such deliberately created constraints. However, the writers referred to above, giving credence to the received wisdom, have concluded that half a loaf is not the bread they expected from a definition of freedom and have, consequently, renounced their allegiance to the negative camp. Let us look at a few noteworthy examples.

In a paper called 'Does Equality Destroy Liberty?' R. Norman argues for the claim that, so far from being antithetical, *freedom* and *equality* are in fact interdependent values. As Norman believes that the negative picture of liberty cannot do justice to this truth, he proposes a definition, 'stressing the positive fact of choice rather than the mere negative fact of non-interference'; according to this freedom means the 'availability of, and capacity to exercise, meaningful and effective choice'.[23] Now, Norman is surely right in taking the axe to certain overly-narrow accounts of liberty and pointing out that 'the dividing line between natural and human impediments leaves a great deal more on the human side of the line than might at first appear'.[24] But why assume that a broader and more sophisticated negative-liberty theory cannot account for this? I have argued, for example, that poverty can be a constraint upon freedom to the extent that identifiable people can be held accountable for it through their negligence, violation of positive duties, etc. There

[22] See, e.g., M. Levin, 'Negative Liberty', in E. F. Paul and J. Paul (eds.), *Liberty and Equality* (Oxford: Basil Blackwell, 1985), pp. 85 and 95.
[23] R. Norman, 'Does Equality Destroy Liberty?', in K. Graham (ed.), *Contemporary Political Philosophy. Radical Studies* (Cambridge University Press, 1982), p. 87.
[24] Ibid., pp. 95–6.

is no need to cry out for a *rapprochement* of negative and positive theories to explain that. It should also be noticed that Norman's own definition fails to meet either of the two criteria which I invoked as touchstones of positive-liberty theories: what it demands is only the 'capacity' for effective choice, not its exercise, and there is no mention of internal bars that could constrain the agent's own freedom. There is, however, some confusion in Norman's paper as to the distinction between ability and freedom. He takes a man who unexpectedly inherits a fortune and suddenly becomes aware of new ways of living to be on a par with a man who experiences liberation upon release from prison.[25] Thus, although nothing in what Norman says exceeds the natural boundaries of a negative account, he may in the end be guilty of the same mistake as Berlin in his most permissive mood, seeing constraints on freedom as potentially emanating from all the alterable consequences of people's actions, and thus shrinking unduly the domain of mere inability.

I. Hunt states in a recent paper that he essentially agrees with Norman's position, and this is unfortunately the case, although Hunt's analysis is considerably more subtle.[26] Hunt stresses the importance of both positive and negative liberty; not as 'two types of freedom', but rather as 'two kinds of condition of freedom: the presence of enabling conditions of our capacity to pursue our interests; and the absence of countervailing conditions of such a capacity'.[27] His overall conclusion is that when positive and negative freedom are properly distinguished in this way, 'both are necessary and desirable for freedom in its fullest sense', namely, freedom as our capacity to pursue our interests in the absence of some humanly corrigible obstacle (once again *la* Berlin at his most permissive).[28] Alert to the objection that his distinction is illusory or useless, because the absence of enabling conditions and the presence of countervailing ones can both be considered constraints on freedom in a negative model such as Miller's, Hunt responds that these conditions still differ in an important way 'at a causal explanatory level'.[29] So it may well

[25] Ibid., p. 96.
[26] See I. Hunt, 'Freedom and its Conditions', *Australasian Journal of Philosophy*, 69 (1991).
[27] Ibid., 300. [28] Ibid., 288. [29] Ibid., 297.

be, but the question remains of what could be the possible relevance of referring to such an explanatory level for conceptual or substantive debates about freedom . If it does not in the end serve to distinguish between constraints and non-constraints in a way that differs from common negative-liberty theories – Hunt seems to acknowledge our earlier insight that causal responsibility is not relevant for such a distinction – then why is he so eager to affiliate himself with positive liberty? And if the presence of enabling conditions and the absence of countervailing ones is as such equally important, how does the mere exercise of distinguishing between them at a causal level in particular cases assist us in settling political disputes?

Finally, let us look briefly at some of the views aired by L. Crocker in his book *Positive Liberty*. Somewhat ironically, Crocker, the only writer to have devoted a whole book to the advocacy of 'positive liberty', turns out to be nothing more than another negative libertarian in disguise. He claims that the largest difference between traditional (negative) libertarian views and positive or 'left' libertarianism is the latter's support for affirmative programmes aimed at removing incapacities and developing human capacities: providing free time, equipment, facilities, and other means to the enlargement of life's possibilities.[30] By contrast, the right libertarian wants only to minimise restraint and coercion. For example, Crocker's blind man, curable with a moderate expenditure, is not, according to the right libertarian, interfered with by those who could afford to pay for a sight-restoring operation but fail to do so.[31] Thus construed, Crocker has, of course, not much difficulty in distinguishing between positive and negative liberty and renouncing the latter. But we have seen that this is simply representing negative liberty in its most implausible, if not caricatural, form. Crocker's own words, however, show that he has no sympathy with positive liberty proper. He says he is 'cautious' in counting internal obstacles as limitations of freedom, since they are not restrictions of 'social liberty'.[32] Moreover, the 'positive liberty' he wants to defend is 'a matter of the presence of options and opportunities,

[30] L. Crocker, *Positive Liberty* (The Hague: Martinus Nijhoff Publisher, 1980), p. 70.
[31] Ibid., p. 2.   [32] Ibid., p. 3.

not a matter of self-mastery or rationality', and the concept of autonomy is really 'quite distinct' from it.[33] I could not agree more, but then I am supposed to be the negative libertarian! Crocker's book is deficient as an account of positive liberty precisely in that it rejects the defining characteristics that distinguish positive from negative liberty. In the end, Crocker upholds nothing more than the by now all-too-familiar version of negative liberty, as that which we would be free to do on some other possible social arrangement,[34] openly declaring his support for Berlin's rendering of it.[35] But there is no reason whatsoever to saddle that view with the name 'positive liberty'.

Crocker's ultimate aim is to find some conceptual apparatus which can underpin the ideological perspective which he calls 'left libertarianism' but would probably be termed 'social democratism' or 'socialism' outside of the USA. However, Crocker is wrong in thinking that a conceptual analysis of freedom will underpin a given ideology. There is, for example, no necessary connection between maintaining a negative account of liberty and upholding so-called libertarian values – witness Hobbes, or the socialist G. A. Cohen who mounts a strong argument for socialism simply in terms of a negative account. Moreover, a right-wing libertarian could plausibly hold that my responsibility view of freedom is correct, and that private property often constitutes a constraint on the freedom of the propertyless. But he could simply add that, on the same account, depriving the owners of their property is also a constraint on freedom, and that for *political* (rather than conceptual) reasons the latter restriction is always, or almost always, more severe and lamentable than the former.

I am not the first writer to argue that everything which can be correctly said about freedom by means of a positive-liberty vocabulary, can be said with even greater clarity within the confines of negative accounts. For instance, the aim of Rodger Beehler's paper 'For One Concept of Liberty' is to demonstrate that the negative concept of freedom is sufficient for the purpose of political and legal discourse.[36] He distinguishes between the

[33] Ibid., p. 4.   [34] Ibid., p. 67.   [35] Ibid., p. 4.
[36] See R. Beehler, 'For One Concept of Liberty', *Journal of Applied Philosophy*, 8 (1991).

positive concept familiar from political and social theory, and the 'street-smart' sense of positive liberty, namely, the one most widely employed in political argument.[37] As to the former, Beehler contends (as I shall do in the following sections) that this should not be admitted as a putative concept of liberty at all, since it dishonours central features of social freedom, for example, by conflating the psychological condition 'lack of autonomy' with the social relation 'lack of freedom'.[38] About the 'street-smart' concept (the one under discussion in the present section) Beehler claims it is in effect the negative concept misdescribed, since it merely duplicates the negative concept within the so-called positive formulation. That is, positive liberty in the street-smart sense treats *not being interfered with* and *possessing the means necessary to act* as though they were distinct, whereas in most relevant circumstances they are the same condition.[39] Thus, Beehler sees, for instance, no reason why the negative concept cannot enable us 'to say all that is necessary about the ways in which a lack of economic resources can nullify formally accorded liberties'.[40]

If this sounds familiar, it is because Beehler seems to be applying the same reasoning as I did; his arguments against the positive-liberty concept of the streets seem to follow the same pattern as my above response to the conceptual-superiority thesis. However, this analogy is partly illusory, for Beehler does not advocate a responsibility view of negative freedom. On the contrary, his paper assumes that traditional conceptions of negative liberty suffice to knock the bottom out of the standard ('street-smart') positive-liberty arguments. It will be helpful, both for the purposes of the present section and those of my study in general, to devote some space to showing why Beehler's assumption is mistaken. The conception of negative liberty to which he helps himself is generally too *narrow* in its identification of the relevant constraining-agents. Somewhat surprisingly, however, it may also at times be too permissive or *broad* in locating such agents.

The first problem we encounter when analysing Beehler's

---

[37] Ibid., 27.   [38] Ibid., 31.   [39] Ibid., 40–1.   [40] Ibid., 27.

arguments is that it is not always clear what exactly his conception of negative liberty involves. 'Throughout, I mean by the "negative" concept of liberty that conception of liberty according to which a person is free to the extent that he or she is not, and will not be, prevented by others from doing what he or she chooses to do', Beehler says.[41] However, this formulation is clearly ambiguous between various conceptions. Does 'preventing' imply intentionality on behalf of the constraining-agents, or something less, such as causal responsibility? Are we prevented from choosing x when x is rendered more difficult to achieve, or only when the option of x-ing has been completely removed?

Fortunately, other points made by Beehler serve to bring out his position more clearly. Thus, he talks about 'coercive threats' as freedom-restricting and stipulates that a person 'who is confronted by threat of harm, confinement, or substantial property loss if he performs some action A may . . . be described as not able to perform A'.[42] In general, the impression conveyed by Beehler's words indicates that he is advocating the common liberal conception: an *intentionality view* of constraints with its typical concomitant: an *ineligibility view* about the weight of such constraints.

Recall then the standard positive-liberty objection which Beehler aims to rebut: it says that traditional accounts of negative liberty, such as his own, fail to explain the existence of paradigmatic relations of constraint, for instance, that of the overprivileged in society to those at their beam-ends. Beehler digs in his heels, arguing that the point of this objection is so far off target that on his very own negative-liberty conception, what a person lacks the money to do, he or she is incontestably unfree to do (assuming the person lives in a society with a money economy):

Just *try* doing in our society what it costs money to do, when you lack the money! Try taking over a television network's transmission for an hour, or a page of a major newspaper for a day – try even just eating in a restaurant, or going to a movie – or studying at university – without having the money to do so. The police will be in the television studio, or

[41] Ibid.   [42] Ibid., 42.

pressroom offices, or at your restaurant table, or on your doorstep, shortly.[43]

Beehler's reasoning is very simple: *B* is unfree to do *x* when *A* (intentionally) prevents *B* from *x*-ing. If one wants to go to university but cannot pay the tuition fee, one is unfree to go there in the straightforward sense that if one attempts to do so one will be interfered with by university authorities, or – if one obstinately refuses to leave the university premises – by the police and courts. Thus, Beehler's traditional negative-liberty conception has no problem whatsoever about explaining how poverty can be a constraint on the freedom of the poor, and there is no reason to give it up for the street-smart conception of positive liberty.

Let us grant for the moment that in case I lack the economic resources to cover the tuition fee, the university clerk who demands that I pay this fee before enrolling has constrained my freedom to enter university. However, at best this constitutes a very uninteresting sense of unfreedom. It is like saying that the race official, who insists that only the first person past the post can be considered to have won a race, has rendered the fallen runner (p. 14) unfree to finish as the victor! It does not mend matters much to add that the university authorities, who decide the exact amount of the tuition fee, or the police, who subsequently remove me from the premises, have also constrained my freedom. All this could be true without our still having located the *primary* constraining-agents – the ones the positive libertarians are after – namely, those who through inattention and mindlessness might have left me indigent: perhaps members of an overprivileged upper-class, perhaps politicians in strategic positions to change an unjust economic order but failing to do so.

The basic question is: *with respect to whom* is the poor person primarily unfree? The answers suggested by Beehler's examples once again bring to light two characteristic weaknesses of the liberal conception. *First*, it only identifies those constraining-agents who deliberately put obstacles in our paths, not the ones who do so through negligence and avoidable omissions. Often the

---

[43] Ibid., 39–40.

primary malefactors – the real *powerholders* – may escape recognition. It would be foolish to think that whenever people with power in society impoverish others, they do so intentionally. More often the poverty is a non-intentional effect, a by-product of other measures, unforeseen by any specific individual among the powerholders because none of them took the trouble to weigh the foreseeable consequences of their actions (see further p. 159). Meanwhile, the liberal conception is notoriously apt at picking out petty constraining-agents: the university clerks, the policemen, etc., the people 'doing their duty'. *Second*, as noted in section 2.1, the intentionality view refuses to accept that *A* can constrain *B*'s freedom unless *A*'s act or omission has *brought about* the obstacle facing *B*. *A*'s carelessly disregarding an already existing obstacle does not constitute a constraint, at least not until *B*'s direct request for assistance to remove the obstacle is met with a rebuff by *A*. What a splendid way to exculpate ourselves from blame for not helping those starving masses in Ethiopia: they are not unfree *with respect to us!*

I conclude from all this that Beehler's conception of negative liberty is much too narrow. It does not explain the *way* in which poverty can be a constraint on freedom in a manner which might convert positive libertarians, or be of relevance for political philosophy. If the choice were only between negative liberty on Beehler's pristine account and positive liberty in the street-smart sense, we would be forced to opt for the latter.

The claim that a poor person is rendered unfree to enter university by university authorities forced to charge tuition fees, by office clerks doing their jobs, or 'by the existing institutional arrangements of police and courts'[44] would at best be deemed platitudinous by positive libertarians. If these persons count as constraining-agents, they do so in a secondary sense only. Here the insights of positive liberty may tally with those of the responsibility view of negative liberty. The responsibility view would not confine its attention to those who intentionally put obstacles in the poor person's way, but would rather search for those who, intentionally or not, have contributed to his misery.

_____

[44] Ibid., 40.

There is even reason to believe that the responsibility view would at times be more restrictive in identifying the petty (secondary) constraining-agents than the intentionality view. This can be brought out by considering another of Beehler's examples of constrained persons: those who cannot enter university because they are intellectually incapable of academic work.[45] At first sight one might think Beehler is simply conflating *ability* and *freedom*. Surely these persons may be free, although unable, to go to university. However, Beehler's point is that lack of intellectual, physical, psychological, or moral capacities can be considered constraints on freedom in social situations 'in which possession of the requisite capacity is a necessary *enabling* condition qualifying a person to be accorded *by other persons* admission to some specific activity, enterprise, or whatever. Non-possession of the capacity makes the person lacking it not free to undertake the activity in question, because other people control . . . access to the activity or to the means of engaging in it.'[46] So, again we can imagine an unfortunate student trying to enrol at a university, this time only to be told by university authorities that he lacks the intellectual capacities to study there. Is he then unfree with respect to them, as Beehler insists?

That sounds counter-intuitive, and once again the responsibility view comes to our rescue. There seems to be no reason, not even prima facie, to expect universities to be open to all, irrespective of their intellectual capacities. Hence, the people in charge there cannot, in general, be held morally responsible for setting and enforcing some standards of competence for prospective students: that is, they cannot be held responsible for those standards *qua* obstacles to the applicants' choices. For – to repeat a previous example – if we held them responsible in that sense, we would also have to say that everybody who wants to fly to the moon, but cannot, is unfree to do so with respect to people in power – because presumably the 'enabling conditions', qualifying more persons as astronauts, could be realised if enough human resources were devoted to that end. However, this is not, as Miller noted, a 'helpful extension' of the concept of unfreedom (p. 68).

---

[45] Ibid., 35.   [46] Ibid., 37.

Unfortunately, Beehler is stuck in the grooves of a pristine conception of negative liberty, one which is sometimes too permissive, but more often too restrictive, in its identification of constraining-agents. I have shown that while standard 'street-smart' positive-liberty objections hit at Beehler's account, they leave the responsibility view of negative liberty untouched. The latter can, whereas the former cannot, strip the misguided negative libertarians described in this section of their camouflage. This may not be conclusive evidence for the viability of the responsibility view of freedom, but it must count as a big point in its favour.

5.4. PROMETHEAN FREEDOM

I'll put up with everything – police, soldiers, muzzling of the press, limits on parliament . . . Freedom of the *spirit* is the only thing for men to be proud of and which raises them above animals.[47]

These words, expressed by Richard Wagner, represent the natural self-assertion of an oppressed party who tries to bolster his own courage and resilience in the face of adversity: you can lock me up, harass me, and beat me, but at least my spirit remains free – and that is the most important freedom of all. Wagner's words as such give no indication to which definition of freedom the oppressed party adheres, they only show what aspect of freedom he happens to value most and what varieties of constraints (he tries to convince himself) he is ready to tolerate. But the view expressed by Wagner may sometimes fuse subtly with another, and philosophically more important, one: that, to quote Oscar Wilde, 'a man can be totally free even in that granite embodiment of governmental constraint, prison'.[48] Here, the point is not only that a person can put up with so-and-so much unfreedom, but a stronger one, namely, that certain familiar kinds of constraints do not make us unfree at all. In this section, I shall be concerned with a genuine positive-liberty

---

[47] Cf. D. E. Cooper, 'The Free Man', in A. P. Griffiths (ed.), *Of Liberty*. Supplement to *Philosophy* (Cambridge University Press, 1983), p. 131.
[48] Cf. ibid.

theory, a theory of what has been called 'Promethean freedom',[49] 'retreat to the inner citadel', or simply 'inner freedom', and that is supposed to account for the truth embodied in Wilde's statement.

Theories of Promethean freedom assume that man's self is divided into two parts, a 'higher' and a 'lower' self, and that 'real freedom' consists in the *subjugation* of the latter by the former. 'Subjugation' must, however, be given a highly unusual interpretation, as we shall see. In a typical statement of this view, D. Cooper emphasises that the right perspective upon freedom is not the common 'civil' one, but a 'private' perspective which sees freedom as a state of mind, rather than as the state of being free from external constraints.[50]

The classic position of Promethean freedom is represented by Stoicism. A pantheistic system, whose linchpin was fullblown natural determinism, the precarious marriage between causation and moral responsibility was accomplished in early Stoicism by means akin to those employed by modern-day soft determinism: although human behaviour is determined, like other events in nature, an action can be considered free (or one for which the agent is morally responsible) if one of its causes is an act of the agent's will – a volition. So far, there is no mention of a bifurcated self. But, as the centuries passed, this soft determinism gradually developed in Stoic thought into the idea of Promethean freedom, represented, for instance, in the writings of Epictetus. There, the events of the external world are believed to be as inexorably determined as before (human actions included), but now man is seen as having the possibility of escaping from this sphere of necessity into an inward space: a protected area to which the laws of cause and effect have no access. In this haven, man's higher self, his reason, can find shelter – freedom – from the fleeting world of necessity to which his lower, appetitive, self is doomed. Man's destiny is compared to that of a dog tied to a cart. He cannot help being dragged along by the cart, but it is up to him what attitude he takes to this external unfreedom within

---

[49] This term was coined by Cooper, see ibid., p. 132, the reason being that 'Prometheus is the paradigm of the man who, enchained by the ruler of rulers, Zeus, yet remains defiantly free'.

[50] Ibid., pp. 131–2.

the confines of his mind: he may be dragged along grudgingly, or he may trot willingly and happily beside the cart. It goes without saying which attitude is then considered the rational one to take.

Wherever this idea of Promethean freedom manifests itself, I see it as resting on three main assumptions: (*i*) Man is subject to some kind of external necessity that restricts his freedom of action completely, or almost completely. (*ii*) Despite this, his real/higher self can seek refuge in an internal domain where it is free from external determination; however, this inner freedom is of little or no consequence to his lower/physical self. (*iii*) The true and only freedom of man is the recognition of external necessity and the mental attitude that is bound to follow: equanimity, tranquillity, or (sometimes) apathy. We thus see what 'subjugation of the lower self by the higher self' really amounts to, namely, paying no attention to it, flouting it. We subjugate our lower nature by detaching our real selves from it.

Historians of ideas tend to explain the concept of Promethean freedom as a reaction to difficult social conditions which hold little prospect of improvement: times of turmoil or economic exigencies. In such situations, the most available recourse may be an 'inner emigration' to the wonderland where you can find solace from your troubles; nothing can touch you and nobody can hurt you; where you can abandon yourself to a mental life of passive detachment from the outside world.

However, straitened circumstances are not always the spring of this notion. In times of relative economic abundance, Promethean freedom has sometimes laid the foundation not for abject *passiveness*, but for unsurpassed *heroism*. The clearest examples of this are found in what MacIntyre calls 'heroic societies': Homeric Greece and the realm of the Icelandic sagas.[51] Being more at home with the latter, I grant that some of MacIntyre's insights into the world of the sagas are very much to the point. He recognises, for example, that in them *fate* is a social reality and the descrying of it an important social role – and that

---

[51] A. MacIntyre, *After Virtue* (London: Duckworth, 1981), ch. 10.

understanding the workings of fate is in itself considered to be a virtue.[52] But not all the conclusions which MacIntyre draws from this about the 'key features' of heroic society are correct. He claims that a 'man in heroic society is what he does ... he has no hidden depths', and that to 'judge a man therefore is to judge his actions'.[53]

That man's *actions* are the touchstone of his real virtues in a fatalistic society seems very implausible; in the case of the Icelandic sagas, at any rate, it is simply untrue. There, man is not 'what he does' but what he *thinks*: what attitude he takes to the drama of his life, whose script has been written in advance. Gísli Súrsson is, as MacIntyre himself notes, a winner, not a loser at the moment of his heroic death. However, it is not because of the number of men he kills or wounds before he is himself overborne, it is because he is a hero at heart: he has the attitudes and ideas that befit a hero. Björn in *Njáls saga* also fights against the odds when battling with the hero Kári, but even while doing so he is a coward at heart and therefore remains an object of unrelenting derision.

The real magic in the literary style of the Icelandic sagas, which seems to have misled MacIntyre, lies in the fact that the things which really matter, man's 'hidden depths', are never described from the inside, as it were, but must always be deduced from descriptions of the person's outward appearance: his countenance, his clothes, his kinship, the odd remarks he makes, etc. MacIntyre mistakes the charming but cryptic *style* of these epic works for an important philosophical truth about the ideas of the society they describe, and thus comes to see things upside down. In reality, the Icelandic sagas are a classical embodiment of the main features of Promethean freedom. The hallmark of the hero is that before the inevitable battle he sees himself faced by a kind of a positive dilemma: his fate is either to die or to survive. If the former, why not die proudly and courageously? If the latter, what reason is there for holding back, either? As the outcome is already determined, a man's real freedom resides in his soul; and, while everything else fades away

[52] Ibid., p. 117.   [53] Ibid., p. 115.

into death and oblivion, the hero's *reputation*, as judged by the *approach* he takes to his destiny, lives on.

How much of what I have said about the Icelandic sagas applies to the society depicted by Homer and the Greek tragedies is an open question. However, if (as I am inclined to believe) the metaphysics of the ancient Greek epics is similar to that of the sagas, Martha Nussbaum need not be as puzzled as she is about Agamemnon's attitude to his predicament in Aeschylus' *Agamemnon*.[54] Faced with the heavy doom of having his expedition fail unless he offers up his daughter Iphigenia as a sacrifice, Agamemnon at first despairs. But he then begins to arrange his feelings to accord with his fortune, and ends up as a willing victim, slipping his own neck into the 'yoke-strap of necessity'.[55] Nussbaum wonders what moral significance it can have simply to blow with the winds that strike against you, and co-operate inwardly with necessity. She concludes that Agamemnon's moral crisis is defused 'by means that seem arbitrary and strange'.[56] Arbitrary and strange they may seem to us, but, given the background of a Promethean theory of freedom, they are the most natural thing in the world. Was not Agamemnon simply entering the sphere of his real freedom, and leaving behind the realm of necessity, by taking this attitude to his predicament?

Although the idea of Promethean freedom has exercised a strange fascination for people at various times in history, the arguments against it are both numerous and strong. *Firstly*, the idea of locating 'real' freedom in a special realm, beyond the empirical world of causality, in a system that is otherwise deterministic, seems seriously suspect. A modern determinist might reply to it in the following way:

People's deliberations take place within the same spatio-temporal order as other natural events in the world. The thoughts that people have at any time, and the reasoning in which they will engage, is determined by the state of their central nervous system and their environment at that time. There is no reason to suppose that the

---

[54] M. C. Nussbaum, *The Fragility of Goodness* (Cambridge University Press, 1986), ch. 2.
[55] Ibid., pp. 35–6.
[56] Ibid., p. 47.

deliberations of pure practical reason are any less caused by brain events than are those of inclination-tainted deliberation. Moreover, if it were the case that there is a natural causal order, which includes the actions of bodies . . . as well as the coming and going of inclinations, it is difficult to see how the 'actions' of the rational self could . . . fail to violate the laws of the natural causal order.[57]

Secondly, Promethean freedom has the counter-intuitive implication that by removing desires we automatically become freer: if a slave does not desire freedom any more, *qua* slave he is no longer unfree. *Thirdly,* as Berlin has pointed out, Promethean freedom rests on the presupposition that knowledge always liberates, that once something is understood or known, it is conceptually impossible to see oneself as being at the mercy of it.[58] But how does the mere knowledge that I have been locked up in my room make me freer? We might want to insist that knowledge is always better than ignorance, but this does not entail that it always makes us freer. On the contrary, real constraints remain constraints even if they are understood and accepted as such. *Fourthly,* we can ask why apathy at worst, heroism at best, is the natural concomitant of the recognition of necessity. Why not irony, or simply despair? *Fifthly,* and most importantly for the argumentation in this book, Promethean theories grossly violate the condition of social freedom that a man cannot make himself unfree. In fact, they violate it to such an extreme degree as to make the subjugation by one part of myself of another a necessary condition of my own real freedom.

In our society, it may be considered an advantage both to be tall and adaptable. For very short people, adaptability is a special asset. However, no one would be tempted to claim that being adaptable enough is the same as being tall, nor dream of including adaptability in his definition of tallness. Similarly, nothing seems to be gained by equating freedom (a relation between agents) and Promethean self-control (a virtue of an individual) – nothing, that is, except conceptual sloppiness. Learning to meet hardship with insouciance and shortage with

---

[57] R. Lindley, *Autonomy* (London: Macmillan, 1986), p. 24.
[58] See 'From Hope and Fear Set Free', in I. Berlin, *Concepts and Categories* (ed. H. Hardy, London: The Hogarth Press, 1978).

self-abnegation undoubtedly makes us *happier*, but there is no good reason for holding that it necessarily makes us *freer*. Thus, logically consistent or not, Promethean theories have no relevance for a correct analysis of social freedom. They can most favourably be understood as upholding certain virtues, such as self-control, self-abnegation, and equanimity in times of hardship, but as carrying them to the extreme by incorporating them within a framework of ill-founded metaphysics.

5.5. FREEDOM AS AUTONOMY

'Autonomy' means literally, as indicated by etymology ('autos' = self; 'nomos' = rules/laws), the having or making of one's own laws. Before examining the variety of positive liberty, quite fashionable at present, which tries to link autonomy with social freedom, some conceptual clarifications are needed. Furthermore, something must be said about the connection between social freedom and freedom of the will, an issue that has been explicitly avoided in this book so far.

Let us start by invoking a useful distinction between 'autonomy' and 'autarchy'.[59] An *autarchic* person has the general psychological constitution necessary for autonomy, i.e., he is a competent chooser, whether or not he happens to make a reflective choice in a given situation. This means that the autarchic person has the capacity for what Aristotle would call practical reason: he can look for reasons, deliberate on them, and make rational decisions when confronted by a range of options. Remaining faithful to etymology, a *heterarchic* agent would only be (*1*) one who had been deprived of this capacity by another person. However, for the sake of simplification, I shall use 'heterarchy' as a contradictory rather than as a contrary of 'autarchy', so

---

[59] This distinction relies heavily on suggestions from S. I. Benn, 'Freedom, Autonomy and the Concept of a Person', *Proceedings of the Aristotelian Society*, 76 (1975–6), pp. 112–17. However, rather than distinguishing, as I do, between the capacity for, and the exercise of, reflective choice, Benn's aim (at least as further developed in his *A Theory of Freedom* (Cambridge University Press, 1988), chs. 8–9, seems to be to contrast two *capacities*: that of being minimally able to make one's own decisions (however uncritically), and that of being able to make them on the basis of values which are the result of one's own critical evaluation and selection from beliefs and values imparted by one's culture.

that everybody who is not autarchic is to be considered heterarchic. Thus, in addition to (*1*) above, a person could be heterarchic for two reasons: because (*2*) of a natural impediment (mental deficiency, brain damage, psychotic state, etc.) that disqualifies him as a chooser, or because (*3*) he has sold himself into some kind of mental slavery (drug addiction, yielding himself mindlessly to manipulation, etc.). Plainly, what these different causes of heterarchy have in common is that they paralyse or impair the agent's capacity for choice, blocking the possibility of rational decision-making.

A person is *autonomous* when he exercises his autarchy, being, as Rousseau or Kant would put it, obedient to a law that he has prescribed to himself. As in the case of heterarchy, 'heteronomy' and 'autonomy' will be considered contradictories. Hence, a person can fail to be autonomous (and thus be *heteronomous*) in a given situation for three reasons: because (*1*) he is constrained by someone else from reaching an autonomous decision, (*2*) he fails to do so owing to some natural impediment (temporary illness, extreme fatigue, lack of knowledge for which no other person is accountable, etc.), or (*3*) he simply does not bother to make the effort. However, in spite of this, he may remain *overall* a competent chooser. These conceptual points clearly entail that every heterarchic person is necessarily heteronomous, but not vice versa, because, as Benn says, 'a competent chooser may still be a slave to convention, choosing by standards he has accepted quite uncritically from his milieu'.[60] A 'slave to convention' may be a rather strong way of putting it, for the autonomous person must keep his capacity to make independent judgements intact; any possible conformism must simply be caused by the fact that he is too busy, lazy, or complacent to look critically at the issues himself, while he can do so if he wants to. Otherwise, he is not only heteronomous, but also heterarchic, toeing the line of custom like a person under hypnosis.

In sum, the autonomous person actualises that which the autarchic person only has potentially. He is not only capable of reasoning, he reasons; not only capable of choosing, he chooses.

---

[60] Ibid., p. 123.

But being fully autonomous is, of course, impossible for a finite being. Trying to reach a rational decision before every action would not only make our lives miserable but impossible to live. While autarchy is a *principle*, something that we generally expect people to have, autonomy is thus rightly described as an *ideal* that transcends it, a goal thought to be worthy of aspiration although it cannot always be attained.[61]

It might now be worthwhile to bring some of this to bear on the question about the connection between free will and social freedom briefly touched upon in chapter 1. Strawson argued convincingly in a famous paper that there are a number of attitudes and institutions (praise and blame, punishment and reward) which are appropriate only to agents who are in some (non-social) sense *free*, and that a person is considered morally responsible only if he is a possible candidate for such attitudes.[62] Since on my view of social freedom the attribution of moral responsibility plays a major role, we must ask what precisely this other sense of freedom amounts to that is required for judgements about social freedom to be appropriate.

Day has an unequivocal answer, namely, that liberty presupposes *ability*: the truth of 'A is able to D' being a necessary condition both of the truth and also of the falsity of 'A is unfree to D'.[63] That this cannot be the correct answer is, however, shown by the fact that a man with a broken leg, confined to a wheelchair, must be counted as free to run, although he cannot; if there were a law against running, he would be unfree to run in addition to being unable to do so. If this statement seems to go against ordinary usage, let it be an initial reminder of the common need to trim the ragged edges of such usage (see further in ch. 7). For surely, we often want to distinguish in our language between natural and man-made impediments, and, by categorising them all as constraints on freedom, we obliterate that very distinction in the same way as we would obliterate the

[61] Ibid., pp. 123–30.
[62] See 'Freedom and Resentment', in P. F. Strawson, *Freedom and Resentment and Other Essays* (London: Methuen, 1974).
[63] J. P. Day, 'Threats, Offers, Law, Opinion and Liberty', *American Philosophical Quarterly*, 14 (1977), 264.

distinction between cars and bicycles by calling both 'cars'. If only for the sake of conceptual clarification, we are well advised to accept that, just as we are often *unfree* to do what we are *able* to do, we are also often *free* to do what we are *unable* to do.

However, the situation changes drastically if we imagine the man being confined to the chair not because of a broken leg but because of a state of severe mental retardation, or if the 'person' sitting there turns out to be an automaton. Here, I think, we come to the core of the matter: questions about social freedom can be raised only about beings who are *autarchic*, who have the minimal capacity to choose. Otherwise, they are not *freedom-evaluable* in the first place. A person in a coma, let alone by others, is not, as one writer claims,[64] a paradigm case of negative freedom: such a person is neither socially free nor unfree. This is also why we hesitate to call a kleptomaniac socially free or unfree to steal since we are not sure if he is really freedom-evaluable in that respect or not.[65]

In chapter 1, I passed a tentative judgement about free will being in some sense a prerequisite of social freedom. Strawson must be understood as making a similar point, and now we may have pinpointed what this sense is. In fact, I would want to claim that all fruitful discussions about *free will* are discussions about the precise nature and extent of *autarchy*, the capacity to choose. Still, someone might want to leave a space in between 'autarchy' and 'determinism' for Epicurean, or should we say Heisenbergian, freedom of the will, covering decisions that are not causally determined but happen at random. I have no real objection to this use; but note simply that this kind of 'freedom of

---

[64] H. J. McCloskey, 'A Critique of the Ideals of Liberty', *Mind*, 74 (1965), 494.

[65] There is a provocative, if ultimately unconvincing, critique of this freedom-evaluability condition in D. Coole's paper, 'Constructing and Deconstructing Liberty: A Feminist and Poststructuralist Analysis', *Political Studies*, 41 (1993). Coole sees it as functioning as a form of power, suppressing passions, emotions, intuitions, and fantasies in the name of rationality and excluding bearers of these elements (especially women) from reckoning as sufferers of unfreedom. Her point may have some historical justification, femininity having often been associated with irrationality, but there is no reason why an enlightened negative-liberty account need make this mistake (nor for that matter positive-liberty accounts which she criticises for a similar reason); especially not nowadays, in an age which acknowledges the essentially *rational* nature of our emotional life.

the will' would have no relevance to social freedom. If, however, this is the only kind of free will possible, or if determinism is true, all talk of 'social freedom' is meaningless.

To exemplify my conclusion about the connection between autarchy and social freedom, let us imagine a 'typical' situation of a robber, with a gun in his hand, ordering a bank clerk to hand over some money. If the robber is autarchic (but not, for instance, working under hypnosis, or insane), he is morally responsible for his threat and thus constrains the clerk's freedom. If he is heterarchic, he cannot make the bank clerk socially unfree to retain the money, but simply make him unable to do so (as is true of any kind of natural compulsion). Let us assume, however, that the robber is autarchic. The bank clerk is then either autarchic or heterarchic. If he is autarchic (which bank clerks usually are, one would hope), then he is socially unfree to retain the money, since he is constrained, and in this case coerced, to hand it over. If he is heterarchic (for instance, under hypnosis), he is not freedom-evaluable and thus neither socially free nor unfree to retain the money. He could, however, be socially unfree *qua* hypnotised person with respect to the agent who hypnotised him and possibly to those who could have prevented it but did not. All these qualifications may seem to have made the process of judging social (un)freedom a most complicated one; but in reality this is not the case since we can usually presuppose, when going about our daily business, that most of the people we are dealing with are autarchic. The reason for this is, as Benn puts it, that autarchy 'is a condition of human normality, both in the statistical sense, that the overwhelming majority of human beings satisfy it, and in the further sense that anyone who does not satisfy it falls short in some degree as a human being'.[66]

Before leaving the topic of free will and social freedom, a disclaimer is needed. It may seem that I have been upholding a theory according to which free will is a purely procedural concept of rationality, much as H. Frankfurt and G. Dworkin

---

[66] Benn, *A Theory of Freedom*, p. 155.

have done,[67] thus defusing the determinism–free will dichotomy and undermining my own claim that if determinism is true, 'social freedom' is devoid of meaning. This has not been my intention. Briefly, in the Dworkin/Frankfurt model an agent with a free will has not only *first-order* desires for particular actions, but also *second-order* (or even higher-order) desires for having a lower-order desire, or for that desire to be his will. In the latter case (which Frankfurt calls a 'second-order volition'), the agent *identifies* himself with a lower-order desire, and, as long as that process is unhindered, his will is free. But as it is conceivable that the process itself is causally determined (the person being determined to want what he really wants), Frankfurt concludes that his account of free will is neutral with regard to the problem of determinism.[68]

Relating this to what has been said here about autarchy as a precondition of social freedom, it may appear that I, like Frankfurt, have abandoned the traditional requirement of free-will theories that we are 'free to do otherwise'. As long as the *procedure* of rational decision-making is up to standard, it does not matter if our higher-order desires have been implanted in us through manipulative conditioning, hypnosis, or whatever. But, on closer inspection, this cannot be correct, since in my model such a person would not be autarchic but heterarchic. My 'autarchy' requires, as Frankfurt's 'free will' does not, what Dworkin calls 'procedural independence',[69] namely, not only that the person has the capacity to choose on the basis of his higher-order desires, but also that these desires are his own, and that the possibility to choose otherwise is a genuine option for him. Thus, I conclude that Frankfurt has failed to explicate the concept of free will or autarchy correctly. Incidentally, I think that the same applies to all those who seek to rescue free will by flirting with some kind of soft determinism. I do not need to establish as part of my present argument what precisely is meant by 'having

[67] See G. Dworkin, 'Acting Freely', *Nous*, 4 (1970); 'The Concept of Autonomy', *Grazer Philosophische Studien*, 13 (1981); and H. G. Frankfurt, 'Freedom of the Will and the Concept of a Person', *The Journal of Philosophy*, 68 (1971).

[68] Frankfurt, 'Freedom of the Will and the Concept of a Person', 20.

[69] Dworkin, 'The Concept of Autonomy', 212.

the option to choose otherwise' or that 'my desires are my own', although I can say that I am more or less in agreement with modern day indeterminists such as P. van Inwagen on those issues.[70] I should, however, finish this detour into the free-will issue by emphasising the claim that, for social freedom, the capacity for choice is presupposed, and that this capacity requires both (minimal) practical reason and procedural independence.

Now, there is an old tradition in philosophy which wants to equate social liberty – to return to that – with autonomy, or at least see the latter as a necessary condition of the former. More often than not, John Stuart Mill is taken to be one of the strongest proponents of this view, with his emphasis on individuality and the choice between different ways of life. Thus, Gray states that this particular version of positive liberty informs Mill's most liberal work, *On Liberty*.[71] As a first step in challenging the theory of freedom as autonomy, I want briefly to suggest that this may not have been Mill's view at all. What Mill defines as a necessary condition of freedom in *On Liberty* is the *readiness* and *capacity* to make deliberate choices between alternative beliefs and patterns of life, rather than the constant *exercise* of this capacity. Hence, his notion of individuality may best be understood as relating to the concept of autarchy, as I have explained it, not autonomy.

Mill argues that freedom from external constraints is a necessary causal condition of individuality which, in turn, is conducive to, or even constitutive of, real happiness. However, the fact that we are not constrained by others does not guarantee that we are free to choose. Mill is here concerned that we do not undermine our own capacity to choose by what I called earlier 'selling ourselves into some kind of mental slavery'.[72] When he claims that he 'who does anything because it is the custom makes no choice',[73] or that our 'faculties are called into no exercise by

---

[70] See P. van Inwagen, 'Ability and Responsibility', *Philosophical Review*, 87 (1978).

[71] J. Gray, *Liberalism* (London: Open University Press, 1986), pp. 58–9.

[72] Mill would probably want to say that the person who has sold himself into mental slavery is 'unfree' to choose – but it unfortunately implies that the person has constrained his own freedom. On my analysis, however, the person would have made himself 'non-freedom-evaluable'.

[73] J. S. Mill, *Utilitarianism, Liberty, Representative Government* (London: J. M. Dent & Sons, 1931), p. 116.

doing a thing merely because others do it', the emphasis must be seen as lying on the 'merely because'. What he is warning against is not what he calls the 'intelligent following' of custom, but the 'mechanical adhesion to it'.[74] Mill thus furnishes a distinction between two types of conformism.[75] To follow custom *merely* because it is a custom is not to make a choice at all; and even worse, in doing so you gradually undermine your own autarchy, and hence freedom. But to accept and follow custom, however uncritically, for instance because you are too lazy to look for an alternative or too content with the way things are, cannot be explained as a lack of freedom in Mill's view, as long as you can make the effort if you want to. Therefore, it is autarchy but not autonomy which Mill sees as a necessary *conceptual* condition of freedom.

What has confused many authors is the fact that Mill simultaneously argues for a *substantive* point, namely, the special value in modern society of making choices that are not only autonomous but also eccentric or idiosyncratic: 'Precisely because the tyranny of the majority is such as to make eccentricity a reproach, it is desirable, in order to break through that tyranny, that people should be eccentric.'[76] But this does not entail that the non-eccentric, but autarchic, conformist is in any sense less free; it only means that if you stubbornly refuse to bend your knees to custom, you are paying an *extra service* to society.

Admittedly, there are places in *On Liberty* and especially in *System of Logic* where Mill seems to demand that we not only have the opportunity for choice, but that we actually exercise it.[77] Some of these may be accounted for by the fact that Mill is not always very systematic in the presentation of his views; but where this excuse does not suffice, the following observation can be made. Claiming that being a competent chooser sometimes requires activity, does not entail that what this competence amounts to must be autonomy (exercise), not only autarchy (capacity). To take a parallel example, overcoming external obstacles may sometimes be necessary to be (negatively) free to

---

[74] Ibid., 117.
[75] See G. W. Smith, 'The Logic of J. S. Mill on Freedom', *Political Studies*, 28 (1980), 252.
[76] Mill, *Utilitarianism, Liberty, Representative Government*, pp. 124–5.
[77] See quotations and references in Smith, 'The Logic of J. S. Mill on Freedom', 238.

do *x*, but that does not mean that the freedom you end up with is more than the opportunity to do *x*. Similarly here, to remain a competent chooser, different types of activity may be needed to overcome internal or external obstacles which threaten to undermine this capacity, but that does not mean that the competence needed as a precondition of social freedom is more than a capacity to choose (autarchy). There is thus no good reason to think that Mill presupposed actual autonomy as a condition of freedom, or that he equated the two.

Suggesting that John Stuart Mill did not adhere to the view of freedom as autonomy does not, of course, show that this view is wrong. First we should note that, although 'autonomy' is most often used in the way I have suggested, to describe the state of exercising our autarchy, there are some other uses abroad. For example, 'autonomy' is sometimes invoked to refer not to a *state*, but to a *right* of non-interference, often in conjunction with topical discussions about the permissible extent of paternalism. There is no time here to partake of these debates about the *value* of autonomy, but I may be allowed to comment, as an aside, that talk about an inviolable right to autonomy may merely serve to obscure the issue at hand, since Mill seemed in any case well equipped to thwart the menace of paternalism without presupposing any such right. I shall, however, leave this and other more deviant uses of the term out of consideration. The pressing question is still about the possible connection between social freedom and autonomy: whether freedom is a necessary condition of autonomy and/or autonomy a necessary condition of freedom.

Richard Lindley in his book *Autonomy* expounds the former view by making freedom from external constraints the second of the 'two dimensions' of autonomy. Now, it is obvious from the discussion above that freedom from certain constraints is a necessary condition of autonomy, namely, from those that would make the person heteronomous in sense (*1*) above (p. 127): another agent having prevented his exercise of practical reason. But Lindley goes much further, claiming that a prisoner languishing in his cell, although having a strong, well-ordered will and being a clear, rational thinker, cannot be considered autonomous since he is 'able to do hardly anything'. Realising, however, that his own example is counter-intuitive, Lindley tries to rescue it by assuming that, while the man may *be* autonomous, he is at least prevented from *exercising* his auton- omy.[78] The problem is that such a distinction cannot easily be made in the case of autonomy, as it is itself an exercise concept. Even if we take Lindley to mean 'autarchic' when he says 'being autonomous', the counter-intuitiveness is not obviated since his claim would still entail that a person such as Nelson Mandela could not have exercised practical reason in his prison cell. On the contrary, the reasonable thing to say seems to be that, although Mandela may have been arriving at reflective choices all the time about what he would do if he were free, he was in fact prevented from acting on them. Taking rational decisions about what we would want to do and being able to carry them out are surely two distinct things. So, apart from the obvious exception noted above, social freedom does not seem to be a necessary condition of autonomy.

But is autonomy a necessary condition of social freedom? While remaining for the most part faithful to a responsibility view of negative liberty, Connolly sometimes seems to answer this question in the affirmative, for instance, by giving a definition of 'acting freely' according to which X acts freely in doing z when 'he acts without constraint upon his unconstrained and reflective *choice* with respect to z'.[79] Why 'reflective' (which seems here to mean 'autonomous')? We have already seen that autarchy is a necessary condition of freedom in the sense that a heterarchic person is not freedom-evaluable. But autarchy makes a much less extended and intense requirement on rationality than does autonomy, or more precisely, autarchy requires only in potentiality that which autonomy requires in actuality. A heteronomous person is not necessarily unfree. He is not unfree if he does not exercise choice because of a natural impediment (in that case he is merely unable to do so), or because of voluntary conformism (in that case he just does not

[78] Lindley, *Autonomy*, p. 69.
[79] W. E. Connolly, *The Terms of Political Discourse*, 2nd edn (Oxford: Martin Robertson & Co., 1983), p. 157.

bother). In neither of these cases are there obstacles to his choice for which another person is accountable and which prevent him from taking an autonomous decision. Hence, as we see, autonomy is not a necessary condition of freedom, at least not when we consider *particular* free actions.

It could be argued, however, that autonomy is in a more general and indirect sense a precondition of freedom, at least from the point of view of those of us who favour the responsibility view. For if people were *never* able to exercise practical reason, there would be no sense in asking them to give justifications for their actions; without that there would be no concept of moral responsibility and, hence, no social freedom. Moreover, the fact that someone has been known to exercise his capacity for reflective choice may be the only reliable *evidence* for our assuming that he has such a capacity. But neither point entails that individual agents cannot perform particular free actions unless they act upon a reflective choice. By comparison, soccer would not exist if no goals could be scored, but this does not mean that a particular goal-less match counts any less as a game of soccer than a match in which goals are scored.

The theory of freedom as autonomy implies both that agents can constrain their own freedom (by not bothering to take autonomous decisions) and, more generally, that a man is unfree if he does not exercise his capacity for choice. Both these claims seem to conflict with the nature of social liberty. Autonomy designates a set of properties which constitute a human *virtue*, and a very important one at that. But, unlike social freedom, autonomy is not an interpersonal relation. Claiming that *B* cannot stand in a relation of freedom with respect to *A* to do *x* unless *B* acts upon a reflective choice, unnecessarily extends the boundaries of the concept of freedom and thereby obfuscates its point. Instead of clarification, the end-product is conceptual confusion.

5.6. COMMUNAL FREEDOM

There is an Icelandic proverb which says that relatives make the worst enemies. It is particularly noticeable that the differences

between the view I shall call 'communal freedom' and other
positive liberty accounts run at least as deep as those between
communal freedom and negative liberty. With the exception of
K. Graham, who tries to square autonomy and communalism,[80]
the point of departure for most of the communal freedom
thinkers is their rejection of freedom as autonomy (and often of
Promethean freedom as well). Hannah Arendt provides a case
in point. For her there has been an ominous trend toward
transposing the idea of freedom from its 'original field, the realm
of politics and human affairs in general, to an inward domain'.[81]
B. Dauenhauer makes an even more pungent remark when he
claims that if radical human autonomy were indeed realised and
sustained, this would be a defeat for freedom and not a triumph.[82]

The basic idea of these thinkers is this: just as for the negative
libertarian the isolated, self-reliant person becomes a valued
objective, so for the proponents of autonomy man is seen
fundamentally as an atomic individual, and only derivatively as
a social being. On both of these accounts it is thus thought to be
possible and desirable for the agent to achieve radical independence from others to enhance his freedom. It is this vision of the
free, self-subsistent individual that the communal freedom
thinkers aim at vitiating. Against it, they pit the views of
Husserl, Merleau-Ponty, and other modern philosophers of a
similar stripe who claim that persons can only be human, and
consequently free, to the extent that they are citizens of a society:
participants in intersubjectivity. This latter view is then seen as
harking back to crucial elements in ancient Greek thought,
where freedom necessarily involved interplay with other persons.[83]
Nobody can be considered free as a mere individual; on the
contrary, man is only free when he acts within a framework of
communal ties, rules and bonds. Freedom is the *raison d'être* of
politics, not of splendid isolation. Some of these writers even go as
far as stating that, since communal interplay always involves

[80] That is the basic intent of his interpretation of Marx, see K. Graham, *The Battle of
Democracy: Conflict, Consensus and the Individual* (Hassocks: Wheatsheaf Books, 1986).
[81] H. Arendt, *Between Past and Future: Eight Exercises in Political Thought* (Harmondsworth:
Penguin, 1977), p. 145.
[82] B. P. Dauenhauer, 'Relational Freedom', *Review of Metaphysics*, 36 (1982), 82.
[83] Ibid., 81.

different kinds of relationships (of equality, hegemony, sub-
sumption, etc.), man is no less free when he is on the receiving
end of authority and power than when he is himself the leader,
exercising power – so long, that is, as there is mutual *respect* at
work in the relationship.[84] In simple terms, this means that
when you obey a command or yield to a constraint imposed by
another agent, this constraint does not limit your social freedom
if (*a*) you see the need for it, and (*b*) you respect the person
imposing it. In capsule form, we can thus define communal
freedom as stating that freedom is the active participation in
different relationships within a community characterised by
fraternity and mutual respect.

As a first response, it may be asked if the communal freedom
thinkers are not really imagining a wonderland in which the
ducklings of this world have become swans. Are solidarity and
respect actually the main characteristics of modern communities?
In Benn's *Theory of Freedom*, there is a trenchant and insightful
critique of different communitarian models which seems to
indicate that the *mutuality* sought for there can be realised only in
face-to-face relations, not on a larger societal basis, and that
other proposed forms of community are likely either to break
down or turn into a totalitarian nightmare: the immersion of the
individual in the whole.[85] In reply to this, the communal
freedom thinker could claim that, although no present society
comes near to satisfying his criteria, such a society of fraternity
and respect is nevertheless a worthy ideal to aim at. The
problem about this move is that it entails that in the present state
of affairs no social freedom is attainable at all; we would have to
embark on a MacIntyrean project of constructing radically new
forms of community to have any hope of creating a background
against which the notion of freedom could (again?) become
intelligible.

Although simple observations about the societies we live in, or
the nature of human societies in general, may seem to cut
against the theory of communal freedom, there remains something
attractive about it. Understanding its attractions may be the

[84] Ibid., 87ff.   [85] Benn, *A Theory of Freedom*, ch. 12.

first step to realising its shortcomings. *First,* communal freedom emphasises as no other theory the social nature of freedom, its interpersonal form, its situatedness. *Second,* it reminds us of the fact that man is a political animal and that most of the activities which are conducive to our flourishing must necessarily take place within a social context. Moreover, active participation in the society we belong to can be seen as a precondition of being able to enjoy many of the benefits, including *freedoms,* that such an institution has to offer: a person who does not 'join the club' is generally not free to partake in the club's activities. There is every merit in underlining these truths about the nature of social freedom and the nature of man.

It must be remarked, however, that in theories of communal freedom all these laudable ideas are overworked and inflated. The crucial point there is not that pursuing communal life, while involving restraints on what one can do as an individual, nevertheless enlarges one's freedom *overall.* Rather, the claim is that the shirker, the social misfit, the extreme individualist, and others of that ilk render themselves unfree, full stop, by refraining from participation in communal activities. Furthermore, it is assumed that because freedom is a social concept, no obstacle legitimately imposed with the needs of society in mind can restrict our liberty. So, freedom not only requires communal activity; such activity cannot *ex hypothesi* – as long as it satisfies requirements of legitimacy and mutual respect – constrain the participants' freedom in any way.[86] But this is simply a *non sequitur*; the conclusion does not follow from the social nature of freedom explained above. On the contrary, we must be considered unfree to do x when we are restrained from choosing and/or doing x, however necessary and desirable such a restriction may be.

Arendt finds something drastically wrong about the notion that perfect liberty is incompatible with the existence of society.[87] However, she is conflating different points. It is true of man that

---

[86] This seems, e.g., to be Dauenhauer's point, 'Relational Freedom', 87ff. Despite their notorious abuse in communist countries, traces of the same ideas can be found in recent communitarian views which argue, along MacIntyrean lines, that 'genuine freedom' can only be re-established through the creation of new 'intimate' communities. See further in Flathman, *The Philosophy and Politics of Freedom,* pp. 65ff.

[87] Arendt, *Between Past and Future: Eight Exercises in Political Thought,* p. 154.

his nature cannot be realised in isolation; it is also true that
freedom only acquires meaning in interpersonal relationships.
But it does not therefore follow that the commitments you must
accept to be a member of society do not limit your freedom.
They do, however just and democratic the society may be; but
then getting married also necessarily restricts your freedom in
many respects, however much you love your spouse and want to
be united with her or with him in holy matrimony. The truth is
that a person often undertakes commitments which, through
someone else's agency, will restrict his freedom, not because he is
forced to do so, but because he wants to; because he prefers some
other value to certain liberties. Denying this is calling for a
'moralised' definition of freedom according to which you cannot
constrain another person's freedom by anything which you have
a right to do; and in the end communal freedom may come
down to little more than that fallacy.[88]

The fact that nobody can enjoy perfect freedom in a society,
and that there is nevertheless a prima facie presumption against
every restriction of it, may seem to be a paradoxical product of
the responsibility view of negative freedom. But if you are an
enthusiastic soccer player, do you not consider every attack of
the other team as a threat? Yet, would it not be a still greater evil
if they stopped attacking altogether, i.e., stopped playing the
game? In general, there is nothing incoherent about combining
a negative theory of freedom with a desire for an integrated
community of common dependence; then the presumption in
favour of freedom is simply overridden in many cases by other
considerations, deemed to be more important.

The reason why the communal freedom thinkers fail to
acknowledge this possibility may, as Berlin suggests, lie in the
belief that all good things must in the end be compatible and

[88] This could also work the other way round. Thus, J. Gray ('Hayek on Liberty, Rights,
and Justice', *Ethics*, 92 (1981–2)) argues that Hayek's moralised definition of
freedom, according to which man is free when he is not subject to coercion by the
arbitrary will of another, leads him into the path of positive liberty. Gray's point is
well taken, for in Hayek's view, rules possessing certain formal elements (generality,
equality: 'true laws', etc.) cannot restrict liberty, in so much as they cannot be treated
as truly coercive. The communal freedom thinkers could not agree more. See also
Miller's treatment of Hayek's ideas, *Market, State, and Community* (Oxford University
Press, 1989), p. 29.

even entail each other (for instance, the anti-social person must be miserable, so he cannot be free!); a belief that he rightly describes as being attractive but false.[89] Anyway, as far as the idea of communal freedom in general is concerned, I have exposed its principal weakness. A theory which claims that we are only free if we are participating actively in a communal project, that we make ourselves unfree by not doing so, and that certain constraints imposed by society are not real constraints at all, is not a viable candidate for an account of social freedom.

5.7. POSITIVE LIBERTY REASSESSED

At the beginning of section 5.3, two main characteristic elements of typical positive-liberty theories were introduced, and it was proposed that these elements might have a bearing on their standing as putative theories of social freedom. Now, after having examined a whole gamut of positive accounts, the concluding remarks will turn out to do little more than confirm my initial suspicions.

Let us first say something about the connection between positive liberty and paternalism. At the end of section 5.2, it was suggested that positive liberty lent itself more easily to development into rampant paternalism, and even totalitarianism, than did negative liberty. This claim can now be supported by reference to the three main forms of positive liberty. Thus, there is plainly not much in *Promethean theories* which can be used to counter paternalism. At worst, paternalism can be seen as simply one more inconvenience with which the higher self has to put up; at best, if enacted by the higher self itself on the lower self, it is an admirable state of affairs. The proponents of *freedom as autonomy*, with their heavy emphasis on individual rational choice, are somewhat better equipped to resist paternalism (see, for instance, K. Graham's arguments against Lenin's vanguardism[90]). But,

---

[89] Berlin, *Four Essays on Liberty*, p. 167.

[90] See Graham, *The Battle of Democracy: Conflict, Consensus and the Individual*. Marxism, incidentally, is perhaps the paradigm case of a positive-liberty theory since it combines all the three main varieties: freedom as the recognition of necessity (until the world revolution), freedom as the autonomy of agents released from false consciousness, and freedom as the participation in productive activity. This may be

as soon as the autonomous self of the individual begins to be
equated with the rational self as such (shared by all rational
agents), a slide into paternalism begins here, too. *Communal
freedom*, on the other hand, seems to be the variety of positive
liberty most open to paternalism. To be free, man must be an
active member of a community; if he fails to participate or
refuses to abide by its rules, the right course of action may be to
'force him to be free', i.e., coerce him into enjoying his liberties
and, hence, realising his genuine human nature.

If we reflect back upon the characteristic elements of positive
liberty, we have now seen that they do indeed violate two central
features of social freedom: that (*a*) a person cannot be said to
constrain his own freedom, and (*b*) to be free, only opportunity,
not its exercise, is required. What, then, is 'positive liberty'? It
turns out to be a very general term, covering a variety of accounts,
all supposedly having to do with social freedom but in fact
upholding other distinct, if no less respectable, values. Self-
abnegation and self-control can be important virtues, the
frequent exercise of autonomy is also a significant accomplishment,
and some degree of social participation is a necessary feature of
man's eudaimonia. But whether or not you learn to accept the
inevitable with equanimity, and whether or not you care to act
upon a reflective choice, seems to have precious little to do with
the extent of your social freedom. Neither does your reluctance to
engage in a common enterprise *in itself* render you unfree; on the
contrary, as was brought to light in the preceding section, social
participation is bound to curtail your freedom in many respects.

It remains to be seen, then, why in the world we should
interpret the above-mentioned values, which refer to non-social
properties of persons or the exercise of certain capacities, as
aspects of freedom which constitutes the social relation of being
unconstrained by another agent. As against that, it could be
asked: if these ideals are worthwhile, why grumble if someone
wants to call them varieties of social freedom? Does it matter
how we categorise them? The simple answer is that it does. It

due to Marxism's mixed conceptual roots: Hegelian, Kantian, and Aristotelian. But
again, all these values could and should be explained and celebrated without any
reference to social freedom.

confuses social debate, both conceptual and normative, to no end when radically different ideals – properties and relations, capacities and the exercise of capacities – are packed together under the same name. The responsibility theorist Miller must be seen as unduly broad-minded when he writes at the end of his 'Introduction' to a recent anthology of freedom essays that to understand the demands of human freedom, we must draw on all the traditions which have contributed to the debate, including the positive ('republican' and 'idealist') ones. 'To be genuinely free', Miller says here, 'a person must live under social and political arrangements that he has helped to make; he must enjoy an extensive sphere of activity within which he is not subject to constraint; and he must decide himself how he is to live, not borrow his ideas from others'.[91] It may well be true that for a person to be genuinely *happy*, all these three conditions must necessarily be satisfied, but to be genuinely *free*, as I have tried to argue, only the middle one is relevant.

As far as I can see, the most sympathetic interpretation of positive liberty would be to try to argue that it designates *another kind* or *kinds* of freedom than the social one (as freedom of the will is another kind of freedom). For instance, we might then consider Promethean freedom not as a candidate for social freedom at all, but rather as an *idea* about it, namely, that it is not very important whereas another sort of freedom is. I would thus have no *conceptual* disagreement with a proponent of Promethean freedom who claimed, in less extreme a fashion than Oscar Wilde, that while those in jail are unfree in a significant sense, it is not this freedom which really matters (for some reason). Unfortunately, positive libertarians generally do not take this stand: they see 'positive liberty' as *competing* with 'negative liberty' for the correct notion of social freedom. However, I have shown that the paradigmatic positive-liberty theories examined in sections 5.4–5.6 uphold specific values which have nothing to do with 'freedom' in any ordinary sense of the word. So, although positive freedom may be 'positive', 'freedom' seems, indeed, to be a misnomer.

[91] D. Miller's (ed.) Introduction, *Liberty* (Oxford University Press, 1991), pp. 19–20.

CHAPTER 6

Freedom and power

After having put paid to attempts to construct a 'positive' account of social freedom, it is now time to return to the insights of the responsibility view. Earlier in the book it became evident that social freedom had to be accorded a place within a hierarchy of interrelated concepts. At that point, emphasis was placed on tracing its logical links *vertically*: to moral responsibility for the non-suppression of obstacles, and from there, in turn, to the notion of obstacles which we have some good reason to expect people to suppress. It remains to examine whether the responsibility view can shed light on the kinship of freedom to other concepts to which it may stand in more *horizontal* relationships, so to speak: concepts such as power, control, influence, authority, etc. These (along with freedom) tend to be referred to collectively as *power concepts* and be said to share certain basic characteristics such as irreflexivity. Also, their meanings are often seen as partially overlapping.[1] In an exhaustive inquiry into the nature of power concepts, all these claims would merit investigation. However, in order to keep the scope of the present book within reasonable limits, I confine my attention in this chapter to the concept of *power*.

What interests me is, naturally enough, power as a *social* concept and, more specifically, the idea of someone's power *over* another person. I distinguish this from the more general possession of power *to* do things, which need not designate a social concept, and also point out a contrast between the social

---

[1] See, e.g., F. Oppenheim, *Dimensions of Freedom: An Analysis* (New York: St. Martin's Press, 1961); *Political Concepts: A Reconstruction* (University of Chicago Press, 1981).

relations of 'exercising power over' and 'having power over' someone. Rather than producing at the outset any hypothesis on the exact links between social power and freedom, I set out, in 6.1, on a short polemical journey into the thicket of scholarly opinion on power. It gradually becomes apparent that many of the insights that were brought to bear on questions of freedom can also aid us here in cutting away some of the dead wood. Subsequently, in 6.2, I formulate and defend a responsibility view of *exercising power over* which, if correct, attests to an even more intimate relationship between freedom and power than has been suggested by previous writers. Finally, in 6.3, I use the conclusions of this and earlier chapters to examine what is meant by saying that individuals or groups of people have more or less freedom/power than somebody else, i.e., I address the question how we can sensibly talk about different *degrees* of freedom/power.

6.1. CONFLICTING VIEWS

There are voluminous studies on power, just as there are on freedom. However, it is difficult to ascertain with some of them what *kind* of power is being discussed. For example, Steven Lukes quotes in his monograph on (social) power Arendt's view that power is the property of a group of people acting in concert; the antithesis of power being violence.[2] This definition seems so far removed from ordinary usage as to verge on the absurd: so far is it from being the case that an exercise of power is necessarily the sign of the union of minds that most people tend to think exactly the opposite. At first sight, one is tempted to conclude that Arendt's problem is here, as was the case in her treatment of freedom (sec. 5.6), that, being preoccupied with certain ideals about how people should lead their lives or how society should be ordered, she takes important social terms such as 'freedom' or 'power' and redefines them to accord with these ideals. This would be as fruitful an endeavour as trying to conquer inflation by expunging the word 'inflation' from the dictionary. However,

---

[2] Cf. S. Lukes, *Power: A Radical View* (London: Macmillan, 1974), pp. 28–9.

Arendt's definition could, more sympathetically, be understood
to refer, not like Lukes' account to A's exercise of power *over B*,
but to the *locus* of social power (in 'the people'), or something of
that sort, in which case these two accounts would simply not be
about the same thing and, hence, not competing.

Another difficulty is that many of the numerous studies on
power are more sociological than philosophical, tending to
presuppose some definition which is never clearly stated. Still,
there are distinguished philosophers who have contributed to
the discussion, notably Bertrand Russell with his claim that
power is the production of intended effects. In this definition,
the question *who* can produce these effects on *what* is passed over.
More importantly, a question from chapter 2 crops up again:
why place so much conceptual emphasis upon *intention*? What is,
for instance, the significance of the distinction between doing
something deliberately and negligently in this context? Connolly
produces a convincing counter-example to an intentionality
view of power: the story of a white employer in control of scarce
job opportunities who, through inattention and habit, fails to
consider other candidates than lower-class white males. He
could do otherwise if he were to attend carefully to the
consequences of his actions, but he does not. So, he contributes
to the high unemployment of minorities and thereby exerts
power over them.[3] The upshot of the story seems to be that
intention cannot be the decisive factor here.

Nor are we much aided by Weber's suggestion that the fact of
resistance is crucial to attributions of power, since it can be
convincingly argued both that power may pre-empt resistance,
as happens in some of the worst cases of totalitarian control, and
that B can be under A's power although he may on particular
occasions (and at great costs) be able to resist A successfully. As
far as Dahl's definition, that A has power over B to the extent
that he can get B to do something which B would not otherwise
have done,[4] is concerned, it seems to be much too permissive by

[3] W. E. Connolly, *The Terms of Political Discourse*, 2nd edn (Oxford: Martin Robertson &
Co., 1983), p. 106.
[4] Russell's, Weber's, and Dahl's views are cf. S. Lukes' (ed.) Introduction, *Power*
(Oxford: Basil Blackwell, 1986).

including all forms of rational persuasion and fraternal advice. If I tell you that the bridge you are planning to cross is unsafe and you change your mind about crossing it, have I exercised power over you? Or are the students X and Y, the former of whom is required by his teacher to read a book in order to pass an exam while the latter is told that if he is interested in a certain field, he might be well advised to read it, both subject to their teacher's power when picking up the book from the library? The answer seems to be *no* to both these questions: acting on good advice does not show that a person is on the receiving end of a power relation. In light of the discussion in chapter 3, the reason immediately suggests itself that the crucial factor here is that advice or rational persuasion do not erect *obstacles* to persons' choices in the first place and, thus, cannot constitute exercises of power over them. If that is so, we may already have spotted one similarity between the exercise of power over somebody and the restriction of his freedom.

The observations up to this point will already have indicated why I question the fruitfulness and general viability of Benn's definition of 'power' in *The Encyclopedia of Philosophy*:

A, by his power over B, successfully achieved an intended result r; he did so by making B do b, which B would not have done but for A's wishing him to do so; moreover, although B was reluctant, A had a way of overcoming this.[5]

Having already viewed the intentionality condition with a beady eye, we may look askance at the other conditions, too: Why 'successfully'? Cannot A be said to have exercised power over B, although B may eventually, maybe at great costs to himself, have been able to prevent A from achieving his desired result? Why did B have to do something? Could he not just as well have refrained from doing it? Why is it necessary that B would not have done b but for A's intervention? In case B's parents threaten to disinherit him unless he marries a white girl, is that not to be considered an exercise of power if it so happens that B would have married a white girl anyway? Why does B

[5] S. I. Benn, 'Power', in P. Edwards (ed.), *The Encyclopedia of Philosophy*, VI (London/New York: Macmillan, 1967), p. 424.

have to act reluctantly? Is it not the supreme example of power when the subjects start obeying the powerholder willingly and uncritically, grovelling at his feet?

Perhaps Benn's mistake lies in trying to define power in isolation from other and intimately related concepts. One of Oppenheim's chief aims has always been to lay out a clear-cut taxonomy of all of these. To do so, he relies on one of the fundamental tenets of operationalism: the need to 'reconstruct' the meanings of terms (sec. 7.1). For Oppenheim, *power* incorporates the extensions of both *control* and *unfreedom*. We have already seen how he defines unfreedom (pp. 33, 46); furthermore, on his definition, A controls B's not doing x to the extent that A influences B not to do x or renders it impossible for him to do x. Thus, although unfreedom and control often coincide, freedom is compatible with control in cases of influence, and unfreedom is possible without control when A constrains B by making it punishable for him to do x. Power then covers both what is common and what is specific to these two concepts.[6]

The problem here is the same as with all of Oppenheim's other definitions; they are not based on any argued analysis of how the terms are actually used, or how they should be used in light of the purpose they serve in our language, but simply on a definitional fiat. Let us decide to define them in this way and then we can use them systematically henceforth: such is Oppenheim's philosophy. It seems more or less a coincidence that he chooses to see control as a form of power but not vice versa, as would, for example, be implied by Rescher's account of control,[7] or that *influence* is not chosen as the most general term, as Wrong does in his book on power.[8] Now, I tend to doubt the value of such arbitrary, stipulative definitions, and one of my objectives in writing this book has been to show that we do not have to make do with a definition of that sort in the case of freedom. However, it may well be true that there is no neat division between many of the interrelated power concepts in our

[6] Oppenheim, *Dimensions of Freedom: An Analysis*, chs. 2–6.
[7] N. Rescher, *Essays in Philosophical Analysis* (University of Pittsburgh Press, 1969), pp. 327–53.
[8] D. H. Wrong, *Power: Its Forms, Bases and Uses* (Oxford: Basil Blackwell, 1979), pp. 22–4.

language; in that case Oppenheim should simply be mindful of Aristotle's advice not to look for more precision in subject-matters than they admit of.

One of the most impressive attempts in recent years to give a rational (non-arbitrary) account of social power is that of Lukes in his *Power: A Radical View*. He claims that there are clearly standard cases of the possession and exercise of power about which we can all agree and which give rise to the following core concept: *A* exercises power over *B* iff *A* affects *B* in a (significant/non-trivial) manner contrary to *B*'s interests. However, people's views about the nature of interests differ; therefore, according to Lukes, power is an 'essentially contested concept' (sec. 7.1) with three main contrasting conceptions.[9]

In brief, what he calls the *one-dimensional* ('pluralist', 'liberalist') view is based on a want-regarding principle of interests as publicly revealed and observable policy preferences; he has most power whose preferences are actually shown to prevail. On the *two-dimensional* ('reformist') conception, interests are understood as preferences within or outside the political agenda, which means that power can also be enacted by preventing certain issues from appearing on that agenda ('non-decisions'). The *three-dimensional* ('radical') conception is of an essentially different sort, implying that power may be exercised over people even when their wants have been fully satisfied, as a person's real interests are not what he happens to want, but whatever he would want if he were to become a fully autonomous agent. In the present state of affairs, people's beliefs and desires are constantly being shaped in such a way as to preclude options which they would have preferred and chosen under ideal conditions. Hence, power may be exerted in preventing a conflict of interests from ever occurring, there can be a conflict of interests without a respective conflict of preferences, and neither *A* nor *B* need be aware of the power relation.

Unfortunately, the many virtues of Lukes' account are overbalanced by its defects. Thus, the reference in the original definition to *A*'s necessarily acting *contrary* to *B*'s interests must

---

[9] Lukes, *Power: A Radical View*.

be unfounded, and in fact Lukes himself has now abandoned
it.[10] A dictator who imprisons a dissident has no less exercised
power over him although the imprisonment may turn out to be
beneficial to the dissident's, but detrimental to the dictator's,
interests. Moreover, ordinary notions of political power seem to
admit that a government might exert power in the interests of
all. The most serious weakness in Lukes' position lies, however,
in his holding simultaneously the incompatible views that power
is an essentially contestable concept and that the three-dimensional
view is superior to the other two as shown by rational arguments.[11]
In sec. 7.1 we see why this will not do and also why the essential
contestability thesis itself, which guides Lukes in his analysis, is
wrong.

6.2. A RESPONSIBILITY VIEW OF POWER

Meanwhile, there are elements in Lukes' account which point in
a more promising direction. In the first place, he is surely right in
emphasising that people's wants may be the product of a system
that works against their real interests and that often, in
attributing power, we are working with counterfactuals as to
how people would have acted if not restricted by internal bars
implanted in them by somebody else. Incidentally, in sec. 5.2 we
saw that the existence of such bars poses no problem for a correct
theory of negative freedom. Secondly, after sketching the
conflicting conceptions of power, Lukes remarks that the
identification of the process of exercising power lies in the
relation between power and responsibility – that to locate power
is to fix responsibility for consequences held to flow from the
action, or inaction, of certain specifiable agents.[12] However,
Lukes fails to pursue this insight in a book that is often needlessly
brief and inexact. For example, he does not explain the
connection between this thesis about responsibility and his
original definition of power which states that power is always

[10] See Lukes' Introduction.
[11] See, e.g., B. Barry's criticisms, 'The Obscurities of Power', *Government and Opposition*,
     10 (1975), 252.
[12] Lukes, *Power: A Radical View*, pp. 55–6.

enacted contrary to the victim's real interests. But if the latter is true, A (the powerholder) is likely to be *culpable*, as well as *responsible*, for exercising power over B. In the end, it is anybody's guess if Lukes' monograph was meant to uphold a responsibility view or a moralised account of power. His considered opinion on this question is complicated by the fact that he has subsequently retracted both the contrary-to-interests clause and the suggestion that a direct attribution of responsibility to individual powerholders is possible.[13]

Other writers, notably Connolly,[14] have tried to develop a more straightforward responsibility view of power, but usually without paying much attention to the connection between such a view and a responsibility view of social freedom. For instance, Connolly's assumption seems to be that the meanings of 'power' and 'freedom' are not too intimately related for each of them to be worked out in isolation from the other. At most, it has been suggested that exercises of power are 'one source of restrictions on liberty' and that 'the attempt to distinguish restrictions for which individuals are responsible as a type of unfreedom from other forms of restrictions is likely to spill over into the discussion of power'.[15]

The aim of this chapter is to defend a responsibility view of power as a *social concept* or, more specifically, of power as used in the locution 'to exercise power over' which I take to constitute its pivotal use in social contexts. This view attests to a much closer relationship between power and freedom than has been suggested by previous writers. My claim is that A exercises power over B if and only if A is morally responsible for the non-suppression of an obstacle O that restrict B's options – and hence that the extensions of 'constraining B's freedom' and 'exercising power over B' are to be seen as coinciding. If this is true, the concepts of power and (un)freedom turn out to be not contingently or partially, but rather necessarily and intimately, related.

The first doubt about the viability of such a responsibility view of power may be expressed by the claim that, unlike

[13] Lukes' Introduction.
[14] Connolly, *The Terms of Political Discourse*, ch. 3.
[15] A. Reeve, 'Power Without Responsibility', *Political Studies*, 30 (1982), 79.

'freedom', the primary use of the term 'power' is not to denote a *relation* but rather a *capacity* or a property. Thus, Peter Morriss goes so far as stating that a power-vocabulary should not be used if our basic concern is something other than the capacity for producing events. While granting that the locution 'power over' has a specific use of its own, he claims that it is not the general, and certainly not the main, way in which we talk about power. On the contrary, what lies at the root of all power-talk is having or exercising the 'power to' do things.[16]

It is obvious that the general possession of power to do things does not necessarily designate a social concept: we can have power *to* move stones or other inanimate things as well as having power to affect agents. However, even if A had the power to move a big rock, we would never say that A had or exercised power *over* the rock. Moreover, by claiming that A used his power *to* do *x*, we are not necessarily attributing moral responsibility to A for the non-suppression of an obstacle.

A cannot exercise power over B without his having in some sense the power to do so, while A can have power to do various things without exercising power over anyone. This much of Morriss' insight is true. So, it is natural to assume that the social relation of exercising power over someone requires the capacity or the property which the general term, 'having power to', designates. But exactly the same applies to freedom: obviously, A cannot constrain B's freedom if he does not have the ability required in the specific case to do so. For example, if A is to have B's hands tied up, he must be able to tie them up himself or have the authority and the means of communication to order someone else to do it. The important point here is that people have made considerable headway in analysing 'constraining freedom' as a social relation without the need arising of stating precisely what A's ability must amount to (except perhaps his satisfying the logical condition of being autarchic, i.e., being a person to whom moral responsibility can be attributed). Now, if the language of *constraint* can usefully be employed and analysed without our basic concern being the capacity for producing

---

[16] P. Morriss, *Power: A Philosophical Analysis* (Manchester University Press, 1987), pp. 22–33.

events, it is odd why it should not also be possible to work out a plausible view of 'power over' as a social relation without saying something important first about the general 'power to'.

It is worth noting here that the adjective 'powerful' is sometimes used in the capacity sense and sometimes in the relational sense. We can easily talk about a *powerful* man as one who has the ability to *do* various things, some of which may affect other persons (for instance, make business offers that are too good to refuse). But, as long as his acts do not (overtly or covertly) erect obstacles to their choices, it is odd to say that he exercises power *over* them. On the other hand, 'powerful' is also commonly used to refer to men who do precisely the latter.[17]

Another potential objection to the thesis of extensional equivalence would be this. Consider a small boy who runs away from home and hides in his neighbour's garage for a few hours because he feels his parents have been neglecting him. 'If they think I am lost or dead, at least they'll miss me', the boy thinks. (Who has not harboured similar thoughts as a child!) Now, on a responsibility view of freedom, the boy may succeed in constraining his parents' freedom by being responsible for placing obstacles in their path, since, knowing their concerns, he rightly predicts that they will cancel their plans for the day and look for him. But – and here is the point of the objection – so far is it from being the case that the boy has power over his parents that the only way he can so much as arouse their attention is by constraining their freedom.[18] Hence, power and (un)freedom are not intertwined in the way claimed above.

Combating this objection requires me to draw another distinction, this time between two locutions about *social* power: 'having power over' and 'exercising power over'. In a somewhat trivial sense, we may say that *A* has power over *B* whenever he exercises power over him. However, this is not the way the locution 'having power over' is commonly used. It tends to denote relations of a *dispositional*, rather than *episodic*, nature.[19]

---

[17] In the former sort of case, 'influential' might, however, often be more apt than 'powerful'.

[18] This example is based on one from Q. Gylfason, *Valdsorðaskak* (Reykjavík: Félag áhugamanna um heimspeki, 1982), pp. 28–9.

[19] Wrong, *Power: Its Forms, Bases and Uses*, also makes use of such a distinction.

'*A* has power over *B*' could mean that *A* is generally *known* to exercise power over *B*, at least in a certain (important) respect: 'my wife has power over me in financial matters but I have complete power over her in the kitchen'. Or it may suffice that *A* stands in a strategic position enabling him to erect obstacles to *B*'s choices (although he does not utilise this option for extended periods) for us to say that *A* has power over *B*. In some contexts, '*A* has power over *B*' could even be tantamount to saying that *A* has *authority* over *B*, because of a difference of standing between them which makes *A*'s exercises of power legitimate and/or voluntarily complied with by *B*.

These observations seem to indicate that while the dispositional concept 'having power over' can mean a number of different things, it always depends logically on the more basic and easily definable 'exercising power over'. To return to the story of the lost son, it may be true that he manages to *exercise* power over his parents in a particular case, and that he, nonetheless, does not *have* power over them in any of the dispositional senses: he is not known to exercise power over his parents regularly, has few significant opportunities to do so (if he tries the same manoeuvre again, he will be seen as 'crying wolf'), and has no authority over them. Morriss might reply by saying that in so far as exercising power is exercising a capacity, it would seem the capacity is more basic than its exercise: it is true that we can have a capacity without exercising it, but we can hardly exercise a capacity without first having it. The obvious response there is to point out that the capacity exercised in exercises of power is not the capacity designated by the locution 'having power over' – for having power over is here not a 'capacity' at all, in Morriss' sense, but rather a disposition. The capacity required for exercises of power to take place is simply *power to*: the general ability discussed earlier, which is in no way restricted to social or political contexts.

It is noteworthy that we have no term corresponding to 'having power over' in the case of unfreedom, meaning that *A* has in general the opportunity to constrain *B*'s freedom (in a particular field) or that he frequently does so. To describe such a state, we would simply say that *A* has power over *B*. This is, I believe, one more indication of the logical affinity between 'exercising power over' and 'constraining freedom', the two locutions to which my thesis of extensional equivalence refers.

The case of the neglected boy failed as an objection since, for *A* to be able to exercise power over *B* in respect *r*, it is not necessary that *A* generally has power over *B* in that respect nor, of course, in other and perhaps more important respects. But does not all this have the counter-intuitive implication that everybody can exercise power over everybody else, at least in some respect? It does have that implication but I am not sure this is a defect. Tony Benn, the politician, has advocated what he calls the 'stiletto heel principle': that if you put all your weight on one place, you can go through almost anything.[20] If an individual *A*, however 'insignificant' a person he may be, sets all his energy at hampering or annoying person *B*, he will most likely succeed, however powerful *B* is. He can, for example, send *B* threatening letters which may force him to employ bodyguards, etc. Also, in a certain trivial sense, by being able to *exercise* power over *B*, *A* *has* power over him (which basically means that he has the power *to* exercise power *over* him), but as pointed out above, the locution 'having power over' more typically designates a dispositional relation, parasitic on the point of the episodic 'exercising power over'.

It is, I believe, no coincidence that replies to objections against responsibility views of power tend to be little more than echoes of points that have already been made, or can be made, in defence of the responsibility view of freedom. For example, Gray complains that on Lukes' or Connolly's view, a power relation exists whenever one agent is significantly affected by another. But the problem is, Gray says, that 'significantly affecting' is a feature of many other sorts of social interactions such as love or trade and, hence, not a distinctive characteristic of power relations.[21] The answer is that on a correct responsibility view, an effect on *B* for which *A* is responsible is not a constraint on *B*'s freedom unless it satisfies the logically prior condition of

---

[20] Cf. Morriss, *Power: A Philosophical Analysis*, p. 88.
[21] J. Gray, 'Political Power, Social Theory, and Essential Contestability', in D. Miller and L. Siedentop (eds.), *The Nature of Political Theory* (Oxford: Clarendon Press, 1983), p. 79.

erecting an *obstacle* to *B*'s choices. Not everything which
'significantly affects' *B* counts as an obstacle to *B*'s choices, for
instance not offers or requests. Proposing to a woman or offering
to trade with a person does not *as such* close options or narrow
down possibilities (as obstacles *ex hypothesi* do). On the contrary,
it extends *B*'s (the recipient's) range of options, whether *B* cares
to accept these offers in the end or not (sec. 3.2). So, Gray's
counter-examples cut no ice with a consistent follower of the
responsibility view.

Another point made by Gray is this: if it is true, as Lukes and
Connolly claim, that power relations may be most pervasive and
efficacious when *B* is himself not aware of them, why can the
powerholder *A* not also be the victim of such an invisible force?[22]
The simple answer is that he can. Obviously, *A*'s own freedom to
do *x* can be constrained by another person (*C*) although *A* is
simultaneously exercising power over *B* by constraining him
from *x*-ing. More importantly, the relation of exercising power
over can be symmetrical. *A* can exercise power over *B* while *B* is
simultaneously exercising power over *A* in the same respect. The
whole idea behind nuclear deterrence was, for example, based
on such a symmetrical exercise of power, the superpowers
constraining each other from using nuclear force.

A. Reeve concurs with Gray in rejecting a responsibility view
of power. Let us look at the three main arguments he produces
against it.[23] *First*, he asks, if *A* has power over *B* to the extent that
A fails to remove a restriction, why does *A* not also have power
over *B* to the extent that *A* might introduce a constraint but does
not in fact do so? Here, it is possible to reply that *A* may well
have such power over *B*. However, what I have been aiming at is
not an account of 'having power over' but of 'exercising power
over', and a person who could introduce a constraint but does
not do so is obviously not responsible for an erected obstacle
(since there is no obstacle). Hence, there is no exercise of power
taking place. This does not subvert my earlier point about the
locution 'having power over' being parasitic on the point of
'exercising power over'. For, as Andrew Mason puts it, 'even

though identifying those who have power over others does not involve attributing moral responsibility, we nevertheless seek to identify them because we think that if they exercise this power . . . then their actions will stand in need of justification'.[24]

Second, Reeve asks us to consider the example of a person A who is taking an exam in which only the top 10% pass. By doing as well as he can, and knowing of this regulation, is he not imposing a disbenefit on the weaker candidates and thus (counter-intuitively) exercising power over them? A possible recourse here would be to grant this, but to remind Reeve that on a responsibility view, a big point has not been scored by convincing us that a restriction of freedom is taking place. Often, the prima facie presumption against the imposition of the constraint is easily overridden by other considerations, in this case the need for competitive examinations, the justice of the best getting their rewards, etc.

However, this concession may not be necessary for the responsibility theorist here. Remember that there are different contexts in which we can invoke moral responsibility. We are always morally responsible for our actions with regard to some *effect*, and how this effect is described is determined by our purpose in ascribing responsibility in the given context (pp. 82–3). To return to Reeve's example, while it may be true that A is responsible, in the general sense, for his decision to sit the exam, *qua* voluntary decision, it need not be true that he is responsible for it *qua* act which creates or fails to remove an obstacle to the other students' choices. As a matter of fact, it is difficult to imagine a context in which it would be appropriate to place the onus of justification on A for disadvantaging other students by doing better than they on an open exam. *Thirdly*, Reeve claims that certain sorts of fanatics might rightly be regarded as lacking responsibility, while still exercising considerable power. If Reeve means that heterarchic persons can be considered as agents, exercising power *over* other persons, I have already produced arguments against such claims in section 5.5 to which I need not add here.

[24] A. Mason, 'Power Over Others and the Power to Effect Outcomes', unpublished paper.

Since responsibility views of power are no novelty, my account of 'exercising power over' is not likely to be looked at with scepticism merely because it is a responsibility view, but rather because of the intimate connection it upholds between power and unfreedom. If, as I claim, the extensions of 'exercising power over' and 'constraining freedom' are best seen as coinciding, the question may be asked why we should go against conceptual economy in having two locutions express the same relation. Would the former not more usefully be taken to refer to something else? One answer might be that by using the expression 'to exercise power over' we are picking out precisely those cases of the general *power to* which involve someone's freedom being constrained. Furthermore, these two locutions could be seen as bringing our attention to different aspects of the relation between A and B: 'exercise of power' shifting the focus to the powerholder, A; with 'constraint on freedom' relating more to B and the obstacles that restrict his options.

What alternative could there be to the sort of responsibility view I have been advocating? The most obvious candidate is an *intentionality view* of power. In such a view, A exercises power over B when he intentionally constrains B's freedom. This would be, more or less, in accordance with Russell's and Benn's views mentioned in the previous section. There, one counter-example about a thoughtlessly discriminating employer was taken to show that A can exercise power over B *negligently*. But this might have been altogether too quick. Would it not be more illuminating to say that while the employer constrains the freedom of individuals from minority groups to find jobs by being morally responsible for the obstacles that stand in their way, he does *not* exercise power over them since the relevant intention is missing?

The problem here is much the same as we came across earlier in dealing with the liberal conception of freedom (sec. 2.1): the difference between those consequences which an agent brings about intentionally and those which he brings about non-intentionally seems to be arbitrary from precisely that moral point of view which talk about social power requires. Such a distinction would rob some of the most topical debates about power of their point. For example, an issue of much concern nowadays is the massive environmental pollution created by big corporations. Few environmentalists would go so far as to claim that these consequences are (*a*) (directly) intended by individuals within the corporations. Rather, they would say that these are (*b*) more or less unwanted but intentionally created (foreseen/avoidable) by-products of other measures, or (*c*) non-intentional effects, unforeseen by any specific individual since none of them took the trouble to weigh the foreseeable consequences of the corporate decisions. However, in (*c*), as well as (*a*) and (*b*), individuals within the corporation could possibly be held responsible for the pollution; and it seems most implausible to hold that only in (*a*) and (*b*) the corporation could be exercising power over people affected by the pollution.[25] To take another example, whether or not we are feminists, most of us will accept that there have been numerous cases in history of men exercising power over women. Surely, we will have to agree that the most insidious, but at the same time the most thorough-going, instances of such relations have taken place when men have not been aware of them, i.e., when they have exercised power over women through their own mindlessness or inattention.

Someone might want to deny that the difference between intentional and non-intentional actions in this context is arbitrary by pointing out that 'exercising power over' is an *exercise concept*.[26] For an *exercise* of *A*'s power over *B* to take place, *A* must be actively engaged in restricting *B*'s options, and for that, *A*'s actions must be intended or at least intentional.[27] I agree that 'exercising power over' is an exercise concept, but I do not accept the objector's subsequent conclusion. For a relational concept to be an exercise concept, it is not necessary that *A* or *B*

---

[25] I deliberately interpret the intentionality view as applying both to effects that are directly and obliquely intended. However, a narrower conception is possible which would accept only the former, and thus be even more open to my criticisms. Much depends here on how the intentionality theorist understands the principle of double effect, see A. Duff, 'Intention, Responsibility and Double Effect', *The Philosophical Quarterly*, 32 (1982).

[26] On the difference between exercise concepts and opportunity concepts, see, e.g., C. Taylor, 'What's Wrong with Negative Liberty', in A. Ryan (ed.), *The Idea of Freedom: Essays in Honour of Isaiah Berlin* (Oxford University Press, 1979), pp. 177ff.

[27] This is also more or less T. Ball's view, 'Power, Causation and Explanation', *Polity*, 8 (1975), 211.

are 'active' in some elementary sense (their minds, bodies, etc.), but that the relation between them is 'actual' as opposed to 'potential'. By a 'potential relation' I mean one in which B stands prima facie with respect to any A, simply in virtue of A's existence. For instance, 'being free' is rightly considered an opportunity concept rather than an exercise concept, because B is free to do x with respect to any A whatsoever that is not responsible for the non-suppression of an obstacle which restricts B's options. By contrast, 'constraining freedom' is an exercise concept, for there the relation between A and B must be 'actual': there must *in fact* be an obstacle impeding B for the existence of which A can be held responsible. But why further assume that the 'actuality' of the relation necessarily implies A's exercise of some *specific* mental or physical capacity?

The same considerations apply to 'exercising power over'. For instance, A does not exercise power over B when B merely responds, perhaps mistakenly, in anticipation of an expected obstacle, although we might want to say in such a case of anticipatory surrender that A *has* power over B in one of the dispositional senses explained above. 'Having power over' in that sense would then designate an opportunity concept. This also tallies with my answer to Reeve's first point above: for an exercise of A's power over B to take place, an obstacle must be present and the possibility to hold A responsible for it – i.e., the relation between them must be 'actual' instead of 'potential' – but it does not follow that there is any need for intentionality on A's part.

The final objection I shall consider is that the link I wish to uphold between power and unfreedom is of a completely *trivial* nature; that what I have done is simply to pick out one locution of power among many and tailor it to meet my needs so that in the end it could not fail to have the same extension as 'constraining freedom'. Here, I deny both the claim that the locution 'exercising power over' was picked out arbitrarily and that it was given a trivial, stipulative definition.

First, I have argued above for the superiority of my responsibility view (and hence equivalence thesis) to previously proposed accounts of power. I believe to have shown how my proposals can ameliorate shortcomings inherent in all the older accounts. *Second*, I have not followed in Oppenheim's footsteps in laying out an operationalist taxonomy of power concepts (sec. 6.1). By contrast, I have tried to show through *argued analysis* that the expression 'exercising power over' is the most basic one when dealing with power as a *social* relation (but not as ability to do things in general). Moreover, after trying to sort out how this particular expression could most usefully be defined to convey our purpose in ascribing to an agent *A* an exercise of power over another agent *B*, the conclusion proved to be in accordance with my original suggestion: that we exercise power over somebody when we constrain his freedom, and vice versa.

To some this may not sound like an earthshaking conclusion. However, at a time when studies of (un)freedom, on the one hand, and power, on the other, *qua* moral or social concepts, continue to appear with regularity, it is worth pointing out that the two concepts do make more harmonious bedfellows than can be inferred from the bulk of the current literature.

6.3. DEGREES OF POWER AND FREEDOM

The course of discussing the relationship between freedom and power may direct our attention to one more potentially thorny issue. Recall the thread of my argument in sec. 3.1, according to which *B*'s freedom to do *x* with respect to agent *A* is an all-or-nothing affair. Either *A* makes *x* less eligible for *B* or not. If he does, the mere 'weight' of the actual obstacle is irrelevant to attributions of unfreedom: an obstacle, of whatever weight, for which *A* is responsible, makes *B* unfree to do *x* with respect to *A*. However, even if *B* is unfree to do *x*, he can be free to do numerous other things which may be more important than *x*. Then, in the previous section, I argued that the locution 'having power over', although not having a single technical meaning, is commonly used to denote the general tendency or ability of an agent *A* to constrain *B*'s freedom in a certain respect. Hence, *A* can have power over *B* in one respect (financial matters) while the reverse holds in another (the kitchen), and it was even shown that the power relation could be symmetrical (nuclear deterrence).

Also, it must be remembered that freedom relations and power
relations are in no way confined to the political or economic
arena. It is within the domain of more intimate (and less easily
calculable) 'face-to-face' relationships of family, friendship, the
workplace, sexual relationships, and marriage that such issues
are most immediately faced by most people.[28] If all this is true,
the question arises whether we can impart any sense to the
common claims that A is in general freer than B, that A has more
power than B or that society S_1 is freer than society S_2. In other
words, is there any *aggregate net* freedom and power?

Most of us have an intuitive feeling that there must be some
way of calculating and comparing different freedoms on a single
scale, for how else could we, for instance, say that Icelanders
have enjoyed more freedom than Albanians in the post-war era?
Berlin is trying to capture this intuitive idea when he says that
what we are referring to in speaking about the degree of freedom
enjoyed by men or society is the width or extent of the paths
before them, the number of open doors, as it were, and the
extent to which they are open: 'The more avenues men can
enter, the broader those avenues, the more avenues that each
opens into, the freer they are.'[29] This sounds convincing, but to
continue with the same metaphor, it cannot be denied that we
may consider ourselves much *less* free after a dozen new, broad
'avenues' have been opened to a destination we do not care about
if, simultaneously, the one possible avenue to our personal 'promised land' has been narrowed down slightly. So, the question is
whether all we can say about the degrees or totality of freedom
and power is bound to be a matter of mere personal preference.

While relatively little has been written on this totality
problem, there are notable exceptions. For instance, Oppenheim
spends considerable time unravelling the different 'dimensions
of freedom'. While holding on to the thesis that there is 'no such
thing as "liberty in general"',[30] he concedes that people often
try to compare the different types of actions that an agent is free

---

[28] This last truth is pointedly expressed by R. Beehler, 'A Neglected Aspect of Liberty',
   Cogito, 7 (1993), 40.
[29] I. Berlin, *Concepts and Categories* (ed. H. Hardy, London: The Hogarth Press, 1978), p. 192.
[30] Oppenheim, *Dimensions of Freedom: An Analysis*, p. 127.

or unfree to perform. The four dimensions he discerns are (*a*) *probability*, (*b*) *degree of deprivation*, (*c*) *scope*, and (*d*) *domain*. *B* is with respect to *A* more unfree to do *x*, (*a*) the greater the probability that he will be prevented or punished, (*b*) the higher the negative utility for him of being constrained, and (*c*) the smaller the number of ways *A* leaves him free to go. Furthermore, (*d*) the greater the number of actors *A* can make unfree, the more powerful is he. Oppenheim then concludes that one actor has more total power or freedom than another if he has more power or freedom as judged by each dimension; or alternatively, if he scores higher than another on one dimension while they are equally powerful or free as judged by the others. Also, one actor has more total power or freedom than another if he is more powerful or free as judged by the *most significant* dimension. But what is the most significant of these dimensions? Here, Oppenheim's uncompromising operationalism comes to a halt; there are no general operational criteria to be found, and the concept of a *free society* is thus 'essentially a valuational one . . . unsuited for the purposes of scientific inquiry'.[31]

Wrong gives a somewhat similar account of the dimensions of power, although for him there are only three. Power is (*a*) *extensive* if the power subjects are many, (*b*) *comprehensive* if the powerholder can move them by a variety of means, and (*c*) *intensive* if he can push them far without a loss of compliance. Wrong then makes certain plausible suggestions about the contingent interrelationships of these dimensions, for example, that the more extensive the power is, the less comprehensive and intensive it is likely to be. However, as far as the totality problem is concerned, the most he can do is to make the general remark that total or absolute power usually means power that is high both in comprehensiveness and intensity.[32]

A possible recourse is simply to abandon oneself to *subjectivism*, as implied by Flathman's claim that a free society is (roughly) one in which it is true of the preponderance of persons that they are not unfree to act in respects that matter most to them,[33] or to

---

[31] Ibid., p. 207.   [32] Wrong, *Power: Its Forms, Bases and Uses*, pp. 14–20.
[33] R. E. Flathman, *The Philosophy and Politics of Freedom* (University of Chicago Press, 1987), p. 311.

the sort of *relativism* implied by Connolly's account, according to which power is greater, the more important interests it touches, while judgements about the importance of interests are inherently controversial.[34] Apparently, this could warrant Taylor's 'diabolic defence of Albania': that the Albanian society is (or was till recently) freer than the American one since there are fewer traffic-lights (although less concern for human rights) in the former than the latter.[35] However, for those of us who are neither moral subjectivists nor relativists, such claims do not constitute a satisfying end-result.

It might be helpful to distinguish here between two questions: (*a*) 'Is S_1 a free society?' – and (*b*) 'Are you freer in society S_1 than S_2?' When we talk about a free society, we are usually referring to one in which social freedom is a fundamental ideal, secured in the constitution and laws. In such a society, the major principle is that one freedom shall only be constrained to protect another (and more important) freedom. In this sense, we can have many different free societies, though Albania would, until recently, hardly have counted among them. Meanwhile, question (*b*) can easily be asked about two 'free societies', S_1 and S_2. Both could be 'free' in the above sense, but in all societies some freedoms have to be restricted, and it is a natural question to ask whether the freedoms protected in S_1 or S_2 by restricting others are the right (the most important) kinds of freedom. A proper answer to such a question requires judging the relative importance of each particular freedom in our lives.[36] In the end, that answer should,

---

[34] Connolly, *The Terms of Political Discourse*, p. 127.

[35] Taylor, 'What's Wrong with Negative Liberty', p. 183.

[36] There is an odd little argument in W. Norman's paper 'Taking "Free Action" Too Seriously', *Ethics*, 101 (1991) which is supposed to show that questions about the value of free action cannot be answered in a meaningful way, lending support to his overall conclusion that what political philosophers should be concerned with is not 'free action' but rather 'free persons'. The argument goes something like this: 'What is the value of being free to do *x*?' cannot be meaningfully answered unless the particular activity *x* is specified. Meanwhile, it is not generally thought that the question 'what is the value of freedom?' is meaningless. Hence, there is a good reason to believe that the 'free action' interpretation of the question is not what we have in mind (p. 513). Norman's mistake lies in considering the question 'what is the value of freedom?' an unambiguous one. Such a question would normally be posed in a certain *context* (e.g., the context of discussing dissidents' freedom of expression) in which case the context would instantiate the activity component *x* ('what is the value of the freedom to do *x*, namely, to express yourself freely in society *S* without state intervention?'). If asked in

I believe, not depend on contingent individual preferences or the relative judgement of the majority of people about the nature of their interests, but rather on certain *objective* truths about human eudaimonia: about that which makes human life worth living. These 'objective' truths would be *substantive* truths, based on facts about the nature of human beings, not *conceptual* ones. But that is another story, not to be further sketched in this work.

To recap, my response to the totality problem discussed in this section is that while an analysis of freedom and power may help us to locate 'free societies', questions about net aggregate freedom and power require judgements about the *most important* freedoms and the *best* states of affairs. As I have repeatedly pointed out, such questions cannot be answered within the limits of a conceptual analysis of freedom and power.

a more general sense, the question about the value of freedom would probably be taken to mean 'what is the value of living in a free society?' – with 'free society' being understood somewhere along the lines I suggested above. In either case, Norman's conclusion is a *non sequitur*.

CHAPTER 7

Observations on method

The last chapter of the main body of this study will be devoted to questions of method. That is, after having, so to speak, delivered the goods, I plan to scrutinise the methodology which has, to a large degree implicitly, been employed in the course of the discussion. The spur to the study was my dissatisfaction with the fact that debates about freedom seldom get off the conceptual ground; the opposing parties do not agree to start with on the meaning of that about which they could disagree, and the opportunity for a fruitful discussion is lost. It may be called naive or old-fashioned, but my belief was (and still is) that an account of social freedom could be proposed which would commend itself to any rational thinker and serve as a natural point of departure for substantive debates.

Admittedly, arguments have so far been launched, and conclusions reached, with a certain complacency toward the methodological hazards which are often taken to bedevil conceptual studies. It must be said that the development of my arguments would have been somewhat more cautious if I had felt genuinely intimidated by these hazards. I have not. However, I can envisage someone objecting that I have been so absorbed in creating a piece of workmanship that I have plunged ahead without giving serious thought to the question whether the tools being employed were appropriate. The purpose of the ensuing discussion is both to rebut such an objection and, if possible, to secure further the foundations of the responsibility view for which I have been arguing, by placing them within a sound methodological framework.

However, before proceeding further, a note of warning should be sounded. May ruminating over questions of method, whether as a prelude to or a sequel to prosecuting them, not be redundant? Is not a method best known by its fruit? The idea behind these misgivings is simple enough. Either you convince the reader that the position you stake out is a tenable one, in which case any further justification is superfluous, or he views your attempts as much cry and little wool, in which case a lengthy discussion of your methods will strike him as that of a bad shearer blaming his sickle.

These considerations suggest that all studies of the present kind could be pruned of methodological considerations. But such a conclusion may be altogether too quick. Admittedly, it is true – to take another example – that we do as a rule run worse, not better, if we think too much about our feet.[1] However, it must not be forgotten either that advances in running techniques, so amply apparent at any Olympic Games, have been partly brought about by experts who have devoted a great deal of attention to the workings of the human foot. So, however convincing the argumentation of the preceding chapters may have been, it does not seem superfluous to ask whether it has been based upon arguments appropriate to a conceptual moral inquiry, and whether I have perhaps been taking assumptions for granted which require justification. I would go so far as saying that despite all the 'running' I have done so far, my results will be unsatisfactory until I have shown that they were arrived at in an appropriate way.

I have already, at the very beginning of the book (p. 3), introduced four conditions of a fruitful conceptual study: (*1*) respect for *common usage*; (*2*) internal and external *coherence*; (*3*) *serviceability* and *non-relativity*; and (*4*) its accounting for *conceptual contestedness*. Before sketching, in sections 7.2 and 7.3, the outline of a proper method for conceptual studies, accommodating conditions (*1*)–(*4*), let us, in 7.1, cast a quick glance over the theoretical terrain in order to ascertain to what extent these four conditions have been satisfied by some well-known methodologies

---

[1] See Ryle's comment, 'Ordinary Language', in V. C. Chappell (ed.), *Ordinary Language* (Englewood Cliffs: Prentice-Hall, 1964), p. 39.

of late – and to ask what effect non-compliance with one or more
of them has had on the viability of these methodologies.

In moral philosophy, there are conceptual studies and conceptual
studies. Let us start by trying to fish out two truths from this
somewhat platitudinous remark: the first concerning quantity
and the second concerning quality.

The quantitative truth is that despite the demise of so-called
conceptual *analysis*, conceptual *studies* of social concepts are still
legion. The qualitative one is that not all of these studies are
equally good. For instance, some of them are characterised by
what we might call 'Procrustean butchery'. The modern-day
Procrustes provide us with sleight-of-hand definitions of social
terms which we are invited to use henceforth, simply because it
suits the purpose of their butchery, however much these
definitions rub up against our ordinary usage. Many opposing
theorists, unfortunately, go to the other extreme of merely
describing how 'we in our neighbourhood' (people sharing the
same philosophical persuasion, or language, or belonging to the
same community as the theorist) prefer to use a particular term,
without giving us any good reason why 'we', the readers, should
agree with 'them'. If these two extreme methods are both
equally to be avoided, it seems in order to ask where exactly they
go wrong – and then try to improve upon them.

The terrain of philosophical method is a field mined with
proverbial controversies. I shall enter the minefield of these
debates only in so far as they bear on my four conditions of a
fruitful conceptual study. The first method worth considering is
operationalism, the spectre of which still haunts us, despite the
alleged death of the rest of its positivist family. Indeed,
operationalism has recently been revived with some force in
Oppenheim's copious writings on political concepts, many of
which have been mentioned in previous chapters.

The Encyclopedia of Philosophy defines operationalism as 'a
program which aims at linking all scientific concepts to
experimental procedures and at cleansing science of operationally

undefinable terms, which it regards as being devoid of empirical meaning'.[2] Confronted with the morass of everyday, non-technical expressions, operationalists see no alternative but to construct a new vocabulary: a precise sense has to be given to these vague expressions in order to make them serviceable for scientific purposes. Oppenheim's demand, for instance, is that each political concept be associated with a precise and definite testing operation, an operation that can be repeated and employed by different people, regardless of their preferences, and which can be used for making predictions about future events (in this case the behaviour of agents). Since neither everyday language nor previous scientific usage has fixed the meaning of terms such as 'freedom' or 'power', they may be defined in whatever way best serves this purpose.[3]

Generally, operationalists are contemptuous of so-called *political philosophy* which they consider hopelessly speculative and inexact. However, they believe it can and should be replaced by *political science* which, by replicating the methods of natural science, constitutes a dispassionate study of the facts as they are, without metaphysical overtones. Most important for our purposes is the claim that political concepts should be purged of all value connotations; that science can only *describe*, not *evaluate*. When we start disagreeing about values, we have exceeded the bounds of science but, according to operationalism, political concepts have a descriptive content which can be isolated and operationalised, apart from all value commitments.

Thus, as Oppenheim's causal-responsibility theory has already brought home to us (sec. 2.3), operationalists view freedom as a descriptive concept to which evaluative connotations have only contingently become attached, and as a concept whose proper use can be determined without any prior agreement on broader issues, such as responsibility. As in other cases, meaningful disagreement about this particular concept presupposes an

---

[2] G. Schlesinger, 'Operationalism', in P. Edwards (ed.), *The Encyclopedia of Philosophy*, v (London/New York: Macmillan, 1967), p. 543.

[3] This is the main working hypothesis both in F. Oppenheim's *Dimensions of Freedom: An Analysis* (New York: St. Martin's Press, 1961) and his *Political Concepts: A Reconstruction* (University of Chicago Press, 1981).

agreed definition in non-valuational terms; the question whether freedom can become a subject of empirical science is simply the question whether there are experimental data to which the term 'freedom' can be linked.[4] We have seen that Oppenheim takes a positive answer to that question for granted.

Now, to be fair to Oppenheim, while he acknowledges that his approach 'moves against the tide of current theory',[5] he also wants to distance himself from some of the dogmas associated with positivism. He is not a behaviourist, nor does he believe that value judgements are 'meaningless'. Most importantly, he accepts that political science cannot in a strict sense be value-free, in so much as ideological commitments tend to influence the choice of topics and hypotheses to be tested.[6] This last concession is frequently made by modern-day operationalists, acknowledging the Popperian insight that 'hard facts' do not lie unproblematically before our gaze; our interests and values steer the process of discovery. But this does not change the fact that once a topic has been chosen, a field has been demarcated, the investigation can proceed within its confines in a value-free manner. Charles Taylor has called this position the 'mitigated positivist view'.[7]

Having been told that political concepts such as freedom can be operationalised, it still remains to ask which rules are to govern this procedure, and how much account should be taken of ordinary usage. In the end, the general rule of procedure for an operationalist is simply that of fulfilling the requirement of fruitfulness for scientific inquiry (practicality, predictability) as explained above. It is here that Oppenheim's *reconstructionism* comes into the picture. Although we should, as a rule, not depart further than necessary from current English, the tools of ordinary language are often too blunt and value-infected to be of use for scientific investigation. What we need to do is to construct a language 'as free as possible of the imperfections of ordinary usage, or rather to reconstruct its basic concepts'.[8] The

[4] Oppenheim, *Dimensions of Freedom: An Analysis*, p. 4.
[5] Oppenheim, *Political Concepts: A Reconstruction*, p. 2.
[6] Ibid., pp. 198–9.
[7] C. Taylor, 'Neutrality in Political Science', in P. Laslett and W. G. Runciman (eds.), *Philosophy, Politics and Society*, III (Oxford: Basil Blackwell, 1967), p. 27.
[8] Oppenheim, *Political Concepts: A Reconstruction*, p. 177.

similarity to Wittgenstein's approach in the *Tractatus* is plain, and indeed acknowledged by Oppenheim: language is not 'in order as it is'; rather, we need to construe a logically perfect language.

That the method of operationalism is far from the mainstream would hardly count as a vice if the method had something substantial to recommend it. Unfortunately, it does not. The specious, but lasting, appeal of operationalism may be due to its fulfilling conditions (2)–(4) rather easily: it does not so much straddle those hurdles as simply throw them aside. Operationalism thus achieves coherence and non-relativity by mere stipulation, by 'Procrustean butchery', while completely ignoring the primary condition of taking account of ordinary usage. Oppenheim might object, claiming that his definitions are explicative, not stipulative, rendering the meanings of terms more precise and exact. But there are as many ways to make meanings more exact as there are to skin a cat, and if no criterion is invoked other than precision, the explicative nature of his 'reconstructions' does not obviate their being stipulative. The main problem is that, by being a law unto himself, Oppenheim banishes our ordinary concepts of 'freedom' and 'power' from political discourse, rather than reconstructing them: for his 'reconstructed' notions have radically different points from the 'unreconstructed' ones of ordinary discourse. The former serve primarily explanatory/ predictive purposes in elegant theory construction, and not moral purposes at all.[9]

The linchpin of Oppenheim's 'new' reconstructionism is simply the old positivist description–evaluation distinction at its most primitive. That, however, leaves the operationalist with a millstone round his neck in the form of an irresolvable dilemma: the further his reconstructions are removed from common usage, the more he is bound to lose contact with the people to which he speaks; on the other hand, the closer they are to it, the more the false appearance of normative neutrality dissolves.[10]

[9] For a more detailed criticism of Oppenheim's method, see A. Mason, 'The Reconstruction of Political Concepts', *International Journal of Moral and Social Studies*, 4 (1989).

[10] W. E. Connolly, *The Terms of Political Discourse*, 2nd edn (Oxford: Martin Robertson & Co., 1983), p. 224.

Finally, it should be noted that if the responsibility view of freedom and power espoused in the present book holds good, the analysis of these concepts has little if any bearing on predictions of human behaviour – which means that one more operationalist ideal goes by the board. A constrained agent may yield to the restriction, but he may also strengthen his will and act in the face of adversity. The mere knowledge that he is unfree to do x does not provide us with any rigorous means of predicting his resulting behaviour. It is, by the way, not clear how such a prediction would be possible on Oppenheim's own operationalist definition of freedom, at least not in so far as his punishability condition is concerned (p. 46). Even if we know that an act is punishable, and an agent therefore in Oppenheim's model 'unfree' to perform it, how can we say in advance whether he will refrain from it or not? But then, as Connolly points out, power and unfreedom are bound to be disappointing concepts to predictivists because predictivism itself provides a defective model of social inquiry.[11]

Operationalism's false appearance of normative neutrality was created by ignoring the first condition of a sound conceptual study. Maybe some advantage can still be reaped from a method that, although having fallen on no less hard times of late than positivism, at least puts all its emphasis on satisfying that very condition. I am there referring to a way of approaching philosophical questions commonly known as *ordinary language analysis* (hereafter dubbed *OLA*), practised by Oxford philosophers such as Austin and Ryle from the forties onwards, and described by one of its more favourable critics as 'piecemeal philosophical engineering'.[12] It is vital to distinguish it from the methods and attitudes of the later Wittgenstein and his followers in Cambridge who are also sometimes called 'ordinary language philosophers'. To appreciate this difference, a few words must first be said about the latter.

The Cambridge type of ordinary language philosophy has its origin in Wittgenstein's repudiation of his earlier views in his later works, and especially in the so-called 'game theory' of

---

[11] Ibid., p. 101.
[12] A. Ryan, 'Freedom', *Philosophy*, 40 (1965), 93.

language which superseded the 'picture theory' of the *Tractatus*. In contrast to Wittgenstein's earlier commitment to the search for a logically perfect language, the main contention of his later works is that ordinary language is all right as it is. Philosophical problems arise not because our language is faulty or imperfect, but because we (philosophers more often than laymen) subtly misuse language. For example, we extend or restrict the ordinary uses of words, gradually straining or contorting their meanings, until we begin to doubt the unhesitant application of these same words in ordinary discourse. Thus, all sorts of perplexities and difficulties are generated. The aim of philosophy is first and foremost a *therapeutic* one; by pursuing it we determine how our language is actually employed, examining the rules that govern the use of various expressions, and as we gradually realise where and how we went wrong, we rid philosophy of conceptual confusion. Its problems turn out to be pseudo-problems which are to be dissolved rather than solved. On this view, philosophy 'may in no way interfere with the actual use of language', it simply 'leaves everything as it is'.[13]

The Oxford philosophers did not share Wittgenstein's therapeutic view of their subject; they did not believe that all philosophical problems were bogus or that every sentence in the language was necessarily 'in order as it is'. However, what they did believe in was the possibility of clearing up or even solving a number of philosophical problems through the analysis of ordinary language. In answering questions by dint of *OLA*, particular linguistic expressions are compared with particular situations, or as Austin described it, we proceed 'by examining *what we should say when*, and so why and what we should mean by it'.[14] That is, we set up scenarios, described in the language which we and the readers share, and then ask what anybody (including ourselves) would say about these situations with a given question or purpose in mind. In this way we utilise the richness of ordinary language with all its subtle distinctions,

---

[13] L. Wittgenstein, *Philosophical Investigations* (translated by G. E. M. Anscombe, Basil Blackwell, 1968), p. 49e [paragraph 124].

[14] J. L. Austin, 'A Plea for Excuses', in V. C. Chappell (ed.), *Ordinary Language* (Englewood Cliffs: Prentice-Hall, 1964), p. 46.

developed through the experience of generations of language
speakers, to clarify the problems at hand and, at best, to bring a
conceptual dispute to a conclusion.

It has often been said that the Achilles' heel of *OLA* is its
conceptual and linguistic conservatism. The idea is that *OLA*
biases political theory in a conservative direction by forestalling
radical departures from existing forms of thought. Williams thus
argues against Austin that he is committed to the view that all
worthwhile distinctions have already been drawn – and by
demanding that we should always look at how things work
before we make changes, he effectively prevents any changes
being made.[15] I do not think this is a fair objection, for Austin's
point was not that language could not be made to work in new
ways; he simply pointed out that a lot of distinctions had already
been drawn in the course of many generations and that these
were 'likely to be more numerous, more sound . . . and more
subtle . . . than any that you or I are likely to think up in our
armchairs of an afternoon'.[16] So, although Austin believed that
it should generally be left to necessity, not to a particular
philosopher, to be the mother of invention, he did not hold any
neo-Darwinistic view about the nature of the distinctions in our
language.[17]

The fact that people are advised to be cautious in drawing
new distinctions is not enough to sustain a charge of conservatism.
However, this charge still crops up at a deeper level. Thus,
Marcuse claims that since *OLA* takes exclusively as its subject
matter the 'totalitarian scope of the established universe of
discourse', it can merely reinforce the values of the society from
which the language evolves.[18] Again, I think the opponents of
OLA are tilting at windmills. Just as a student may use the very
terms and expressions he picked up from the lips of his teacher to
criticise him later on, the concepts of ordinary language,
although first learnt within pre-established language games,

---

[15] Cf. Ryan, 'Freedom', 99.
[16] Austin, 'A Plea for Excuses', p. 46.
[17] See Ryan, 'Freedom', 99–101.
[18] Cf. A. Wertheimer, 'Is Ordinary Language Analysis Conservative?', *Political Theory*,
4 (1976), 405.

may later be used to criticise those very practices or institutions. For example, Lukes and Connolly do not seem to have any difficulties in arguing for a 'radical' conception of interests, as superior to a more 'conservative' one, by employing tools of ordinary language.[19] Generally, in times of political or social instability, people tend to be rebellious and their use of language radical, but it is radical because it is used to argue for radical views, not because the rebels have managed to transcend any limits of *OLA* in defining terms. Claiming that ordinary language is inherently conservative, in the sense of reinforcing prevailing values, is like claiming that water is in its nature a 'peaceful' substance since it is more often used to quench our thirst than to drown people in. As far as freedom and power are concerned, I see no reason to believe that my analysis of these concepts has functioned in any regulative or conservative manner, nor that it would necessarily assume a different form in a radical society than a quiescent one (propagandism and abuse apart).

It may still be urged that despite all its meticulous clarifications, its ingenious ways of passing the first hurdle above, *OLA* has in the end no means of resolving problems of incoherent or divergent usage. For instance, we obviously do not all say the same things in the same situations; usages do differ. Austin's reply in his famous paper 'A Plea for Excuses' is to point out that they do not differ nearly as much as one would think: 'The more we imagine the situation in detail, with a background of story . . . the less we find we disagree about what we should say.'[20] The point here is that often when we think we want to say different things of the *same* situation, we have actually imagined the situation slightly differently. However, Austin concedes that nevertheless, '*sometimes* we do ultimately disagree',[21] and that considerations other than those of common usage are likely to be of relevance 'if our interests are more extensive or intellectual than the ordinary'.[22] Ryle has no compunction about admitting

---

[19] See Connolly, *The Terms of Political Discourse*, ch. 2; the radical concept of interests is the foundation of S. Lukes' analysis of power, *Power: A Radical View* (London: Macmillan, 1974).
[20] Austin, 'A Plea for Excuses', p. 48.
[21] Ibid.
[22] Ibid., p. 49.

this either: 'Sometimes the stock use in one place is different from its stock use in another . . . Sometimes, its stock use at one period differs from its stock use at another',[23] etc.

It has been fashionable for a while to take potshots at *OLA*. I wonder if some of the harshest criticisms of this method have not been misplaced. That *OLA* cannot do more than to unpack an existing linguistic practice at a particular time and place is not an *objection* against its method; this was all it ever pretended to do (at least in theory, if not always in practice where the handmaid was sometimes allowed to give herself the air of a mistress). Austin himself never claimed that *OLA* was the only source of fruitful discussion. He explicitly said that 'ordinary language is *not* the last word: in principle it can everywhere be supplemented and improved upon and superseded. Only remember, it *is* the *first* word.'[24]

Despite its obvious limitations, *OLA* vastly surpasses operationalism as a methodology for conceptual studies. Contrary to the latter's 'I-am-the-king-of-the-Romans-and-above-grammar'-attitude, *OLA* insists that a study of 'what we . . . say when' serves as a natural starting-point for all conceptual inquiries. Indeed, I tend to agree with Alan Ryan that 'everyone who appeals to the propriety of departing from ordinary language is under the necessity of making out a case for this departure'.[25] There is often a good reason for doing so, in order to achieve coherence and non-relativity; *respect* for common usage not being the same as eventual *obedience*. Notwithstanding that the opponents of *OLA* are right in that uncritically submitting to the arbitrament of ordinary language, while neglecting to look for the *point* (sec. 7.2) of the concept under scrutiny, is a mistake, the question remains whether examining common usage cannot be considered a necessary step *en route* to establishing this point. I believe it can.

Although appeals to 'ordinary language' are now, surprisingly, considered *passé* by most philosophers, the same cannot be said for appeals to our moral *intuitions*. They are widely used to elicit verdicts about the correct descriptions of various scenarios. But

---

[23] Ryle, 'Ordinary Language', p. 26.
[24] Austin, 'A Plea for Excuses', p. 49.   [25] Ryan, 'Freedom', 99.

if the objective there is also to find out what is the proper thing to say in or of a given situation, how does this differ in practice from *OLA*? The differences might run less deep than many philosophers are inclined to think. Still, there are some: the considered moral intuition of a rational agent is not the same as any spontaneous verdict of ordinary language, and the appeal to intuitions tends to presuppose a certain methodology, namely, Rawls' *reflective equilibrium*.

The general method of reflective equilibrium has been too widely discussed recently to need much rehearsing here. Applied to conceptual studies, it involves, as always, an interplay: constant mutual adjustments between the abstract and the concrete; between theory on the one hand, use and intuition on the other. The latter serve only as provisional starting-points that are to be measured for consistency, tested by criticism and reflected on in the light of the former. To take *freedom* as an example, people have certain intuitions about the concept, frequently brought to light in judgements about particular situations, whether artificial (such as the office stories in sec. 2.3) or real. It appears that people share at least certain criteria for freedom; they understand freedom-talk, even if they lack a developed, articulated definition. The right way to start a conceptual inquiry into freedom, according to the method under discussion, is to propose such a definition, one that seems at first sight best to support our intuitions. Then, by going back and forth, sometimes altering the details of the general theory in question, sometimes withdrawing the judgements based on our intuitions and bringing them into conformity with the proposal, we eventually arrive at a definition that is both formally coherent and yields results which 'match our considered judgments duly pruned and adjusted'.[26] This process gradually leads to a state of reflective equilibrium, the state reached 'after a person has weighed various proposed conceptions and has either revised his judgment to accord with one of them or held fast to his original convictions'.[27]

The basic justification for this method in Rawls' work is

[26] J. Rawls, *A Theory of Justice* (London: Oxford University Press, 1973), p. 20.
[27] Ibid., p. 48.

simple enough: there is no other way to proceed. If we reject this method, we are forced to rely either on Cartesian self-evident truths or try to win acceptance for some stipulative definition. But both of these have been done many times without much success. By contrast, the fundamental insight here lies in accepting the fact that to solve any disagreement, we must proceed from certain shared assumptions. We look for possible bases of agreement and try to expand and develop them by mutual adjustment. Naturally, we have to make some compromises along the way, but we are bound to be satisfied with the end result, knowing it to be the best we can hope for.

Rawls' reflective equilibrium is clearly superior to *OLA* as a general methodology for moral inquiries. It explains both the prima facie plausibility of common beliefs and linguistic practices *qua* considered intuitions, and why and how radical departures from these are sometimes called for in order to achieve coherence. In fact, the reflective equilibrium is first and foremost a *coherence method*. Put compendiously, the reason why it surpasses *OLA* is simply that it passes two of the aforementioned hurdles instead of merely one. But what about the third and the fourth?

Plato poses a crucial question in the *Republic* when he asks: 'If a man starts from something he knows not, and the end and the middle of his argument are tangled together out of what he knows not, how can such a mere consensus ever turn into knowledge?'[28] The problem about a coherence method such as Rawls', where a general account is made to match intuitions by mutual adjustments, is that it seems ultimately liable to a charge of relativism. Rawls' reflective equilibrium is 'tangled together' out of things that are not in themselves certain or objective. The output depends on the input: hence, it is possible that different groups of rational agents using this method all end up with different conclusions, depending on the intuitions and proposals with which they started. For example, the definition of freedom, however 'duly pruned and adjusted', might in the end vary between communities. Rawls himself is fully aware of this fact. As has become clearer in some of his more recent writings, his

---

[28] Plato, *The Republic* in E. Hamsten and H. Cairns (eds.) *The Collected Dialogues* (Princeton University Press, 1963), 533c.

aim was never more than to reveal and refine the general principles which *we* (and this explicitly means we in Western liberal democracies) are inclined to use.[29]

It seems then that the much-discussed modification of Rawls' original reflective equilibrium from 'narrow' to 'wide', incorporating not only a set of moral principles and considered moral judgements, but also a set of relevant background theories, did not much help to thwart the menace of relativism. But this should not surprise us, for Rawls' insistence that the background theories themselves would have to be largely justified in terms of their fit with considered moral judgements, must make his wide reflective equilibrium vulnerable to a charge of circularity.[30] Rawls' stumbling-block may well be his blatant anti-naturalism, his refusal to accept the idea of moral truths as grounded in facts 'out there' (see further in section 7.3). Because of the lack of a procedurally independent background theory, reflective equilibria are extremely under-determined by their starting-points. In default of any clear-cut guidelines as to which of the original judgements should eventually be retained, and as a result of the subsequent acceptance that 'there is no single *best* way of cohering the relevant phenomena',[31] the temptation will be strong to tailor the background theory to accommodate as *many* of the original judgements as possible. The end-product is then likely to be one of unreasonable charity: witness Swanton's attempt to formulate a coherence theory of freedom along Rawlsian lines. By collocating most of the possible *endoxa*, the conceptions of the 'many or the wise', about freedom to be found, Swanton ends up with a definition which is even more permissive than MacCallum's schema (criticised in sec. 1.1); accepting as constraints on freedom all kinds of flaws, breakdowns, and restrictions on practical activity that limit the potential of human beings as agents. Thereby, Swanton is lead to embrace,

---

[29] See references in R. J. Arneson, 'Symposium on Rawlsian Theory of Justice. Recent Developments. Introduction', *Ethics*, 99 (1989).

[30] See the thrust of D. W. Haslett's paper, 'What is Wrong with Reflective Equilibria?', in J. A. Corlett (ed.), *Equality and Liberty: Analyzing Rawls and Nozick* (London: Macmillan, 1991).

[31] C. Swanton, *Freedom: A Coherence Theory* (Indianapolis: Hackett Publishing Co., 1992), p. 13.

inter alia, not only all the positive-liberty conceptions which we have found good reasons to reject, but also the most far-fetched virtue conceptions of freedom, according to which one is not fully free unless one leads a virtuous life![32]

The general method applied in most of the more interesting conceptual studies of late, such as Miller's account of freedom, is essentially that of Rawls (and, of course, of countless other philosophers, early and late, who have used the same method without giving it a catchy name). However, I still nourish the hope – some would say the fond hope – that a method can be found which, while retaining the insights of Rawls' reflective equilibrium, also satisfies conditions (3) and (4) above.

How, then, can the fact of seemingly endless conceptual disputes be accounted for? John Locke tried to do so by upholding what might be called the *miscommunication thesis*. Generally, people fail to reach agreement in conceptual disputes because, while they 'fill one another's heads with noise and sounds',[33] amounting to the same spoken words, they do not refer to the same underlying concepts. Starting from the premises of his empiricist epistemology, where all words are supposed to describe ideas in the mind of the speaker (in the case of moral concepts the ideas of simple and mixed modes), Locke claimed that by reducing our terms to 'determined collections of the simple ideas they do or should stand for', all disputes would 'end of themselves, and immediately vanish'.[34] More specifically, with moral terms this is all the easier since they do not refer to any real existences in nature but are simply given by definitions. Unfortunately, Locke's simple remedy is based on the empiricist picture theory of meaning, now generally discredited.[35]

An initially more promising approach is that of the recently fashionable *essential contestability thesis* (hereafter *ECT*), first

[32] Ibid., pp. 32ff.

[33] J. Locke, *An Essay Concerning Human Understanding*, II (Oxford: Clarendon Press, 1914), p. 106.

[34] Ibid., p. 151. An interesting modern application of Locke's view is to be found in P. Morriss' treatment of the 'different concepts' of power (*Power: A Philosophical Analysis* (Manchester University Press, 1987), pp. 205ff.).

[35] See further in A. Mason, 'Locke on Disagreement Over the Use of Moral and Political Terms', *Locke News*, 20 (1989).

formulated by W. B. Gallie.[36] Relating its insights to the thread of our discussion so far, the basic idea would be this: it may be that even after all the mutual adjustments of the *reflective equilibrium*, we do not come up with a uniquely definable, authoritative definition. But this does not mean that we will still rationally be talking at cross purposes about a concept such as freedom, and hence failing to satisfy conditions (*3*) and (*4*). Although the criteria employed in freedom-talk are truly disparate, they are nevertheless elements in a common *underlying concept* which gives the discussion its unity. It is at least in a partial sense the *same* freedom that forms the bone of contention. For instance, whatever our eventual answer is to the question how correctly to define freedom, the answer must be such that a student in Tiananmen Square could have recognised it as a description of what he was fighting for.[37]

Thus, the proponents of the *ECT* claim that there are certain concepts (not only in political philosophy, but also in ethics, aesthetics, religion, etc.) which have no clearly definable standard or correct use, but of the elements of which each party has its own 'interpretation' or 'weighing' that it contends is the only proper one, with a stock of convincing arguments. These concepts are, then, not only *contested* (as a matter of fact), or *contestable* (no logically coercive reasons having yet been found for preferring one set of criteria to others), but *essentially contestable*: there is not and never will be any warrant for the belief that any one interpretation is the best one, i.e., there will always be good reasons for disputing the propriety of any of its uses.[38] What exactly is the nature of these concepts? They must (*1*) be appraisive, (*2*) describe an internally complex achievement, (*3*) the explanation of worth be initially unsettled in many respects, (*4*) the achievement persistently vague and modifiable in light of changing circumstances, and (*5*) the contested use guarded both defensively and aggressively by its proponents.

---

[36] See W. B. Gallie, 'Essentially Contestable Concepts', *Proceedings of the Aristotelian Society*, 56 (1955–6).

[37] This sensible point is made by D. Miller (ed.), *Liberty* (Oxford University Press, 1991), in his Introduction, p. 2.

[38] See J. Gray's clarifications of the ECT, 'On the Contestability of Social and Political Concepts', *Political Theory*, 5 (1977), 338–9.

The proper use of the essentially contestable concepts then involves endless disputes, sustained by perfectly respectable arguments, although not resolvable by such arguments.[39]

Plainly, if the *ECT* is not to collapse into full-blooded relativism or to be explained away by a Lockean you-are-really-dealing-with-different-concepts strategy, something must be added, namely, good reasons must be adduced for the assumption that all users at least tacitly agree that *one and the same* concept is at stake, not a multiplicity of overlapping concepts. This is precisely Gallie's point: only by insisting that the same concept is being disputed can we see and keep sharply focused the differences between the conflicting interpretations. What we need, then, is a *common core* around which the different uses revolve. But where can it be found and how can it be explained?

A number of possibilities have been suggested, the first one by Gallie himself, who adds the condition that the concept at stake be derived from an 'original exemplar' whose authority is acknowledged by all contestant users. Unfortunately, the actual historical examples given by Gallie of his 'original exemplars' are not very plausible.[40] The second possibility is that of giving the overarching concept by a schema or canonical form, such as MacCallum's definition of freedom, where disagreements in the end concern only the proper ranges of the variables, which each party can interpret according to the criteria of freedom it holds. However, as we have already seen in MacCallum's case, such formal definitions tend to be so vague that unanimity is gained only at the expense of the specificity required to constitute a single concept. Others have tried to invoke Rawls' concept–conception distinction.[41] The common element in different *conceptions* of freedom is then to be encapsulated by a specification of the *concept*, sufficiently restrictive for a single concept, but sufficiently broad to allow a number of interpretations.

To make a long story short, I shall suggest that the whole

---

[39] Gallie, 'Essentially Contestable Concepts', pp. 171–80.

[40] Gallie's own examples are art, democracy, social justice and Christianity. Their invocation has been criticised by, e.g., E. Gellner, 'The Concept of a Story', *Ratio*, 9 (1967).

[41] Rawls, *A Theory of Justice*, pp. 5–6.

thesis of essential contestability is wrong, since the thinking behind it is either *circular* or *paradoxical*. The proponents of the *ECT* tend to concentrate on particular types of concepts: aesthetic, moral, or political. If asked what is so special about these, opposed for instance to concepts such as 'table', 'kettle', or 'cancer', the answer seems to be that the former are appraisive or normative whereas the latter are not. But why should normative concepts be different from non-normative ones? Well, because normative disputes must be essentially irresolvable! Hence, we are caught in a vicious circle. On this reading, the *ECT* does nothing but reintroduce the description–evaluation distinction in a new fancy form. Proponents of the *ECT* may, however, deny that there is anything special about normative concepts as such. They may claim that the *ECT* is true of a large number of concepts, and that the moral and political ones simply happen to be among them. But then another objection applies, this time in the form of a dilemma: either the alleged 'common core' of these concepts must itself be essentially contestable or not.[42]

If it *is*, the 'common core' is no longer common and the *ECT* has collapsed, at worst into a Kuhnian incommensurability thesis, leading to traditional relativism,[43] at best into a Wittgensteinian *cluster theory* of meaning, based on the idea of family resemblances. As 'resembling' or 'being related to' are not transitive relations, for Wittgenstein two games such as football

---

[42] See Gray, 'On the Contestability of Social and Political Concepts', 337–43 and C. Swanton, 'On the "Essential Contestedness" of Political Concepts', *Ethics*, 95 (1985), 816.

[43] Kuhn represents the other extreme stance according to which concepts (political or non-political) are inextricably bound to a particular conceptual framework. A strong (and what seems to me the correct) reading of his *The Structure of Scientific Revolutions*, 2nd edn, enlarged (University of Chicago Press, 1970) attributes to him a thoroughgoing relativism: these frameworks are incommensurable (the 'same' terms in different frameworks having irreducibly different meanings), and the transfer of allegiance from one to another cannot be forced by logical arguments; it is more like a gestalt-switch or a conversion experience (ch. 10). On a weaker reading, based mainly on his 'Postscript', there can be better or worse reasons (although no final proofs) for accepting or rejecting a framework. But this concession is immediately diluted, if not abandoned, with the claim that although 'good reasons for choice provide motives for conversion and a climate in which it is more likely to occur', no set of good reasons can in the end definitively prescribe such a conversion (p. 204). The irrational element of historical coincidence and the effects of propagandism seem to be more important after all.

and chess may have nothing in common except their relation to a third game, tennis, which is like football played with a ball and like chess played by two persons. Similarly, two instances of unfreedom would not, *ex hypothesi*, need to have anything else in common than some resemblance with a third instance, perhaps one commending a wider measure of assent as an example of unfreedom. On this view, no definition of freedom as such is required or possible. Somewhat understandably, some *ECT*-theorists conflate the *ECT* with such a cluster theory by wanting to hold simultaneously that most concepts in politics are essentially contestable and that they are 'cluster concepts'.[44] But, of course, if the latter is true, they would not have any common core which could be contested.

However, to turn to the second horn of the dilemma, if the common core of the essentially contested concepts is itself *not* essentially contestable, it is hard to see why the different conceptions should be essentially contestable either, since the best conception could, at least in principle, be picked out by comparison with the proper non-contestable core. It has, indeed, been pointed out before that Gallie's own reference to some non-contested, unambiguously defined exemplar implies that a criterion for terminating disagreement really exists, thereby betraying his own thesis.[45] If my claim here is seen as question-begging – the point of the *ECT* being that this kind of picking out cannot be done – my answer would be that it must be incumbent on the *ECT*-theorists to show us *why* it cannot be done. If, for instance, the unessentially contestable common core of a concept of freedom does not allow us to separate freedom from autonomy or social from metaphysical freedom, it seems much more likely that the common core is simply too vague to constitute a single concept of freedom than that the different conceptions 'surrounding' the core are themselves essentially contestable. There is no use here in comparing the interpretation of a concept with the interpretation of a literary work, saying that the same 'incontestable' work of literature can give rise to various essentially contestable interpretations, for –

[44] Connolly for one makes this mistake (*The Terms of Political Discourse*, pp. 18–22).
[45] Gellner, 'The Concept of a Story', 53.

contrary to studies of concepts – what we are after in literary interpretations is their *message* rather than their *reference*.

So, whether or not the supposed common core of the essentially contestable concepts is itself considered essentially contestable or not, the *ECT* seems to misfire. It is of no surprise that in the latest versions of the *ECT* the common-core assumption has simply been abandoned. For instance, Christine Swanton notes how the *ECT* smacks of incoherence, but she still wants to rescue it.[46] Her method is to drop the common-core assumption. She claims that we may sensibly speak of contested conceptions referring to the same ideal without assuming that there is a core concept common to these conceptions. A necessary condition of communication is only that people share some judgements about some cases, enabling arguments to get off the ground, for instance, by analogy or counter-arguments. In the case of freedom, we would thus only need to agree on a reasonable number of sample instances of utterances containing 'free' to be able to say that we were arguing about the *same* kind of freedom. Further, although political disputes are not resolvable by inductive or deductive arguments (proofs), they can still be rationally resolved in specific cases by giving good reasons. This strategy is meant to save a writer like Lukes from accusations of inconsistency in claiming simultaneously that the concept of power is essentially contestable and that one of its conceptions is superior to the others (p. 150). On Swanton's account, although there is no best wheat, we can separate the wheat from the chaff, i.e., some conceptions may be shown by rational arguments to be better than others although there is no *best* conception. The problem about Swanton's recourse is that once the common-core assumption has been dropped, little remains of the *ECT* as a specific thesis. She may be making some interesting observations on the nature of ethical arguments, but I fail to see their potential contribution to a defence of the *ECT*.[47]

---

[46] See, e.g., Swanton, 'On the "Essential Contestedness" of Political Concepts'.

[47] The same applies to A. Mason's paper, 'On Explaining Political Disagreement: The Notion of an Essentially Contested Concept', *Inquiry*, 33 (1990). His is, indeed, an ingenious account of how a belief in one conception can be warranted by reasons which exclude various other options, without this conception necessarily being the best available one. (See also Mason's book, *Explaining Political Disagreement* (Cambridge

The real dilemma of the essential contestability thinkers is that they both want to have their cake and eat it. They want to claim at once that debates about the meaning of for instance 'freedom' or 'power' relate to the same, non-relative concept, and that they are rationally irresolvable. Deep down, most of them are nothing but old-fashioned relativist wolves in sheep's clothing. Thus, in an article by Lukes, it is claimed that there are no distinctively moral criteria of rationality that are not internal to a particular moral belief system: 'moral judgments may be incompatible but equally rational, because the criteria of rationality and justification . . . are themselves relative to conflicting and irreconcilable perspectives'.[48] This is a typical statement of relativism, since what we end up with, in the case of a moral concept such as freedom, would not be a definitional dispute about a common concept but rather, as John Gray puts it, 'a conflict between adherents of mutually unintelligible world-views'.[49] However, if you believe in relativism, why not say so – why call it 'essential contestability'?

The standing of the *ECT* is of particular relevance to this book since most earlier proponents of the responsibility view have described freedom as an essentially contestable concept. Only in Connolly's book, however, is this claim worked out in any detail. His somewhat bleak conclusion is that no definition of freedom can be advanced that precisely distinguishes constraints on freedom from other limitations; what can be produced is at most a flexible set of considerations.[50] The reason is that disagreements over where to draw this line are in the end 'contests over the extent to which a presumption of social responsibility should obtain for the obstacles themselves'.[51] But since ascriptions of responsibility are in many cases open to reply and objection, we are left with a 'grey area' in which no conclusive arguments are

University Press, 1993).) Such an account may well save Lukes' face, but not *qua* follower of the *ECT* as a specific doctrine about a common core around which different conceptions revolve.

[48] S. Lukes, 'Relativism: Cognitive and Moral', *Proceedings of the Aristotelian Society*, suppl. vol. 48 (1974), p. 178.

[49] Gray, 'On the Contestability of Social and Political Concepts', 342.

[50] Connolly, *The Terms of Political Discourse*, p. 167.

[51] Ibid., p. 166 (emphasis omitted).

available. The question whether a particular obstacle in this grey area constitutes a constraint on freedom is, however fervently debated, rationally irresolvable; this is why Connolly insists on talking about 'paradigms' of freedom or power instead of definitions.[52]

What Connolly would have to say about my efforts in this book is something like this: I was right in trying to solve disputes about the nature of freedom by moving to another level, that of responsibility. In doing so I clarified the issue considerably and have perhaps successfully demarcated the concept of freedom. But to say that settled decisions at one level can help to set limits to conceptual controversies at another level, does not mean that such decisions can eliminate these controversies completely. In the present case, my definition of freedom rests upon the concept of responsibility; but responsibility is itself an essentially contested concept. Hence, while the basic concept of freedom can (contrary to relativism) be fixed, it admits of varying interpretations, for different notions of responsibility support different understandings of freedom, even within the fixed terms of the definition.

Now, it seems to me that by granting this, the basis of freedom-talk, which I so rejoiced in finding, is not so firm after all. I discovered, so to speak, the back of the elephant on which the earth rests, only to find that the elephant itself is floating in mid-air. In that case, whatever conclusiveness and finality my efforts have produced are counteracted to such a degree as to rob the responsibility view of most of its value. But this is so, of course, only if Connolly's argument holds water. We must now consider whether it does.

Connolly's argument takes up Gallie's idea of the 'original exemplar'. Let us say that there is a general consensus on the extension of a concept such as *genocide* (the complete extermination of a nation or a racial group) when it is originally invented or defined. Then, as time goes by, new situations arise that deviate in some way from the original case(s) which occasioned its formulations; perhaps the extermination is not complete, or it is a foreseeable but not an intended consequence of some political

---

[52] Ibid., p. 217.

decisions. Now, some parties will want to revise the criteria of
the concept and continue to apply it to those new situations also,
while others claim that such revisions are unwarranted. Both
support their case with good reasons, and an irresolvable
conflict emerges.[53]

Even granting, for the sake of argument, that Connolly's
analysis of the genocide example is right, the question remains
whether the same applies to the concept of responsibility.
Connolly wants to maintain that there, also, a historical shift has
occurred. In olden times when responsibility was on the agenda
of conceptual inquiries, philosophers could restrict their attention
to specific relations between individuals: the responsibility of the
shopkeeper towards his client, the lord towards his tenant, etc.
But in modern societies, we have to move from considerations of
individual relations to those involving collectivities: organisations,
ethnic groups, and, especially, large corporations. May it not be
that the traditional language of responsibility is now insufficient
to characterise the conditions in which we live? May it not be
that we are unable to discover within this traditional language
an answer to the question whether a collectivity is responsible
for – to take one example – the gradually debilitating effect of
environmental pollution on the inhabitants of a given community?
Connolly's answer to such questions is an unequivocal *yes*, and
that is why the concept of responsibility is, at least in modern
societies, an essentially contestable one.[54]

There are, it seems, on Connolly's view two possible reasons
for an irresolvable conflict over the use of a given concept. Either
its point is vague, for example the point of responsibility, or
there are some insurmountable difficulties in determining how
to fit the concept to particular situations, for instance, the
behaviour of collectivities. In response to the first of these
reasons, I could simply rehearse my analysis from section 4.3,
showing that the point of moral responsibility is at least
reasonably clear. But Connolly's claim is presumably the other
one: it is not so much the point of responsibility that is contested
– a point which Connolly says is based on certain deeply

<hr>

[53] Ibid., p. 28.   [54] Ibid., ch. 5.

embedded 'shared ideas'[55] – but rather the extent and manner to which various cases meet this point.

Again, this second line of objection can be interpreted in two ways. Either the problem is an intrinsic one with respect to typical, important cases, or it merely involves borderline cases and factual uncertainties. It must be realised that the boundaries of the sets of things to which our concepts refer are generally difficult to fix precisely. We can always expect to come across examples that puzzle us because they represent situations previously unheard of, or because they lie near the boundary of the concept. (This will be explained in more detail in the following section.) Such contingencies give rise to contestedness, but not to one which justifies the more radical interpretation. What we do in such situations is to put both the example and the point of the concept under further scrutiny. Generally, we come up with a conclusive answer; at worst we are left with some controversial but atypical borderline cases. New information and better arguments, of course, can also make us change our mind. Oppenheim is, for example, right in pointing out that the question whether the situation of workers in the nineteenth century constitutes an example of unfreedom is primarily a matter of factual, not conceptual, controversy.[56] The question to be answered is whether there were good reasons to expect others to suppress the obstacles facing the workers, or whether the obstacles were perhaps the products of non-suppressible economic forces – and that is simply a factual question.

What we have been describing so far are situations of contestedness which is merely factual and/or innocuous. So, Connolly must be relying on the more radical interpretation, namely, that there is an *intrinsic*, irresolvable problem in determining whether certain (typical, important) cases fall within the province of responsibility. But that contention is notoriously difficult to swallow when we have seen how clear the point of the concept of responsibility is. Why can we not simply use the test of moral responsibility for the non-suppression of obstacles and ask: is this a case of an obstacle that an agent could

---

[55] Ibid., p. 192.
[56] Oppenheim, *Political Concepts: A Reconstruction*, p. 87.

plausibly be expected to suppress? As we have seen (sec. 4.6), the existence of collectivities does not, for instance, as such undermine the viability of this test. So, however hard I try, I altogether fail to see where the intrinsic contestability could lie in judging these typical, important cases. In sum, the less radical interpretation of the second argument merely leads to factual and/or innocuous contestability, while the more radical one, used by Connolly, seems to be wrong, at least as far as the concept of responsibility is concerned.

At the end of this brief critique of a number of different methodologies our pumpkin has not yet turned into a coach. That is, we have not hit upon a way to satisfy conditions (*3*) and (*4*) of a sound conceptual study: those of non-relativity, and the plausible explaining, or explaining away, of conceptual disagreement. It may be time to pause and take stock.

7.2. CONCEPTUAL REVISION AND OPEN TEXTURE

Kovesi's *Moral Notions* is a gem, too often overlooked by students of social philosophy. Some of the things Kovesi has to say about the nature and formation of concepts are particularly pertinent to our discussion at this point. What, for instance, makes an object fall under the concept of a table? Kovesi's agreeably Aristotelian answer is that what turns an object into a table is not that it has some specific perceivable properties but that it fulfils a certain *function* or satisfies a sociological *need*. The features we look for in deciding whether an object is a table or not are those which constitute the object's being the sort of thing which serves the purpose tables were invented to serve. The point of talk about *tables* is thus to designate objects that fulfil a specific function, important to human life, enabling us to sit, eat, read, write, etc., in a convenient way, given the shape of the human body. The point of talk about *murder*, on the other hand, is to classify a type of action: the wrongful taking of human life. Terms such as 'murder', which group together the morally relevant facts of certain situations, Kovesi calls 'moral terms', and their meanings 'moral concepts'.[57]

---

[57] See J. Kovesi, *Moral Notions* (London: Routledge and Kegan Paul, 1971), ch. 1.

Most noteworthy in Kovesi's subsequent analysis is that the difference between moral and other notions does not appear to coincide with a difference between evaluation and description. The real difference can rather be seen as lying in the formal elements, the divergent reasons for collocating certain features, aspects and qualities, and for grouping them together. Thus, whereas we always describe from some point of view, we can never be said to do so from a perspective we could call *the descriptive* point of view. In the case of moral concepts, such as 'murder', we describe from the moral point of view, but that point of view is in no way less descriptive than the perspective employed in classifying an object as a table or a kettle. It is simply *another* perspective; we are drawing attention to features of another sort.

Kovesi's considerations suffice to bring out the nature of the misunderstandings that have flourished so long on the basis of the description–evaluation distinction. Evaluation is not the icing on the cake of hard facts: in the case of moral notions we cannot, so to speak, peel away the layers of evaluation until we touch bottom – the neutral descriptive content. We do not *first* have hard facts and *then* load them with normativity. That is, although we have facts such as a man picking up a gun and shooting someone which are, to use Anscombean terminology, 'brute relative to' murder, there is nothing in the nature of the brute facts *themselves* that tells us which of them to collocate under the heading 'murder'. There is an independent *moral* rationale behind the concept of murder which determines the acts brought together under that heading. If we remove the rationale, we are not left with the descriptive criteria for murder minus evaluation: we are simply left with nothing at all. To take another example, by removing the evaluative element from the notion of tidiness, we strip ourselves of the possibility of grouping together various instances of untidiness. Why would ink spots and coffee stains on this page both be considered untidy? Surely ink and coffee are chemically different! An attempt to specify 'tidiness' in chemical ('tidiness-neutral') terms would fail for the same reason as an attempt to specify 'murder' in morally neutral terms: there is nothing left to specify as the *same*.[58] As Kovesi puts

---

[58] See J. M. Brennan, *The Open-Texture of Moral Concepts* (London: Macmillan, 1977), pp. 54–5.

it most forcibly: 'Moral notions do not evaluate the world of description but describe the world of evaluation.'[59] All notions are formed for some reason, and they 'describe' from some point of view.

Kovesi's arguments conclusively undermine the common assumption that moral and social concepts have some special logic of their own, as a result of which their definitions are susceptible to irresolvable disputes. More specifically for our present purposes, his arguments help to vindicate my treatment of freedom as a moral, or value-loaded concept. I would, indeed, go as far as Crocker who claims that to 'attempt a "value-neutral" account of liberty is at best only superficially more sensible than to give a "biology neutral" account of fish'.[60] It seems to me, in line with Kovesi, that the point of employing the term 'freedom' is to group together actions that are similar to one another in a morally relevant way.

Unfortunately, however, although the threat of the *specifically* relative nature of moral concepts has been averted, the threat of *general* conceptual relativism still hangs over our heads. It could be that our intuitions about the point of all, or most, concepts differ and that an inquiry which aims at a single definition for any given concept is doomed to failure. Even if all concepts are formed for a purpose and have a point, why does this point have to be the same for everyone? Might not, for instance, the point of 'freedom' happen to coincide with that of 'autonomy' among some language speakers in some societies; or the point of 'table' with that of 'bed'?

Now, it is true that on a map there often seem to be numerous ways up each mountain; nevertheless, a mountain may actually be of a sort such that, for a rational mountaineer, there is but one best path to its top. Let us say that the 'mountain' we are supposed to climb is to define the term 'table'. What we do, as Kovesi suggests, is to search for a function or a social need that the term is meant to fulfil. If someone insists on reserving the term 'table' for four-legged objects fulfilling this need, we point out the arbitrariness of the distinction; why not also three-legged

[59] Kovesi, *Moral Notions*, p. 119.
[60] L. Crocker, *Positive Liberty* (The Hague: Martinus Nijhoff Publisher, 1980), p. 9.

ones? For what reason, that is, should the language of 'table' be thought to mark out this particular distinction? If, on the other hand, the definition is so broad as to include tables and beds, we would say: 'If you use "table" in this way, you will have no uses left to refer specifically to objects you put your plates on at dinner, as distinct from those you sleep on at night', etc. The notion of a table has become bloated beyond good sense. Maybe we could think of some use for a portmanteau concept of a 'bable' (bed + table) but its point could surely not be the same as that of a table.

This example brings out what I take to be a very important truth, already anticipated in chapter 1 (p. 4). All satisfactory inquiries into the nature of concepts (at any rate those relating to the empirical world) will be *critical* inquiries. What we should be aiming at in a good conceptual study is conceptual *revision* rather than mere *analysis*. It must be shown why the point of the given concept *is* or *should be* of interest to people, given their human nature, and how the term designating the concept must be defined so as to correspond to this point. Much the same applies here to 'freedom' as to 'table' in the example above. In my inquiry into freedom, I claim to have found a rationale behind a concept which should be of interest to us as humans: the concept of not being constrained by another agent. It is a negative concept in the sense that we are free to do x, as long as there is no agent responsible for the non-suppression of an obstacle to our doing x; and it involves a prima facie moral presumption of illegitimacy in that it places the onus of justification on the constraining agent. I have pointed out that the term '(social) freedom' is frequently, though not always, used to convey the meaning of this concept in English (so does 'Freiheit' in German, 'frihed' in Danish, 'frelsi' in Icelandic, etc.); many, if not most, of our common usages and intuitions are in harmony with it.

The crux of the critical method in this particular case has been to argue that the term 'freedom' must be defined in such-and-such a way for its use to be internally coherent, and to distinguish it from the meanings of other terms which may be just as important, but which do not have exactly the same extension as freedom. For instance, if we define 'freedom' more broadly than I have proposed, it starts to take up a role admirably filled by other terms ('autonomy', 'ability', etc.); and if we define it more narrowly (for instance, as involving only intentionally created constraints), then the definition becomes arbitrary from precisely that moral point of view which indicates the purpose of freedom-talk (why not also negligently created ones?).

I have claimed that it is a necessary condition of the fruitfulness of substantive debates that people agree on the meaning of those ideals about the value of which they can then disagree. My arguments have been designed to show that one particular definition of 'social freedom' is best fitted to serve as the basis for substantive political debate, even if this definition should not always prove to be in strict accordance with the common usage of people in a given society. We do, indeed, sometimes need to 'trim the ragged edges' of ordinary usage – knock the corners off this usage, finegrain that distinction – to satisfy our intellectual demands of coherence and non-arbitrariness, but that is in no way mysterious: definitions are *created* to serve a purpose, they are neither *discovered* nor fall into our lap by chance. Let me re-emphasise that what I have come up with in this book is not an arbitrary, stipulative definition of freedom. I have tried to show that freedom-talk has a particular point or purpose in human relations, and have argued critically for a particular definition of '(social) freedom' that best conveys this point. In the end, I claim to have proposed a definition that is *objective* in the sense of being objectively useful to those interested in certain relations between agents, relations which are of widespread importance for human beings.

While aiming at non-relativity, it must be remembered that the boundaries of the sets of things to which our concepts refer do not typically constitute tight-shut compartments and are difficult to fix precisely (p. 189). This feature of our quest for definitions has been admirably captured by Friedrich Waismann in his analysis of the *open texture* of most of our concepts.[61] Although the

---

[61] See F. Waismann, 'Verifiability', *Proceedings of the Aristotelian Society*, suppl. vol. 19 (1945), pp. 119–25.

point, or formal element, of a moral concept (freedom) or a
non-moral one (table) may be a clear-cut and indisputable one,
the incompleteness of empirical data makes it impossible to give
an exhaustive enumeration of all the material features which the
formal element may assume. That is, the set of tables or freedoms
is open, and not closed as in the case of geometrical terms. In the
latter case, we can, for example, give a strict rule which
prescribes the necessary and sufficient properties of a rectangle;
we can give a complete definition which anticipates and settles
once and for all every possible question of usage. By contrast,
one cannot specify exactly what shapes, sizes, materials, etc.,
potential tables can be made of, and, although we have roughly
formulated the necessary and sufficient condition under which a
situation constitutes an example of unfreedom, we have not
defined freedom with absolute 'geometrical precision'. The
point is that it may be a matter of doubt whether a certain
situation precisely satisfies these conditions. For example, in
Miller's fourth office story (p. 30), we may debate whether the
passer-by could still have been expected to pay more attention
to the cries of the locked-in person, although he knew all about
the janitor's daily rounds. In addition to such borderline cases,
situations of an unforeseeable nature can arise, perhaps owing to
a new technology – situations which could not be taken into
account when formulating the original definition of the term but
which nevertheless call for categorisation as instances of freedom
or unfreedom. Also, in the future we may have to emend or
refine our definition of moral responsibility (and hence of
freedom) to do justice to such phenomena as artificially intelligent
robots, or Martians. Still, Aristotle for one would remind us not
to feel too disheartened, since this just is all the precision the
subject-matter admits of. We must plough with such oxen as we
have, and the nature of moral philosophy is simply different
from that of, say, geometry – for better or for worse.

However, what is disconcerting is the impression which this
explanation of the open texture of concepts may create, namely,
that I am now sailing dangerously close to the thesis of essential
contestability which I renounced in the previous section. Do the
open-texture model and the *ECT* not in the end come down to

the same thing? I think not. On the open-texture reading, a concept such as freedom has a clear core; according to the *ECT*, different interpretations of the concept only share a vague common core. On the latter thesis, most conceptual disputes are intrinsically unsolvable; on the former they are, in principle, decidable, since there is an objective control to the inquiry: an independent criterion by which competing answers can be measured. That, of course, is the formal element of the concept, its point, which, *ex hypothesi*, none of the parties to the dispute can change. Furthermore, there is a method by which this formal element can be brought to bear on the questionable cases – namely, just that process of critical clarification and refinement which should be the chief method of conceptual inquiries.

The open-texture model thus affords us, whereas the *ECT* does not, the sense of objectivity, of rational decidability, which alone can satisfy our intellectual demands for the subject of ethics in general, and our practical need of finding an authoritative basis for the co-ordination of our social practices. This idea is emphatically expressed by Stanley Benn, in arguing against the *ECT*:

To the extent that we embark on the task of winning assent by rational argument rather than by mind-bending manipulation, we are committing ourselves to the belief that there is no inherent impossibility about the enterprise, and though agreement may be hard to reach, we never know that it could not be found by still more patient exploration.[62]

It is this prospect of success by 'patient exploration' which makes the open-texture model so much superior to a thesis of rational irresolvability; with the trowel of patience we dig out the roots of truth. If this model helps us to achieve compliance with the all-important condition (*3*) of fruitful conceptual inquiries, as I have suggested, what more can we ask of it?

It may be helpful to conclude this discussion of the contestability/decidability of (moral) concepts with a short, if somewhat oversimplified, summary of the main proposals dealt with so far. According to (*a*) *the miscommunication thesis*, a moral concept has a clear point, and any possible disagreement would be caused by a

---

[62] S. I. Benn, *A Theory of Freedom* (Cambridge University Press, 1988), p. 151.

deliberate or accidental failure to communicate; according to (*b*) *the open-texture model*, the concept has a clear point, but it may give rise to disputes over borderline cases; according to (*c*) *the essential contestability thesis*, the concept has a point but a vague one which can support various interpretations, mutually conflicting in a rationally irresolvable way; according to (*d*) *the cluster theory*, the concept has no point or essence but designates a family of properties (a 'cluster'), some of which must be satisfied by a potential member of the set; according to (*e*) *the incommensurability thesis*, the concept may have a point, but only one that is specific to a particular community or paradigm; no inter-paradigmatic (non-relative) agreement is attainable.

As always, there are horses for courses. So, although moral concepts do not, in my view, fall under (*a*) and (*e*), other concepts may: geometrical ones under (*a*), aesthetic ones under (*e*), perhaps. It may also be that some general moral and political concepts fall under (*d*) (the cluster idea seems to fit well with a term such as 'politics'); but after examining the *ECT*, I doubt that (*c*) is a relevant category for the understanding of moral concepts. My main suggestion, however, is that most of the important and historically controversial moral and social concepts fall under (*b*). They are concepts with a point – an essence – but at the same time an open texture. They give rise to disputes, but only disputes that are, in principle, decidable by the methods of critical conceptual inquiry. Their 'contestability' is not an essential one.

7.3. RETURN TO NATURALISM

As I have presented it, the method of patient critical clarification, or conceptual revision, within the framework of an open-texture model, satisfies conditions (*3*) and (*4*) set down in chapter 1 and section 7.1. It yields non-relative definitions of moral concepts, while simultaneously explaining the continued possibility of a *non-essential* conceptual disagreement which rests on the incompleteness of empirical data. Moreover, this method neatly tallies with a resurgent Aristotelianism whose outstanding characteristic is its down-to-earth *naturalism*, in which human beings are seen as a natural kind among other natural kinds in a broadly teleological world. Whether we like it or not, this world is a net; the more we stir in it, the more entangled we become. Instead of escaping from its contingencies to the realm of possible worlds in our conceptual inquiries, the method I have suggested accepts the fact that the set of criteria associated with our philosophical concepts inevitably reflects contingent assumptions. As Nicholas Rescher has put it, these criteria are 'fact coordinated'.[63] In our world, things have purposes, whether naturally or as given them by us: consequently concepts have points. The aim of conceptual studies is to argue critically what these points *are* and/or what they *should be*, in the light of our existing knowledge of ourselves and our world.

Still, a proponent of Rawls' reflective equilibrium might object that I have not really been proposing an alternative methodology. Rawls' method is also critical; it is an attempt to rationalise our concepts within a system of concepts and their relations, correcting concepts to fit the system and the system to fit the concepts. Moreover, although it perhaps does not come out so clearly in Rawls' own discussion, such an enterprise requires attention (in order to be reflective) to what a system of concepts is intended to do. This may all be true. However, what I have been trying to add to the Rawlsian insights is a Kovesian emphasis on the functional nature of concepts. Notions such as 'table' or 'freedom' fulfil a certain *function* in human life. I have suggested that it is possible to bring out what this function is, and hence to show how the terms 'table' and 'freedom' would most usefully be defined. In other words, I have tried to add the crucial *naturalistic* link to Rawls' methodology which was found missing in section 7.1: the acknowledgement that conceptual moral truths can be grounded in facts 'out there' which are independent of particular conceptions of the good.[64]

---

[63] N. Rescher, *The Strife of Systems* (University of Pittsburgh Press, 1985), pp. 50–6.
[64] This use of Kovesi's ideas may seem to contrast sharply with Brennan's characterisation of him as a non-naturalist (*The Open-Texture of Moral Concepts*, pp. 66ff.). Much depends here on how we define 'naturalism'. If Brennan means by it the theory that value words are definable in terms of specific 'brute facts', such as colours, feelings, etc., he is surely right that Kovesi's account is antagonistic to it. However, there are more plausible forms of naturalism, such as Aristotle's view that what is *good* for man is

Plainly, Kovesian 'functionalism' does not constitute a methodology in and of itself. It is not that functions are given and obvious: they have to be argued for and adjudicated like everything else. While I differ from Rawls in my meta-methodological commitment to the non-relative nature of such arguments, I freely admit that to pass hurdles (*1*) and (*2*), something like Rawls' reflective equilibrium is needed. In fact, Rawls has never claimed any originality for this method, and it is of no surprise to find it having been used – broadly speaking – in, for instance, Aristotle's *Nicomachean Ethics*. We set down the appearances ('*endoxa*'), work through the puzzles of contradictions in our usage and beliefs, and then formulate a new account which we bring back to the appearances, trying to retain the truth of the greatest number and the most authoritative of these.[65] Admittedly, there is *at the outset* simply no other rational way to proceed than to jump – alas, temporarily – onto Rawls' bandwagon.

However, Rawlsians will still not be satisfied. They will doubtless complain that, while I have concentrated on the mutual adjustments between theory and common usage, with the notion of a function as some sort of a gobetween, I have neglected to put the enterprise of conceptual revision into broader perspective. Just as there are no brute facts which lie unproblematically before our gaze – all facts are theory-laden – so functions are not isolable independently of *conceptual schemes*, and definitions are helpful only in so far as they aid in the production or in the understanding of a general theory. Even granting the importance of functions, objectors will argue, a given function may be expressed *by one or by several* terms or concepts. It may be either an arbitrary matter, or one decidable by reference to factors beyond the expression of this particular function. Perhaps a number of different decisions can be made to appear plausible, each one, of course, requiring systematic adjustments in our conceptual scheme, or even a transfer to

what conduces to his flourishing (his all-round growth as a human being), and there is absolutely nothing in Kovesi's view to make it incompatible with such naturalisms. On the contrary, we may discern in his view arguments which reinforce naturalism, in as much as Kovesi maintains that values are facts of a certain kind.

[65] For a discussion of Aristotle's methodology, see M. C. Nussbaum, *The Fragility of Goodness* (Cambridge University Press, 1986), ch. 8.

another scheme (general moral theory, political ideology, etc.). The upshot of all this is, they would urge, that unless you want to lean naively, like Hope on her anchor, on the idea of one function–one concept, you have failed to avert the possibility of general conceptual relativism, to which Rawls wisely bows.

To be sure, modern-day naturalists have no reason for rejecting the theory-ladenness of concepts. However, that does not mean that their naturalism has been undermined in any way. They can, for example, advise us, as Michael Bishop does in a recent article, to adopt that conceptual revision which plays a role in the best available theory on the subject, namely, the one which provides more pragmatic and epistemic benefits than the alternatives.[66] At any given time, there is bound to be a best available moral theory (the theory which most satisfactorily captures the existing knowledge of our nature and the role of morality) and within such a theory, there is bound to be a best available definition of a given moral or social concept.

It is crucial not to confuse theory-ladenness with arbitrary theory-choice here. We are beings with an essence which cannot be accounted for by simply any theory or ideology you happen to choose. Thus, as Gordon Graham has noted in a different context, 'politics being what it is, there are always certain facts which the advocate of any ideology cannot, or would not, wish to ignore'.[67] The idea is of political debates taking place within a framework of social concepts which are themselves fixed by certain basic facts about human beings and their environment, and where the factually fixed points limit the possible elasticity of any rationally constructed 'conceptual scheme'. We can easily imagine a world in which these facts do not hold, since they are contingently but not logically true; but that world is not ours to live in. *Our world* being what it is and *we* being what we are, it is not a matter of arbitrary choice how the morally relevant facts of our existence are grouped together. If we accept this, we see that the theory- and context-dependence of moral

---

[66] See M. A. Bishop, 'The Possibility of Conceptual Clarity in Philosophy', *American Philosophical Quarterly*, 29 (1992).

[67] G. Graham, *Politics in its Place: A Study of Six Ideologies* (Oxford: Clarendon Press, 1986), p. 74.

terms does *not* in itself exclude the application of moral considerations across cultural or ideological borders.

'But are these any more then mere assertions?' the objector might ask. 'Your case against the "general conceptual relativism," which you considered the major threat to your enterprise, started by pointing out that "a mountain may actually be of a sort such that . . . there is but one best path to its top." However, you have not given us any good reasons to believe that the "mountains" under discussion here are actually of this sort; you have not bridged the gap between "may" and "is".' And the objector might conclude by noting that, given the endless disputes about the proper extensions of social concepts, it is highly unlikely that they, of all concepts, would lend themselves to the kind of naturalistic revision described above.

To respond conclusively to this objection, I would have to offer sample definitions of more social concepts than merely 'freedom', and 'power', showing how these could be arrived at through naturalistic reasoning. It is not within the scope of the present book to supply this further step. However, it is fully in the spirit of naturalism to insist that the proof of the pudding will be in the eating. The viability of the proposed methodology depends solely on whether it can be made to work: that is *the point* of such a naturalism. I have already given reasons to suggest *why* and *how* it can be thought to work, and examples of definitions of 'freedom' and 'power' which I believe have been made to work. The rest is left to further inquiry. This may not seem to be a sufficiently potent medicine to cure the 'general conceptual relativists' of their ailment. However, we could also remind them of the way in which the tide has recently turned in discussions of substantive moral relativism. Such relativism flourished as never before among laypeople and philosophers from the beginning of this century, generated in part by the findings of 'classical' anthropologists who reported on the bizarre and mysterious ways of life on the 'peripheries'.[68] Until recently, the most promising strategies to counter moral relativism were thought to be conceptual ones, showing how the relativist

---

[68] See an enlightening discussion of the changing trends in anthropology in T. McCarthy, 'Doing the Right Thing in Cross-cultural Representation', *Ethics*, 102 (1992).

was involved in some sort of a logical or moral paradox. Unfortunately, these strategies did not work; relativism proved to be demonstrably un-self-defeating. With the recent revival of virtue-based ethics, however, a new and more successful strategy has emerged, dismissing moral relativism on contingent grounds: it simply cannot be that there is an unending choice of ways of social life for members of a species sharing roughly the same nature, the same virtues and vices. Thus, factual objections have taken over from conceptual ones. In the preceding discussion, I have tried to apply this new way of looking at substantive questions to conceptual disputes: may it not be that naturalism holds the key to a refutation of relativism in that sphere as well?

For some reason, naturalistic reasoning continues to fall on many deaf philosophical ears. Such philosophers simply cannot understand how factual considerations can help us in solving or dissolving conceptual puzzles. A case in point is the steadily growing mountain of literature on John Stuart Mill's 'conceptual blunders', his alleged failure to realise that the principle of liberty is at odds with the principle of utility, and that his ranking of higher and lower pleasures is inconsistent with the utilitarian idea of pleasure as the satisfaction of any desire.[69] What these writers overlook, I believe, is Mill's uncompromising naturalism. For him, it is simply a matter of fact that an area of private action can be cordoned off where utilitarian considerations, other than those embraced by the principle of liberty, are *in fact* always outweighed. Similarly, it would simply be a true *empirical judgement* for Mill that a person who has known real love would not sacrifice it for any amount of chocolate offered, even if the love were also attended by more discontent than the chocolate.

According to Thomas Nagel, 'objectivity is the driving force of ethics . . . [and] of science'.[70] The picture I have been suggesting is one which would have the same lines drawn on the conceptual canvas as a Mill or a modern-day advocate of virtue

[69] One recent example is E. S. Anderson, 'John Stuart Mill and Experiments in Living', *Ethics*, 102 (1991).
[70] T. Nagel, *The View From Nowhere* (New York: Oxford University Press, 1986), p. 8. Cf. F. D'Agostino, 'Transcendence and Conversation: Two Conceptions of Objectivity', *American Philosophical Quarterly*, 30 (1993), 87.

theory would draw on the substantive one. This is a picture which satisfies our intellectual demand for objectivity; not objectivity *qua* transcendence or a 'view from nowhere', but rather *qua* human justifiability, a view from our vantage-point as natural rational beings in *this* world.[71] Let us by all means, as I granted earlier, recognise the possibility of alternative conceptual schemes and alternative methodologies in other worlds, inhabited by rational beings with natures different from ours, but for our present purposes the vantage-points of those beings are irrelevant to us, since, *ex hypothesi*, we do not have them.[72]

The Rawlsian objector's conflation above of theory-ladenness with arbitrary (or at least inherently controversial) theory-choice exemplifies a defect which, more than any other, tends to mar analyses of moral and political concepts. This defect is the promiscuous running together of two distinct theses: (*a*) that social theorising cannot avoid being a normative activity; and (*b*) that moral and social theory is beset by an ineradicable conceptual relativism which prevents it from yielding any definitions capable of compelling rational assent.[73] This chapter has been an attempt to show that while (*a*) is definitely true, (*b*) may be nothing but an industriously propagated legend.

My conclusions about the normativity of moral concepts do not commit me to the views, espoused for instance by Connolly, that by analysing a concept of politics I have implicated myself in politics; that explicating a concept such as freedom is 'not a prelude to . . . but a dimension of politics itself',[74] and that by adopting any definition I am taking a stand in an ideological debate. What leads Connolly astray is the historically frequent use of seriously flawed 'definitions' of moral terms for propagandistic purposes. For example, just as it is easier to win a football game by pointing out that the opposing team is fielding an illegal player than by scoring goals, so it is 'easier' to claim that

---

[71] D'Agostino ('Transcendence and Conversation: Two Conceptions of Objectivity') admirably explains these two different understandings of objectivity.

[72] Ibid., p. 103 (drawing on insights from Rescher).

[73] J. Gray, 'Political Power, Social Theory, and Essential Contestability', in D. Miller and L. Siedentop (eds.), *The Nature of Political Theory* (Oxford: Clarendon Press, 1983), p. 77.

[74] Connolly, *The Terms of Political Discourse*, p. 3.

the starving masses in Ethiopia are 'free', if their situation is not the result of deliberate actions, than to grant that they are unfree, and then (perhaps) produce good reasons for not helping them. Such reasons can often be found, for instance in cases of imperfect responsibility (sec. 4.3); but these would be *substantive*, political or moral, reasons, not *conceptual* ones. It goes without saying that people's values conflict, i.e., their views on what is to count as the good life and the well-structured society. The reason may partly be that aiming at eudaimonia involves an essential trade-off between equally important but mutually incompatible values. Thus, politics is rightly described by Connolly as the 'sphere of the unsettled';[75] but that is not because our conceptual inquiries are irresolvable and our concepts vague, but because people, employing the same concepts, differ over substantive issues.

My conclusions in this chapter clearly support an optimistic view as to the general prospects of conceptual inquiries in political philosophy. By a painstaking investigation into more and more of its concepts and their interrelations, we should be able to dissipate gradually the confusions that have surrounded their application. In this, I concur with Gray in endorsing a 'classical conception of political philosophy as an intellectual activity capable of yielding determinate results and, so, of assisting reflective agents in their search for a good society'.[76] In other words, I have been espousing a variant of what Mason calls 'the imperfection conception' of political disagreement: that when conceptual political disagreements arise, at least one party to the dispute is mistaken; and that with sufficient time, patience, and logical skills, such disputes could be settled to the satisfaction of any reasonable person who is sincerely engaged with them.[77]

Nevertheless, it could still be argued that there is an unbridgeable gap, not between facts and values, descriptions and evaluations, but between *moral facts*, on the one hand, *moral prescriptions* on the other. Knowing what is good does not commit

---

[75] Ibid., p. 227.
[76] Gray, 'On the Contestability of Social and Political Concepts', 346.
[77] See Mason, *Explaining Political Disagreement*, pp. 2ff.

us to aim at the good; even less does an understanding of the definition of freedom commit us to lessen the burden of unfreedom. If I am an evil-minded person, I may utilise my knowledge to increase the world's misery and injustice. If, however, I am noble-minded, being clear about the meaning of freedom may assist me in analysing and arguing against particular instances of unfreedom in the world around me; and in that endeavour, perhaps, this book will help.

CHAPTER 8

Concluding remarks

A distinguished philosopher once remarked that there could be no general theory of *holes* since holes are dug for different purposes: by children in the sand, by gardeners to plant lettuce, etc.[1] My book should have brought to light that there can be no general theory of *freedoms* either. The most we may hope for is to clarify the concept of a specific *kind* of freedom by looking at the purpose it can most usefully be made to serve. Indeed, this has been my aim here, namely, to arrive at a definition of *social freedom*. In the case of that particular concept, people have often used the term 'social freedom' as a shopping trolley which could be packed with anybody's chosen selection of separate goods. By contrast, I have tried to show how an open-textured and normative, but yet authoritative, definition can be arrived at through naturalistic reasoning: a definition that catches the point which the term should reasonably be made to convey and is not unduly relativistic.

It would be lighting a candle to the sun to rehearse here the various arguments employed in the course of my discussion; – my polemic targets being as many as was deemed necessary to reach out to the perplexity of the issues at hand – these are to be found in the relevant chapters. What I shall do instead is to summarise my conclusions in brief compass as follows:

Social freedom is a moral concept, logically distinct from other freedom-concepts although it presupposes free will *qua* 'autarchy'.

[1] Cf. P. Morriss, *Power: A Philosophical Analysis* (Manchester University Press, 1987), p. 45. The 'distinguished philosopher' is Alasdair MacIntyre in his book *Against the Self-Images of the Age* (London: Duckworth, 1971).

This book has argued for a 'responsibility view' of negative social freedom, held to be superior to other negative-freedom conceptions. According to this view, social freedom designates a triadic relation between an autarchic agent A, another autarchic agent B, and some choice/action x. B is socially free to do x *iff* he is not constrained by A from doing x. A constrains B when A is morally responsible for the non-suppression (imposition, non-prevention of imposition, non-removal) of an obstacle that impedes, to a greater or a lesser extent, B's choosing/doing x. A is morally responsible for the non-suppression when the onus of justification can be placed on him, that is, when it is appropriate to ask him, in the given context, why he did not suppress the obstacle, and that, in turn, is when there exists an objective reason – however overridable – satisfying a minimal criterion of plausibility why A could have been expected, factually or morally, to suppress the obstacle. This entails that the same situation could constitute a constraint on freedom in Society$_1$ and not in Society$_2$, but as the rational arguments used to show what a person can appropriately be called upon to justify in either society would be of the same nature and mutually understandable, my responsibility view is not relativistic. Indeed, I have specifically argued that it is methodologically possible to construct an authoritative definition of freedom which is normative and critical but non-relative. The irreflexive nature of the relational concept of social freedom implies that 'internal bars', for which no other agent is responsible, cannot constrain our own freedom; nor is there a necessary connection between autonomy (*qua* specific exercises of autarchy) and freedom. Accounts of positive liberty assume that (*a*) a person can constrain his own freedom, and (*b*) freedom is an exercise-, not an opportunity concept. Hence, they are not to be seen as accounts of social freedom, but rather as upholding other, logically distinct, values.

Much of this study has been taken up with answers to possible objections. It is fitting to end it with four more. *First*, someone might claim that I have continually overstated my differences with previous versions of the responsibility view to provide a focus for my own thesis. To answer that, I could do no better than to direct the objector back to the various places where important dissimilarities with the views of Benn and Weinstein, Miller, and Connolly manifested themselves. To be sure, I pledged my allegiance at an early stage in this study to a responsibility view of freedom. There, I took my stand upon sound precedents since such a view has been upheld recently by the above-mentioned writers as well as other notable contributors to debates about freedom and power. However, coming across a prima facie plausible account at the start of a conceptual inquiry is merely a promise of merit which further investigation can either ratify or annul. The natural way to proceed was to examine whether every cranny could be blocked through which doubts and objections to this original account might enter. I found it wanting in various respects. None of my predecessors had, as far as I could see, (a) defined the notion of an obstacle with adequate precision, (b) given a satisfactory account of moral responsibility for obstacles, (c) discussed the connection between freedom and power, (d) distinguished sharply enough between negative- and positive-liberty theories, or (e) provided any good reasons for or against the common claim that definitions of freedom are bound to be essentially contestable. The present study has been an attempt to ameliorate these shortcomings and, thus, to place the responsibility view of freedom on a firmer footing.

Second, I have taken it for granted from the start that the responsibility view is a negative account of freedom, whereas Gray, for example, categorises it as a positive account.[2] His reasons, also mirrored in Patrick's thesis,[3] are that such a view accepts the reality of internal bars and is connected with the idea of the autonomous individual. However, I have repeatedly pointed out that (a) a correct negative-freedom theory also takes account of internal bars, and (b) the responsibility view does not presuppose actual autonomy as a necessary condition of freedom. Here, Gray is simply wrong.

---

[2] J. Gray, *Liberalism* (London: Open University Press, 1986), p. 59.
[3] M. Patrick, 'Liberty and Liberalism', M.Phil. dissertation (University of St Andrews, 1988), chs. 4–5.

Third, it might be asked why I frequently evade embattled topics by saying that they relate to substantive, not conceptual, issues. If, as I have claimed, there is no gap between description and evaluation, and evaluative (moral) terms often embody a presumption against this or that, what is left of the distinction between the conceptual and the substantive? The answer is that by a 'substantive' issue I am referring to an issue where different arguments or values have to be weighed against one another. For example, the term 'social freedom' embodies a presumption which places the onus of justification on the constraining-agent(s). That is a *conceptual* truth which people of every political stripe would be wise to acknowledge. Thus, as G. Cohen has realised,[4] socialists and capitalists can and should start their debates from a conceptual common ground. However, if they want to argue for the superiority of their respective substantive, moral systems while employing a common definition of freedom, they need to bring other concepts and arguments to bear on the discussion. How are the values of merit, efficiency, private property, etc., to be weighed against the presumption involved in freedom-talk? These are what I call *substantive* questions and they require a whole moral theory which cannot be supplied here. Conceptual studies cannot perform the actual bricklaying, but they can provide the bricks.

Fourth, it might be urged that I have deprived the concept of freedom of its real significance in political debate, since it no longer seems decisive or conclusive to describe a state of affairs as involving unfreedom if different freedoms have to be weighed against each other all the time and a loss in freedom can be offset by a gain in other values. Here, I can do no better than to quote Miller who points out that although a charge of unfreedom does not settle a political debate, by invoking it we are *making a move* in a political argument.[5] Conceptual truths do not settle substantive issues but they can contribute to our discussion of them.

More specifically, however, the objection might be that an analysis of '*B* is unfree with respect to *A* to do *x*' is in itself

---

[4] G. A. Cohen, 'Illusions about Private Property and Freedom', in J. Mepham and D. H. Ruben (eds.), *Issues in Marxist Philosophy*, IV (Brighton: Harvester Press, 1981), p. 235.
[5] D. Miller, 'Constraints on Freedom', *Ethics*, 94 (1983), 69.

irrelevant to the all-important task of establishing whether the obstacle created by A is unjustified or not (i.e., whether A is culpable for the obstacle's non-suppression). Such a dispensability or red-herring argument concerning analyses of free action is forcibly expressed by Wayne Norman. He asks us to consider the following two arguments:

> A.   1.   R creates obstacle O for P.
>
>   2.   O renders P unfree to x.
>
>   3.   (Conditions C)
>
> Thus   4.   O is unjustified (i.e., R is culpable for
>   creating O).
>
> B.   I.   R creates O for P.
>
>   II.   (Conditions C)
>
> Thus   III. O is unjustified.[6]

Norman's point is that since we still need conditions C to tell us whether R's creating an obstacle for P is in the end unjustified or not, the inclusion of premise 2 in A is irrelevant; it adds nothing to argument A which is not included in argument B. I must say, in response, that Norman has a rather restricted view of the scope of political debate about obstacles to action if he thinks that the only important move in such arguments is the drawing of final conclusions about the eventual justifiability of obstacles. We can envisage an argument analogous with Norman's showing us that the concept of *stealing* is dispensable in moral debate, since knowing that R's taking away P's possessions falls under that concept does not enable us to conclude that R is culpable for his action – for arguably there may be cases where stealing is justifiable in extreme situations. The concept of a *lie* would then fall by the wayside, too, along with many others. It may well be that some general terms 'can' (in a trivial sense) be expunged from our moral vocabularies, but what is the use if the respective concepts are still relevant to our making moves in moral debates and will continue to be expressed in some more long-drawn and cumbersome ways? It is hardly in the interest of conceptual

---

[6] W. J. Norman, 'Taking "Free Action" Too Seriously', *Ethics*, 101 (1991), 509.

economy to replace '*B* is unfree' each time it would occur in such a debate by 'there is an obstacle to *B*'s doing *x* which another agent *A* has failed to suppress; moreover, there is a good reason why *A* should not have failed to do so; now go ahead and give me some reasons why this non-suppression was still justified!'

A person in *Brekkukotsannáll*, a novel by Halldór Laxness, the Icelandic Nobel laureate, remarks that most questions can be answered if they are correctly put. In this book I have tried to *put correctly* a question about the meaning of social freedom and to find an adequate answer to it.

Bibliography

Anderson, E. S., 'John Stuart Mill and Experiments in Living', *Ethics*, 102 (1991): 4–26.

Anscombe, G. E. M., *Intention* (Oxford: Basil Blackwell, 1976).

Arendt, H., *Between Past and Future: Eight Exercises in Political Thought* (Harmondsworth: Penguin, 1977).

Aristotle, *Nicomachean Ethics* (translated by Irwin, T., Indianapolis: Hackett Publishing Co., 1985).

Arneson, R. J., 'Symposium on Rawlsian Theory of Justice. Recent Developments. Introduction', *Ethics*, 99 (1989): 695–710.

Austin, J. L., 'A Plea for Excuses', in Chappell, V. C. (ed.), *Ordinary Language* (Englewood Cliffs: Prentice-Hall, 1964).

Baldwin, T., 'MacCallum and the Two Concepts of Freedom', *Ratio*, 26 (1984): 125–42.

Ball, T., 'Power, Causation and Explanation', *Polity*, 8 (1975): 189–214.

Barry, B., 'The Obscurities of Power', *Government and Opposition*, 10 (1975): 250–4.

Beehler, R., 'For One Concept of Liberty', *Journal of Applied Philosophy*, 8 (1991): 27–43.

'A Neglected Aspect of Liberty', *Cogito*, 7 (1993): 40–7.

Benn, S. I., 'Freedom and Persuasion', *The Australasian Journal of Philosophy*, 45 (1967): 259–75.

'Power', in Edwards, P. (ed.), *The Encyclopedia of Philosophy*, VI (London/New York: Macmillan, 1967): 424–7.

'Freedom, Autonomy and the Concept of a Person', *Proceedings of the Aristotelian Society*, 76 (1975–6): 109–30.

A Theory of Freedom (Cambridge University Press, 1988).

Benn, S. I. and Weinstein, W. L., 'Being Free to Act, and Being a Free Man', *Mind*, 80 (1971): 194–211.

'Freedom as the Non-Restriction of Options: A Rejoinder', *Mind*, 83 (1974): 435–8.

Berlin, I., *Four Essays on Liberty* (Oxford University Press, 1969).

Concepts and Categories (ed. Hardy, H., London: The Hogarth Press, 1978).

Bishop, M. A., 'The Possibility of Conceptual Clarity in Philosophy', *American Philosophical Quarterly*, 29 (1992): 267–75.

Brennan, J. M., *The Open-Texture of Moral Concepts* (London: Macmillan, 1977).

Cavell, S., 'Must We Mean What We Say?', in Chappell, V. C. (ed.), *Ordinary Language* (Englewood Cliffs: Prentice-Hall, 1964).

Chamberlin, R., 'A Philosophical Investigation of Political Liberty and Education', Ph.D. dissertation (University of Bristol, 1986).

Christman, J., 'Constructing the Inner Citadel: Recent Work on the Concept of Autonomy', *Ethics*, 99 (1988): 109–24.

Cohen, G. A., 'Illusions about Private Property and Freedom', in Mepham, J. and Ruben, D. H. (eds.), *Issues in Marxist Philosophy*, IV (Brighton: Harvester Press, 1981).

Cohen, M., 'Berlin and the Liberal Tradition', *The Philosophical Quarterly*, 10 (1960): 216–27.

Connolly, W. E., *The Terms of Political Discourse*, 2nd edn (Oxford: Martin Robertson & Co., 1983).

Coole, D., 'Constructing and Deconstructing Liberty: A Feminist and Poststructuralist Analysis', *Political Studies*, 41 (1993): 83–95.

Cooper, D. E., 'The Free Man', in Griffiths, A. P. (ed.), *Of Liberty*. Supplement to *Philosophy* (Cambridge University Press, 1983).

Crick, B., 'Freedom as Politics', in Laslett, P. and Runciman, W. G. (eds.), *Philosophy, Politics and Society*, III (Oxford: Basil Blackwell, 1967).

Crocker, L., *Positive Liberty* (The Hague: Martinus Nijhoff Publisher, 1980).

D'Agostino, F., 'Transcendence and Conversation: Two Conceptions of Objectivity', *American Philosophical Quarterly*, 30 (1993): 87–108.

Dauenhauer, B. P., 'Relational Freedom', *Review of Metaphysics*, 36 (1982): 77–101.

Day, J. P., 'Threats, Offers, Law, Opinion and Liberty', *American Philosophical Quarterly*, 14 (1977): 257–72.

'Is the Concept of Freedom Essentially Contestable?', *Philosophy*, 61 (1986): 116–23.

'On Häyry and Airaksinen's "Hard and Soft Offers as Constraints"', *Philosophia* (Israel), 20 (1990): 321–7.

Demos, R., 'Lying to Oneself', *Journal of Philosophy*, 57 (1960): 588–95.

Dilman, I., 'The Freedom of Man', *Proceedings of the Aristotelian Society*, 62 (1961-2): 39–62.

Duff, A., 'Intention, Responsibility and Double Effect', *The Philosophical Quarterly*, 32 (1982): 1–16.

Dworkin, G., 'Acting Freely', *Nous*, 4 (1970): 367–83.
'The Concept of Autonomy', *Grazer Philosophische Studien*, 13 (1981): 203–13.
Elfstrom, G., 'Dilemmas of Intervention', *Ethics*, 93 (1983): 709–25.
Feinberg, J., *Social Philosophy* (Englewood Cliffs: Prentice-Hall, 1973).
The Moral Limits of the Criminal Law, III: Harm to Self (New York: Oxford University Press, 1986).
Flathman, R. E., *The Philosophy and Politics of Freedom* (University of Chicago Press, 1987).
Frankfurt, H. G., 'Freedom of the Will and the Concept of a Person', *The Journal of Philosophy*, 68 (1971): 5–20.
Gallie, W. B., 'Essentially Contestable Concepts', *Proceedings of the Aristotelian Society*, 56 (1955–6): 167–98.
Gardiner, P., 'Error, Faith and Self-Deception', in Glover, J. (ed.), *The Philosophy of Mind* (Oxford University Press, 1976).
Gellner, E, 'The Concept of a Story', *Ratio*, 9 (1967): 49–66.
Graham, George, 'Doing Something Intentionally and Moral Responsibility', *Canadian Journal of Philosophy*, 11 (1981): 667–77.
Graham, Gordon, *Politics in its Place: A Study of Six Ideologies* (Oxford: Clarendon Press, 1986).
Graham, K., 'Regulative Political Theory: Language, Norms and Ideology', *Political Studies*, 33 (1985): 19–37.
The Battle of Democracy: Conflict, Consensus and the Individual (Hassocks: Wheatsheaf Books, 1986).
Gray, J., 'On the Contestability of Social and Political Concepts', *Political Theory*, 5 (1977): 331–47.
'On Liberty, Liberalism and Essential Contestability', *British Journal of Political Science*, 8 (1978): 385–402.
'On Negative and Positive Liberty', *Political Studies*, 28 (1980): 507–26.
'Hayek on Liberty, Rights, and Justice', *Ethics*, 92 (1981–2): 73–84.
'Political Power, Social Theory, and Essential Contestability', in Miller, D. and Siedentop, L. (eds.), *The Nature of Political Theory* (Oxford: Clarendon Press, 1983).
Liberalism (London: Open University Press, 1986).
Gylfason, Þ., *Valdsorðaskak* (Reykjavík: Félag áhugamanna um heimspeki, 1982).
Haight, M. R., *A Study of Self-Deception* (Sussex: Humanities Press, 1981).
Hart, H. L. A., *Punishment and Responsibility* (Oxford University Press, 1968).
Haslett, D. W., 'What is Wrong with Reflective Equilibria?', in Corlett, J. A. (ed.), *Equality and Liberty: Analyzing Rawls and Nozick* (London: Macmillan, 1991).
Hobbes, T., *Leviathan* (Harmondsworth: Penguin, 1968).

Hunt, I., 'Freedom and its Conditions', *Australasian Journal of Philosophy*, 69 (1991): 288–301.

Husak, D. N., 'The Presumption of Freedom', *Nous*, 17 (1983): 345–62.

Inwagen, P. van, 'Ability and Responsibility', *Philosophical Review*, 87 (1978): 201–24.

Kenny, A., *Freewill and Responsibility* (London: Routledge and Kegan Paul, 1978).

Kovesi, J., *Moral Notions* (London: Routledge and Kegan Paul, 1971).

Kristjánsson, K., 'Böl og bölsvandi', B.A. dissertation (University of Iceland, 1983).

'Freedom as a Moral Concept', Ph.D. dissertation (University of St Andrews, 1990).

'For a *Concept* of Negative Liberty – but which *Conception?*', *Journal of Applied Philosophy*, 9 (1992): 221–31.

'Freedom, Offers, and Obstacles', *American Philosophical Quarterly*, 29 (1992): 63–70.

'Social Freedom and the Test of Moral Responsibility', *Ethics*, 103 (1992): 104–16.

'What is Wrong with Positive Liberty?', *Social Theory and Practice*, 18 (1992): 289–310.

'"Constraining Freedom" and "Exercising Power Over"', *International Journal of Moral and Social Studies*, 7 (1992): 127–38.

Þroskakostir (Reykjavík: Rannsóknarstofnun í siðfræði, 1992).

'Moral Concepts: Normativity without Relativity', unpublished paper presented at the 10th Inter-Nordic Philosophical Symposium in Finland (1993).

'Social Concepts: Normativity without Relativity', *Res Publica*, 1 (1995): 71–89.

Kuhn, T. S., *The Structure of Scientific Revolutions*. 2nd edn, enlarged (University of Chicago Press, 1970).

Levin, M., 'Negative Liberty', in Paul, E. F. and Paul, J. (eds.), *Liberty and Equality* (Oxford: Basil Blackwell, 1985).

Levine, A., 'Foundations of Unfreedom', *Ethics*, 88 (1977–8): 162–72.

Lindley, R., *Autonomy* (London: Macmillan, 1986).

Locke, J., *An Essay Concerning Human Understanding*, II (Oxford: Clarendon Press, 1914).

Lucas, J. R., *Responsibility* (Oxford: Clarendon Press, 1993).

Lukes, S., 'Methodological Individualism Reconsidered', *The British Journal of Sociology*, 19 (1968): 119–29.

Power: A Radical View (London: Macmillan, 1974).

'Relativism: Cognitive and Moral', *Proceedings of the Aristotelian Society*, suppl. vol. 48 (1974): 165–89.

'On the Relativity of Power', in Brown, S. C. (ed.), *Philosophical*

Disputes in the Social Sciences (Brighton: Harvester Press, 1979).
Lukes, S. (ed.), *Power* (Oxford: Basil Blackwell, 1986).
MacCallum, G. C., 'Negative and Positive Freedom', *The Philosophical Review*, 76 (1967): 312–34.
McCarthy, T., 'Doing the Right Thing in Cross-cultural Representation', *Ethics*, 102 (1992): 635–49.
McCloskey, H. J., 'A Critique of the Ideals of Liberty', *Mind*, 74 (1965): 483–58.
McCluskey, J. B., 'The Nature and Value of Political Liberty', Ph.D. dissertation (University of Miami, 1986).
MacIntyre, A., *Against the Self-Images of the Age* (London: Duckworth, 1971).
'The Essential Contestability of Some Social Concepts', *Ethics*, 84 (1973): 1–9.
After Virtue (London: Duckworth, 1981).
MacPherson, C. B., *Democratic Theory: Essays in Retrieval* (Oxford: Clarendon Press, 1973).
Martin, M. W. (ed.), *Self-Deception and Self-Understanding* (University Press of Kansas, 1985).
Mason, A., 'The Reconstruction of Political Concepts', *International Journal of Moral and Social Studies*, 4 (1989): 245–58.
'Locke on Disagreement Over the Use of Moral and Political Terms', *Locke News*, 20 (1989): 63–75.
'On Explaining Political Disagreement: The Notion of an Essentially Contested Concept', *Inquiry*, 33 (1990): 81–98.
Explaining Political Disagreement (Cambridge University Press, 1993).
'Power Over Others and the Power to Effect Outcomes', unpublished paper, n.d.
Mill, J. S., *Utilitarianism, Liberty, Representative Government* (London: J. M. Dent & Sons, 1931).
Miller, D., 'Constraints on Freedom', *Ethics*, 94 (1983): 66–86.
'Linguistic Philosophy and Political Theory', in Miller, D. and Siedentop, L. (eds.), *The Nature of Political Theory* (Oxford: Clarendon Press, 1983).
'Reply to Oppenheim', *Ethics*, 95 (1985): 310–14.
Market, State, and Community (Oxford University Press, 1989).
Miller, D. (ed.), *Liberty* (Oxford University Press, 1991).
Morriss, P., *Power: A Philosophical Analysis* (Manchester University Press, 1987).
Nagel, T., *The View From Nowhere* (New York: Oxford University Press, 1986).
Norman, R., 'Does Equality Destroy Liberty?', in Graham, K. (ed.),

Contemporary Political Philosophy. Radical Studies (Cambridge University Press, 1982).

Norman, W. J., 'Obstacles and Constraints', unpublished seminar paper (London School of Economics, 1985).

'Taking "Free Action" Too Seriously', *Ethics*, 101 (1991): 505–20.

Nozick, R., *Anarchy, State, and Utopia* (Oxford: Basil Blackwell, 1971).

'Coercion', in Laslett, P., Runciman, W. G., and Skinner, Q. (eds.), *Philosophy, Politics and Society*, IV (Oxford: Basil Blackwell, 1972).

Nussbaum, M. C., *The Fragility of Goodness* (Cambridge University Press, 1986).

Oppenheim, F., *Dimensions of Freedom: An Analysis* (New York: St. Martin's Press, 1961).

Political Concepts: A Reconstruction (University of Chicago Press, 1981).

'"Constraints on Freedom" as a Descriptive Concept', *Ethics*, 95 (1985): 305–9.

Parent, W. A., 'Some Recent Work on the Concept of Liberty', *American Philosophical Quarterly*, 11 (1974): 149–67.

'Freedom as the Non-Restriction of Options', *Mind*, 83 (1974): 432–8.

Parfit, D., *Reasons and Persons* (Oxford: Clarendon Press, 1984).

Partridge, P. G., 'Freedom', in Edwards, P. (ed.), *The Encyclopedia of Philosophy*, III (London/New York: Macmillan, 1967), 221–5.

Paton, H. J., *The Moral Law: Kant's Groundwork of the Metaphysics of Morals* (London: Hutchinson & Co., 1976).

Patrick, M., 'Liberty and Liberalism', M.Phil. dissertation (University of St Andrews, 1988).

Pettit, P., *Judging Justice* (London: Routledge and Kegan Paul, 1980).

'Consequentialism and Respect for Persons', *Ethics*, 100 (1989): 116–26.

'A Definition of Negative Liberty', *Ratio*, 2 (1989): 153–68.

Plato, *The Collected Dialogues*, Hamsten, E. and Cairns, H. (eds.) (Princeton University Press, 1963).

Rawls, J., *A Theory of Justice* (London: Oxford University Press, 1973).

Raz, J., *The Morality of Freedom* (Oxford: Clarendon Press, 1986).

Reeve, A., 'Power Without Responsibility', *Political Studies*, 30 (1982): 77–86.

Rescher, N., *Essays in Philosophical Analysis* (University of Pittsburgh Press, 1969).

The Strife of Systems (University of Pittsburgh Press, 1985).

Ryan, A., 'Freedom', *Philosophy*, 40 (1965): 93–112.

Ryle, G., 'Ordinary Language', in Chappell, V. C. (ed.), *Ordinary Language* (Englewood Cliffs: Prentice-Hall, 1964).

Schlesinger, G., 'Operationalism', in Edwards, P. (ed.), *The Encyclopedia of Philosophy*, v (London/New York: Macmillan, 1967), 543–7.

Shaw, W. H., 'Intuition and Moral Philosophy', *American Philosophical Quarterly*, 17 (1980): 127–34.

Smith, G. W., 'The Logic of J. S. Mill on Freedom', *Political Studies*, 28 (1980): 238–52.

Steiner, H., 'Individual Liberty', *Proceedings of the Aristotelian Society*, 75 (1974-5): 33–50.

Strawson, P. F., *Freedom and Resentment and Other Essays* (London: Methuen, 1974).

Swanton, C., 'On the "Essential Contestedness" of Political Concepts', *Ethics*, 95 (1985): 811–27.

Freedom: A Coherence Theory (Indianapolis: Hackett Publishing Co., 1992).

Szabados, B., 'The Self, Its Passions and Self-Deception', in Martin, M. W. (ed.), *Self-Deception and Self-Understanding* (University Press of Kansas, 1985).

Taylor, C., 'Neutrality in Political Science', in Laslett, P. and Runciman, W. G. (eds.), *Philosophy, Politics and Society*, III (Oxford: Basil Blackwell, 1967).

'What's Wrong with Negative Liberty', in Ryan, A. (ed.), *The Idea of Freedom: Essays in Honour of Isaiah Berlin* (Oxford University Press, 1979): 175–93.

Ten, C. L., *Mill on Liberty* (Oxford: Clarendon Press, 1980).

Waismann, F., 'Verifiability', *Aristotelian Society*, suppl. vol. 19 (1945): 119–31.

Wertheimer, A., 'Is Ordinary Language Analysis Conservative?', *Political Theory*, 4 (1976): 405–22.

Coercion (Princeton University Press, 1987).

White, D. M., 'Negative Liberty', *Ethics*, 80 (1969-70): 185–204.

'The Problem of Power', *British Journal of Political Science*, 2 (1972): 479–90.

Wittgenstein, L., *Philosophical Investigations* (translated by Anscombe, G. E. M., Oxford: Basil Blackwell, 1968).

Wrong, D. H., *Power: Its Forms, Bases and Uses* (Oxford: Basil Blackwell, 1979).

Index

Index

221